MW01201067

The Bible Explained

Allen Linn

Copyright © 2017 by Allen Linn

PYRAMID
Publishers

1314 Grandview Circle
Buffalo, MN 55313
763-486-2867
www.pyramidpublishers.com

All rights reserved. No part of this publication may be reproduced, stored in a retrieval system, or transmitted, in any form or by any means, electronic, mechanical, photocopying, recording, or otherwise, without the prior written permission of the author.

Printed by Lightning Source
1246 Heil Quaker Blvd.
La Vergne, TN USA 37086
ISBN – 978-0-9851514-9-2

Cover Design by Alexander Galutsky
Interior Design and Layout by Just Ink Digital Design
Printed in the United States of America

Unless otherwise noted, Scripture quotations are from The Holy Bible, New International Version™, NIV™. Copyright© 1973, 1978, 1984, 2011 by Biblica, Inc.™ Used by permission of Zondervan

CHAPTER ONE
The Beginning and Meaning of All things
God

God was before anything else existed. The Eternal One, without beginning. He created time, space, and matter. He is the cause of all causes and is Himself uncaused. He alone had no beginning. He has eternally existed. Only He is self-existent, all else exists through Him.

We are created and are creatures of time; everything we know had a beginning. The concept of origin can only apply to created things and separates God from all else. We cannot grasp the concept of the Uncreated and Eternal because our minds themselves are created and our minds are uncomfortable outside the realm of the familiar.

God is independent of space, time, and matter. He is the source of all life. Life can only come from life. If there was ever a time when there was no life, there could be none now. If we could go back, we would eventually come to the original source of life, and this source must be eternal or there could be no life now. God's self-existence is stated in Exodus 3:14 in His words to Moses, *I Am who I Am;* God alone owes His existence to no one.

As the self-existent One, God possesses all things and we possess nothing except for what He gives us. This applies to everything, from our natural physical lives, to the spiritual benefits through Christ.

God is ETERNAL: *From everlasting, you are God* (Psalm 90:2). When we try to conceive of eternity, our minds race backward and forward in time; but God is not a creature of time, as we are, and we must think in terms of time.

God is INFINITE and OMNIPRESENT. These are closely related. Infinite means that God is not limited by time and space. Omnipresent means that He is present in all His fullness everywhere in time and space.

God is TRANSCENDENT. In Isaiah 57:15 God is called *the high and lofty one who inhabits eternity.* God is infinitely exalted above His created universe. This refers to the quality of Being. God is not merely the highest in an ascending order of beings from the lowest insect to the highest archangel. That is pre-eminence, but transcendence is far more.

God is not only infinitely greater than all creatures – He is infinitely apart from them. He is as high above the highest archangel as He is above the gnat. The gulf between the archangel and the gnat is finite, while the gulf between them both and God is infinite. Everything else is created; he alone is uncreated. There are ultimately only two categories: that which is God and that which is not God.

God is SOVEREIGN. This simply means that God is free to do as He pleases, always. He alone is independent of everything. He is absolutely sovereign because He is absolutely free, all-powerful and all knowing. No one can compel Him or hinder Him; His authority is absolute.

God is omnipotent (Almighty). "Omni" means unlimited; "potent" means power. God has unlimited power. All power is His and no one else can have power that He did not give to them. The power that He gives to others, He still possesses. It all flows out from Him and returns to Him. There is no limit to His power: His potency is absolute. While He delegates power, He does not relinquish it. He gives but does not give away. What He gives still remains His. Since His power is unlimited, He can do anything as easily as anything else. All He does is without effort.

God is ALL KNOWING. He has always known everything past, present, and future with perfect and unerring understanding. Psalm 147:5 declares *His understanding is infinite.* He knows everything perfectly, the end from the beginning. He sees every detail in relation to all other details and is able to bring about His predestined goals. He never has to guess, is never surprised, and is never caught off guard. He never makes a mistake.

God is IMMUTABLE (does not change). *I am the Lord, I do not change* (Malachi 3:6). We change all the time and live in a world of constant change. We may be happy in the morning and irritable at night. We may have changed at 40 from the person we were at 20. God is perfect and His perfection never changes. He is always the same in all His perfection. If he loves us now, He will always love us. When He makes a promise, He always keeps it. This gives stability to our lives. Without this, we would never know if He had changed His mind about a given thing. He loved me yesterday, but does He still love me today? There could never be any assurance. But we can be sure of all His promises because they are as unchangeable as God Himself. What God is He always has been and always will be.

God is HOLY. *Holy, holy, holy, is the Lord of hosts* (Isaiah 6:3). Sinful man can have no real concept of God's holiness. It is incomprehensible and unapproachable. When the best of men are approached by God in the Scriptures, they collapse and melt within themselves in His presence. They are filled with a mysterious fear of the created in the presence of the uncreated. Holy is not merely how He acts but what He is. To be holy He does not conform to a standard, He *is* the standard. Because God is holy, holiness is the necessary moral condition for the well-being of the universe. Whatever is holy is healthy; whatever is evil is diseased. Sin is a disease that can only end in death.

God's first concern for His creation is for its moral well-being. While God's holiness is without degrees, there is a relative holiness which He shares with humankind and angels. God shares His holiness with fallen humanity imparted to them through Jesus Christ. This was His first step in the redemption of the human race, to provide righteousness and holiness through Christ. He must first deal with the cause of sin, and then He will deal with the effects of sin. Both of these are remedied in Christ. Today God's people can rejoice in the fact that they have been saved from sin's penalty, while they look forward to the time when God will remove all the effects of sin.

God is rational and has emotions. He is a Person and has personality. He thinks, loves, He sympathizes, He's faithful, just, gracious, and merciful. That He is rational is shown in His creation, which is an intelligible system. This rationality has a fundamental correspondence between the universe and the human mind He created. This makes science possible. This is why the pioneers of science were Christians. Science is the rational mind responding to a rational universe.

He reveals Himself to the writers of Scripture in an intimate and personal relationship to the world. Human actions arouse His emotions of joy or sorrow. Mankind may grieve or please Him. Scripture abounds with imagery of Him and His people in a husband and bride relationship, or as a Father and His children. He woos His people to respond to Him in love. The love He wants from us is genuine, not as spoiled children who want His gifts more than Himself.

God is JUST – RIGHTEOUS. Justice and righteousness are both translated from the same Greek word. "Just" and "Righteous" are words that describe the way God is. God is not bound by rules or laws that He must follow, as are human judges.

When God is just or righteous, He is simply acting like Himself in a given situation. Everything in all creation is good or evil to the degree that it conforms, or fails to conform, to the unchanging nature of God.

God is LOVE. *For God so loved the world that He gave His only begotten Son* (John 3:16). *Herein is love, not that we loved God, but that He loved us and sent His Son as an atoning sacrifice for our sins* (1 John 4:10). It is the nature of love that it cannot lie dormant but must express itself. *God demonstrates His own love for us in this: while we were still sinners, Christ died for us* (Rom 5:8).

The depth of one's love for the object of his love is revealed by what he is willing to give for their sake. That God's love is infinite is revealed by His willingness to give the greatest gift that even God can give. We can also learn much about God's love through His other attributes: because He is eternal, His love will never end; because He is infinite, His love can have no limits; because He is holy, His love is holy and pure and seeks the best for the objects of His love; because He is incomprehensible, His love is beyond our comprehension. God seeks the good of His sinful creatures whatever the cost. His love, however, is not bestowed upon us because we are good and loveable, for we are not, but for the sole reason that it is God's nature to love His creatures. The reason is found in God Himself.

As self-sufficient and sovereign as He is, God is emotionally identified with mankind and has bound His heart to us forever. This is why He had to create mankind with free will. God does not want a heaven full of robots who love Him merely because they were programmed to do so. As they face the storms and trials of life, the children of God can rest in the knowledge that God seeks their welfare – His wisdom has planned for it, and His power will achieve it.

GOODNESS, MERCY, GRACE. These are manifestations of God's love. Because He is good, His attitude toward His creation is kindness and goodwill. The cause of this goodness is never man's merit, but simply because God is good. God's holiness demands judgment for our sins, while His love carries out this judgment upon Himself, in His Son. This is grace. Grace is giving the opposite of what is deserved. On the cross God dealt with Jesus as though He were the sinner: He gave Jesus the opposite of what He deserved. He deals with the believing sinner as though he were His Son: The opposite of what he deserves. Christ paid the debt that the sinner could not pay and God transfers His merit to the believer who deserves condemnation. It is God's grace that changes a sinner into a saint, a rebel into a son.

God is FAITHFUL. In Revelation 19:11, Christ is presented as triumphantly riding a white horse bearing the names "faithful and true." All the future hopes and joy of God's people rests upon His faithfulness. In the meantime, the weary, the tempted, the anxious, the discouraged can go to the bottomless well of God's promises, knowing that they are as sure as God Himself.

The fact of one of God's attributes leads to the fact of another attribute. If God is self-existent, He must also be self-sufficient. If His Being is infinite, His power and wisdom must be unlimited. If He is unchangeable, He cannot be unfaithful, for that would require Him to change. He cannot cease being who He is, or act out of character with himself. Within the divine nature, there can be no conflict in His attributes. All His actions are in perfect union. He cannot divide Himself and act according to one attribute while the others remain inactive.

What God is like and how we can expect Him to act toward us are vital questions that relate for time and eternity. These attributes describe His very nature. They simply describe God as being Himself. In eternity other attributes may be revealed to His redeemed creation. God has been pleased to reveal His attributes that affect us now.

GOD'S TRIUNE NATURE

The Bible emphasizes that there is one God. *The Lord our God, the Lord is One* (Deuteronomy 6:4).

The Lord Himself is God: besides Him there is no other (Deuteronomy 4:35).

I am the first, and I am the last, apart from me there is no God (Isaiah 44:6).

I am the Lord, and there is no other; apart from me there is no God (Isaiah 45:5).

However, it is also taught that this one God consists of a plurality of Persons. God is a plurality of one. This sounds strange, but it is what the Bible repeatedly teaches. This is taught in the very Scriptures that emphasize that there is One God. For instance, Deuteronomy 6:4 uses two Hebrew words to emphasize this: *The Lord* (Jehovah—singular), *our God* (Elohim—plural) *is one Lord* (Jehovah—singular).

Deuteronomy 4:35 reads: *The Lord* (Jehovah—singular), *Himself is God* (Elohim—plural)*; there is none other besides Me.*

Isaiah 45:5 reads: *I am the Lord* (Jehovah—singular), *there is no God* (Elohim—plural) *besides Me.*

If the Bible wanted to teach a single entity within the Godhead the word "Eloah" would have been used instead of the plural "Elohim."

Note in Genesis 1:26: *God said, "Let US make man in OUR image, in OUR likeness.* In the next verse, we read: *So God created man in HIS own image.* The "US" and "OUR" in verse 26, become "HIS" in verse 27. This singular God consists of a plurality of Persons. This singular God with a plurality of Persons also runs all through the New Testament. Note in John 1:1 we have *In the beginning was the Word* (Jesus Christ), *and the Word was WITH God* (plurality), *and the Word WAS God* (singular).

This plurality is consistently revealed as three Persons. Genesis 1:1 says: *In the beginning God* (Elohim—plural) *created the heavens and the earth.* Here the plural is used, a plurality of Persons. This is why we are told that the FATHER created all things: *The Father from whom all things come* (1 Corinthians 8:6). The Son created all things: *All things were made through Him, and without Him nothing was made that was made* (John 1:3). And the Holy Spirit is the Creator: *The Spirit of God had made me* (Job 33:4).

Likewise, Jesus' resurrection is attributed to the triune God. To the Father: *This Jesus God has raised up* (Acts 2:32). To the Son: *Therefore My Father loves Me, because I lay down my life that I may take it again* (John 10:17). And to the Holy Spirit: *But if the Spirit of Him who raised Jesus from the dead dwells in you, He who raised Christ from the dead will also give life to your mortal bodies through His Spirit who dwells in you* (Romans 8:11).

In John 1:18 we read: *No one has ever seen God. But God the One and only who is at the Father's side has made Him known.* Here we see that no one has seen God in His divine essence but the Second Person of the Trinity; the pre-incarnate Christ is the One who was manifested many times in the Old Testament as the Angel of the Lord. He is God's Revealer. He took the angelic appearance to reveal God. In the New Testament, Jesus Christ was incarnate in human form; he *became flesh* (John 1:14). Jesus Christ, in His earthly life, revealed the Father.

Every visible manifestation of God in the Scriptures was the work of the Second Person of the Trinity. This is what Jesus meant when He said in John 14:9, *He that has seen me has seen the Father.* In John 5:20 Jesus is called *The True God and eternal life.* In Isaiah 9:6 He is referred to as *the Mighty God.* In Acts 5:3 Ananias is said to have lied to the Holy Spirit; in the next verse, verse 4, this is explained as *Lying to God.* In 1 Corinthians 3:16, believers are called the *temple of God.* Why? because the Holy Spirit dwells in them.

These three Persons are coeternal and coequal. They are distinct individuals. Each partakes of the full divine essence. The one God is also three Persons, and they are always together and always cooperating. They are inherently one in the fullness of Deity, in which each one lives in and through the others in a union eternally rooted in infinite love. At the center of reality is a relationship within the nature of God.

The inner life of the Triune God is characterized by a self-giving love which revolves around the others. Scripture declares *God is love* (1 John 4:8). This means that it is His very nature to love. The Persons of the Trinity continuously pour out love to each other and receive love in return.

The universe was created by a fellowship of Persons who have loved each other from eternity. Mankind was created for a mutually self-giving, other-centered love; Our self-centeredness came from the fall and destroys our purpose. The Scriptures do not explain the Trinity, just as they do not explain God. The existence of God is taken for granted, as is His triune nature. It is simply ingrained in Scripture; it's just there.

Christ is the Mediator, and the Preserver, of creation: *For by Him all things were created that are in heaven and that are on earth* (Colossians 1:16). *All things were made through Him, and without Him nothing was made that was made* (John 1:3).

But in these last days He has spoken to us by His Son, whom He appointed heir of all things, and through whom He made the universe. The Son is the radiance of God's glory and the exact representation of His being, sustaining all things by His powerful word . . . (Hebrews 1:2-3).

He is the Mediator of redemption. *For God chose us in Him before the creation of the world to be holy and blameless in His sight (Ephesians 1:4). According to His eternal purpose which He accomplished in Christ Jesus our Lord* (Ephesians 3:11). *He was chosen before the creation of the world, but was revealed in these last times for your sake* (1 Pet. 1:20).

According to His eternal plan, the Father chose the Son in advance as the Redeemer and determined to send Him into the world as heaven's highest gift. *Thanks be to God for His indescribable gift* (2 Cor. 9:15).

He is the Mediator of judgment. *The Father judges no one, but has entrusted all judgment to the Son* (John 5:22).

The fall of mankind was known and provided for. As the Son was the Father's gift to the world, the redeemed world was the Father's gift to the Son. *I have manifested your name to the men whom You have given Me out of the world* (John 9:6). *Father, I desire that they also whom you gave Me may be with Me where I am, that they may behold My glory which you have given Me; For You loved Me before the foundation of the world* (John 9:24).

God's glory is the source and goal of all things: *To the praise of His glory* (Eph. 1:6,12,14), so that *God may be all in all* (1 Cor. 15:28). By virtue of His very perfection, God must want the highest for His creation. Thus, He Himself is the goal. So the source and goal of all creation is the Son, *for by Him all things were created, things in heaven and on earth . . . All things were created by Him and for Him* (Col. 1:16). God's nature is love, the perfect love of John 3:16. Therefore God created mankind for love and the supreme goal is the unfolding of the Being of God as the perfect, holy, and loving one, in the establishment of a fellowship of life and love between the Creator and His creatures.

THE PURPOSE OF GOD'S CREATION

It is God's desire to unfold Himself to His creation and overflow it with Himself. Because He is love, He created mankind as a spiritual personality on whom He could bestow His love. He created us so that He could pour out His love and glory to fill His creation and have it reveal His beauty and majesty. He created mankind in His own image and placed them in a perfect environment to reflect His glory. He created them for Himself. He wanted them to know Him and love Him. He wanted to share Himself with His creation and reveal Himself in His Triune Essence, which is an eternal, loving relationship, to expand His love throughout His creation. He created them in His own image, so they would have the ability to return His love. He created them with free will to return His love willingly, not as mere robots programmed to love Him.

Their sin and fall were foreknown by God and He built into the plan of creation the plan of redemption. The Second Member of the Triune God, Jesus Christ, was appointed as *the Lamb of God slain from before the foundation of the world* (Rev 13:8).

Who has saved us and called us with a holy calling, according to His own purpose and grace which was given to us in Christ Jesus before time began, but has now been revealed by the appearing of our Savior Jesus Christ, who has abolished death and brought life and immortality to light through the Gospel (2 Tim 1:9-10).

In hope of eternal life which God, who cannot lie, promised before time began, but in due time manifested His word through preaching, which was committed to me according to the commandment of God our Savior (Titus 1:2-3).

Jesus' prayer in John 17:1-5 shows God's plan for His redeemed: *Father, the hour has come (He was about to go to the cross), glorify your Son, that the Son may glorify you. You have granted Him authority over all people, that He might give eternal life to all those you have given Him. Now this is eternal life; that they may know you, the only true God, and Jesus Christ whom you have sent. I have brought you glory on earth by completing the work you gave me to do (He anticipates the cross). And now, Father, glorify me in your presence with the glory I had with you before the world began.* Then in verse 24, He continues: *Father, I want those you have given me to be with me where I am, and to see my glory, the Glory you have given me because you loved me before the creation of the world.*

It has always been God's plan that we share in the relationship He has with Christ.

This plan centers in Christ: *According to His eternal purpose which He accomplished in Christ Jesus our Lord* (Eph. 3:11). Because God saw that man's sin would interrupt His purpose for mankind, God chose Jesus to be the Mediator, the "Lamb of God," to pay the penalty for our sin.

It was God's plan to demonstrate the exceeding riches of His grace in Christ through all the ages to come *in order that in the coming ages He might show the incomparable riches of His grace, expressed in His kindness to us in Christ Jesus* (Eph. 2:7).

The earth, the scene of the fall, would also be the scene of Christ's death and resurrection, where He would forever lift the curse from mankind by taking it upon Himself and giving eternal life to all who would believe in Him (John 3:16). Christ's sacrifice for sin as the source of salvation was in the mind of God from eternity. God's plan of redemption stretches from eternity to eternity and Christ Himself is the guarantee of its fulfillment. This is why we are told *all things were Created BY Him and FOR Him* (Col 1:15-16).

CHAPTER TWO
The Creation

Creation begins with God alone. He was the preexisting intelligence and power operating from another dimension. God created all things from nothing, without any preexisting material. He simply spoke the creation into existence.

God's invisible attributes are revealed through His creation, as we are told in Romans 1:19-20: *For since the creation of the world God's invisible qualities – his eternal power and divine nature – have been clearly seen, being understood from what has been made, so that men are without excuse.*

The creation account in chapter 1 of Genesis reads: *In the beginning God created the heavens and the earth. Now the earth was formless and empty, darkness was over the surface of the deep, and the Spirit of God was hovering over the waters. And God said, "Let there be light," and there was light. God saw that the light was good, and he separated the light from the darkness. God called the light "day," and the darkness He called "night." And there was evening, and there was morning – the first day* (Gen 1:1-5).

Only God can call into existence by the sheer power of His Word. As we are told in Heb. 11:3: *By faith we understand that the universe was formed at God's command, so that what is seen was not made out of what was visible.*

Because he was created in God's image, mankind can make things out of existing material, but only God can bring things into existence out of nothing. The physical universe was spoken into existence by the all-mighty and all-wise God!

The ancient myths of creation all begin with matter in some form or another, as do the so-called more sophisticated theories of evolution. They all begin with space, matter, and time. Only the Bible begins with the First Cause: An Eternal, Almighty, Personal God. Only this can explain the intelligent design of creation with life and personality.

In verse 1 "beginning" refers to time. Time had a beginning. Only God is eternal. "Heaven" refers to empty space and "earth" refers to matter that the earth is made of. The planet earth was not yet formed. This formless matter was used to form the planet earth and later other material bodies.

The universe is clearly a place of thought and planning. Only persons can think and plan. If you find yourself in a room with a soda machine, you put your money in and the machine gives you a can of soda. We know that matter cannot think. A person who can think had to design that machine to obey a certain built-in response to the money being inserted. Machines do not think; matter does not think. The stars and planets and other material bodies did not get together and decide which laws they would obey and operate under. A Great Designer did this. As a house is not built simply to look at, but walking through it, one realizes that it was built for people, so also the earth was created for people.

At first the earth was empty, then God designed it for people. As one scientist has said, "It's as though the universe knew we were coming." New parents don't wait until the baby comes to prepare for him or her. Loving hands prepare to make life more enjoyable before the baby is brought home. In God's creation, earth is at the center. Not geographically, but in importance. God first made the earth and then the sun, moon, and stars were made to serve the earth (Genesis1:14).

Moses wrote the first five books of the Old Testament. It is obvious that Moses did not write according to the creation theories of his day. He was *learned in all the wisdom of the Egyptians* (Acts 7:22). Yet Moses' account of creation avoids all the myths of the pagan world of his day.

Now the earth was formless and empty, and darkness was over the surface of the deep, and the Spirit of God was hovering over the waters (Gen 1:2).

Chapter 1 shows a sequence and connects the verse before and after, and tells in detail how God brought form to this matter and filled its emptiness with living beings to inhabit its empty surface. So at the beginning, *the heavens and the earth* referred simply to "space and matter" and the matter was yet unformed and uninhabited. There were no heavenly bodies. The matter was not energized. Light is energy, so darkness was everywhere. What we have in verse two is a water and element mixture referred to as *the deep*. No gravity was in force to form a coherent matter of definite form; no electromagnetic force was in operation, and all was in darkness: *and the Spirit of God was hovering over the waters.*

The word translated "hovering" has the thought of rapid, energizing motion, transmitting energy to the cosmos. The Spirit's energy permeated the universe to make the gravitational and electromagnetic forces that operate on matter, and the formless earth was formed.

Then God said, *"Let there be light," and there was light* (v. 3). After imparting motion and form to the shapeless and lifeless watery matrix, He created light to replace the darkness. *And God saw that the light was good. And He separated light from darkness. God called the light "day" and the darkness He called "night." And there was evening, and there was morning – the first day.*

God divided the darkness into day and night. From the first day, there was established a set period of light and darkness, meaning the rotation of the earth on its axis caused a source of light on the earth even though the sun was not made until the fourth day (1:6). It was after separating the day and night that God completed His first day's work. This is true of each of the six days.

The Hebrew word for "day" is "yom," and it means a literal day of 24 hours unless the context makes it clear that the literal sense is not intended. When distinct limits are used as day and night, or are used in a series of days, the literal sense is always used. Both of these are present in these first verses of Genesis.

Moses was being very emphatic here because all the nations of his day believed in some form of evolution, taking in vast periods of time before life developed from chaos. The creation of visible light waves brings electromagnetic force into operation, completing the energizing of the cosmos.

The angels were created on day one, shortly after the creation of the physical universe, which was to be their sphere. According to Job 38:4-7, the angels were created before the foundations of the earth were laid. *Where were you when I laid the earth's foundation? Tell me if you understand. Who marked off its dimensions? Surely you know! On what were its footings set? Or who laid its cornerstone – while the morning stars sang together and all the angels shouted for joy?* The angels' purpose was to minister to the heirs of salvation. *Are not all angels ministering spirits sent to serve those who will inherit salvation?* (Heb 1:14).

Then God said, "Let there be an expanse between the waters to separate water from water." So God made the expanse and separated the water under the expanse from the water above it. And it was so. God called the expanse "sky" and there was evening, and there was morning – the second day (Gen 1:6-8). Some of the waters, in vapor form, were to be raised above the rotating earth to form a vapor canopy. The word for "expanse" refers to atmosphere. This canopy gave the earth its unique atmosphere. Later on, these waters above were condensed and fell to earth during the great flood.

And God said, "Let the water under the sky be gathered to one place, and let the dry ground appear." And it was so. God called the dry ground "land" and the gathered water he called "seas." And God saw that it was good (Gen 1:9-10). And now the dry land rises from the lower waters. This is what is referred to in Scripture as the foundation of the earth. *"Long ago you laid down the foundation of the earth, and made the heavens with your hands* (Psa 102:25). See also (Job 38:4; Zech 12:1; Isa 48:13).

Then God said, "Let the land produce vegetation: seed-bearing plants and trees on the land that bear fruit with seed in it, according to their various kinds." And it was so. The land produced vegetation: plants bearing seed according to their kinds and trees bearing fruit with seed in it according to their kinds. And God saw that it was good: and there was evening, and there was morning – the third day (Gen 1:11-13).

During this time God was producing a finished product, not developing a process that would take a period of time. The whole universe was fully developed and functioning. Trees were fully developed with fruit and full-grown plants with apparent age. The words "according to their kind" or its equivalent, occur ten times in this first chapter of Genesis. The fully developed universe with the producing of plants and animals and humans "according to their kind" clearly refutes the evolutionary theory that the universe evolved and that living things are interrelated by a common ancestry and descent. One "kind" cannot change into a different kind; apple trees cannot produce oranges; rose bushes cannot produce violets nor turn into violets, etc. It also refutes the theory that these "days" refer to long "ages" since many plants require insects for pollination and insects were not made until the sixth day.

In his love God was preparing a magnificent feast for his creatures to enjoy upon their arrival, unnumbered varieties of luscious fruits and plants bursting with flavor. There was also a plethora of sights, sounds, and tastes, and within these were seeds so they could reproduce themselves.

And God said, "Let there be lights in the expanse of sky to separate the day from the night, and let them serve as signs to mark the seasons and days and years, and let them be lights in the expanse of the sky to give light on the earth." And it was so.

God made two great lights – the greater light to govern the day and the lesser light to govern the night. He also made the stars. God set them in the expanse of the sky to give light on the earth, to govern the day and night, and to separate the light from the darkness, and God saw that it was good. There was evening, and there was morning – the fourth day (Gen 1:14-19).

The reason for the lights was to separate the day from the night, and the light was immediately visible. Certainly, God did not mean for the light to have to travel for millions or billions of years from distant stars to reach the earth. The entire universe was created fully developed from the first. The lights were created for the purpose of giving light to the earth, and they did so immediately.

The vast universe was filled with heavenly bodies of unlimited variety. Even with our mega computers, we cannot fathom the immensity of our seemingly unlimited universe. Even now it is filled with mysterious beauty, but before the fall it would have been beyond our comprehension. The Bible tells us that God *determines the number of stars and calls them all by name* (Psa 147:4).

The heavens declare the glory of God. The creation displays His craftsmanship. Everyone understands the language of creation that tells us of God's wisdom and power and love. This makes people accountable to God. *The heavens declare the glory of God. The skies proclaim the work of His hands. Day after day they pour forth speech; night after night they display knowledge. There is no speech or language where their voice is not heard. Their voice goes out into all the earth* . . . (Psa 19:1-4). *For since the creation of the world God's invisible qualities – his eternal power and divine nature – have been clearly seen, being understood by what has been made, so that men are without excuse* (Rom 1:20).

God said that the moon and sun were to serve as signs to distinguish seasons and days and years. The sun sets the length of days and the moon sets the length of months. The sun takes one day to circle the earth. The moon orbits the earth in about one month. Seasons are determined by the earth's tilt in relation to its revolution around the sun. The earth's tilt away from the sun causes less sunlight in the winter months; the summer months are caused by more sunlight because of the earth's tilt toward the sun. It takes the earth 365 days for its elliptical orbit around the sun –

one year. Sunlight and moonlight and starlight brought a new majestic beauty upon the earth, bathing it in celestial glory.

Then God said, *"Let the water teem with living creatures, and let the birds fly above the earth across the expanse of the sky." So God created the great creatures of the sea and every living and moving thing with which the water teems, according to their kind, and God saw that it was good. God blessed them and said, "Be fruitful and increase on the earth. And there was evening, and there was morning – the fifth day* (Gen 1:20-23).

The earth and air were now ready for life, and God would now remedy the earth being empty of inhabitants.

The waters suddenly swarmed with living creatures. A single drop of water can hold 500 million microscopic creatures. The "great creatures" in Hebrew is "tannim" or "dragons" and refers to large sea creatures, including dinosaurs. God arranged for winged creatures to be flying through the air making melody and the sea teemed with life before the creation of humans.

And God said, "Let the land produce living creatures according to their kinds: livestock, creatures that move along the ground, and wild animals, each according to its kind." And it was so. God made the wild animals according to their kinds, the livestock according to their kinds, and all the creatures that move along the ground according to their kind, and God saw that it was good (Gen 1:24-25).

Here we have the land animals created and described in categories based on their relation to man and his interests. "Livestock" refers to animals that could be used by man for work or as pets. "Creatures that move along the ground," refers to animals that crawl or creep close to the ground and includes insects, smaller reptiles, small mammals, and amphibians such as rabbits, moles, squirrels, etc. "Wild animals" include mammals like elephants and rhinos, lions, and large dinosaurs now extinct.

On the first part of day six, God fills the earth with land animals, reptiles, and insects. God was preparing for man's arrival. There was no sin and death. The animals were here for us to love and care for and they, in turn, would love and help us.

Then God said, "Let us make man in our image, in our likeness, and let them rule over the fish of the sea, over the birds of the air, over the livestock, over all the earth, and over all the creatures that move along the ground." God created man in his own image, in the image of God he created him; male and female he created them (25-27).

"Man" is the generic term for "mankind," both male and female; they were given dominion over the rest of creation. They would be unique from all the other creatures. They would be spiritual, like the angels, and also physical like the animals.

The "image of God" would include the ability to reason, moral awareness, the ability to know God in a personal way and worship Him. Mankind had the divine likeness and represented God. The word for "image" means "likeness," but not exactly.

Mankind was given dominion over the rest of creation. God is the Creator of all the earth. He created mankind to rule under him. He gave them dominion over the earth and commanded them to rule over every living creature. They were to glorify God. They were to do this by expressing his love and care as they ruled for him. Because he loves his creation, he wanted to share his rule with them. They were to have dominion and subdue the earth by sharing and reflecting his love.

God blessed them and said to them, "Be fruitful and increase in number; fill the earth and subdue it. Rule over the fish of the sea, and rule the birds of the air, and over every living creature that moves on the ground." Then God said, "I give you every seed-bearing plant on the face of the whole earth and every tree that has fruit with seed in it. They will be your food, and to all the beasts of the earth and all the birds in the air and all the living creatures that move on the ground – everything that has the breath of life in it – I give every green plant for food." And it was so. God saw all that he had made, and it was very good, and there was evening, and there was morning – the sixth day (Gen 1:28-31).

God appointed man as his steward over the earth. But they sinned and failed in this stewardship and that's why Hebrews 2:8 says, *But we have not yet seen all things put under their authority.* Instead of obeying God and fulfilling His command, they sinned and have not fulfilled their stewardship. However, this stewardship has not been changed and will be fulfilled in the new heaven and earth when the curse is lifted and Christ reigns. This is the purpose for which mankind was created in God's image. We have an eternal purpose to fellowship with God in ruling the universe for His glory.

God filled the earth with food for man and animals for when they spread out upon the earth. There were no deserts or uninhabitable areas. Man and animals were vegetarians and were given every green herb (plants and grasses) and every fruit tree.

Meat was not eaten before the fall. Nothing made by God was unworthy of him; no death, no suffering, or pain, no struggle for existence; nothing out of order; no disharmony at all because there was no sin. All evil comes from man's rebellion against God. At the end of the six days, God had filled the earth and heavens with beauty of all kinds. The sights, smells, tastes, and sounds were breathtaking. There were delicious vegetables, luscious fruits, nuts, seeds, and grains, and hidden within all was the marvelous treasure of seeds so they could reproduce themselves to provide a never-ending food supply. The fragrances of flowers and the sound of birds singing and cooing and the sight of animals playing and frolicking completed the picture.

Thus the heavens and earth were completed in all their vast array. By the seventh day God had finished the work he had been doing; so on the seventh day he rested from all his work. And God blessed the seventh day and made it holy, because on it he rested from all the work of creating that he had done (Gen 2:1-3).

Four times in this section it is made emphatic that God finished all his work and rested or ceased from his work of creating. God is not now creating but is sustaining his creation. The present processes of the universe have changed from creating to preserving; today energy cannot be created because God is no longer creating, and energy cannot be destroyed because he is now preserving his creation.

The creation account in Genesis chapters 1 and 2 do not contradict, as some try to claim, but rather complement each other. Chapter 2 adds details to man's creation, especially the making of Eve. It also gives the setting for man's fall.

This is the account of the heavens and the earth when they were created. When the Lord God made the earth and the heavens – and no shrub of the field had yet appeared on the earth and no plant of the field had yet sprung up. For the Lord God had not sent rain on the earth and there was no man to work the ground, but streams came up from the earth and watered the whole face of the ground (Gen 2:4-6).

This section begins with an introduction to man's creation. It describes the creation just prior to man's creation. At this point of creation, there were no shrubs or plants since there was no rainfall upon the earth and there was no man to cultivate the ground. God set up a system of water springs that watered the ground. This would last until the flood.

The Lord God formed the man of the dust of the ground and breathed into his nostrils the breath of life, and the man became a living being (Gen 2:7).

The basic chemical elements of the earth were used to make our physical bodies. God then energized the man's body with the breath of life. Here we have a very intimate picture of God forming man's body and then breathing directly into it. Man becomes a living being, which refers to his consciousness.

Now the Lord God planted a garden in the east, in Eden, and there he put the man he had formed and the Lord God made all kinds of trees to grow out of the ground – trees that were pleasing to the eye and good for food. In the middle of the garden were the tree of life and the tree of the knowledge of good and evil (2:8-9).

Man was created for God and knowing that man would fall, God planned, through Christ, *the exceeding riches of his grace through all the ages to come* (Eph 2:7). God prepares a special area, a perfect garden with beautiful trees bearing delicious fruit of every kind, for his home. It was called "Eden," which means "delight." It was located "East" of Adam's location to the west. The garden was paradise to the whole world.

Adam was the representative of all his descendants, and he would write the first chapter that would set the course of humanity and human history. They were already commanded to be fruitful and multiply to fill the earth with people. In the midst of the garden were the tree of life and the tree of the knowledge of good and evil – so called because evil would be known when man disobeyed God concerning it and good would be known if he obeyed.

A river watering the garden flowed from Eden; from there it was separated into four headwaters. The name of the first is the pishon; it winds through the entire land of Havilah, where there is gold (The gold of that land is good; aromatic resin and onyx are also there). The name of the second river is Gihon; It winds through the entire land of Cush. The name of the third river is Tigris. It runs along the east side of Asshur. And the fourth is the Euphrates (Gen 2:10-14).

These verses provide more information about the geography of Eden and the primeval water system. The lush Garden of Eden would require an abundance of water. Along with the springs, a water supply came from a river flowing through the garden area.

The Lord God took the man and put him in the Garden of Eden to work it and take care of it. And the Lord God commanded the man, "You are free to eat from any tree in the garden; but you must not eat from the tree of the knowledge of good and evil, for when you eat of it you will surely die" (Gen 2:15-17). Mankind was given dominion over the whole creation. The center of his rule would be a beautiful garden with a perfect world-wide environment. God created mankind for intimate fellowship and Genesis 3:8 tells us that the garden is where God would meet with them.

In every way, God showed his love and care for them. But the garden was about to become a testing area. Mankind was created for a relationship of love, but love must be chosen freely. It would require a morally responsible choice. This is why humans and angels were created with free will. Love, by its very nature, must be voluntary. It must be given freely. A mere robot cannot truly love its maker.

They could eat of every tree, with only one restraint. If mankind was to be morally responsible, he must be given a choice. With clear evidence of God's love all around them, trusting him should have been easy. Eating the forbidden fruit would give experimental knowledge of evil, and good would consist of obeying God's command. The result of disobedience would be death. God is the source of life, physically and spiritually. The result of sin was separation from the source of life. Mankind would die spiritually and begin to die physically.

And the Lord God said, "It is not good for man to be alone. I will make a helper suitable for him." Now the Lord God formed out of the ground all the beasts of the field and all the birds of the air. He brought them to the man to see what he would name them; and whatever Adam called each living creature, that was its name. And Adam gave names to all the livestock, the birds of the air and all the beasts of the field. But for Adam no suitable helper was found (Gen 2:18-20). The intent of 2:19 is to refer back to the creation of the animals in 1:24-25. Some of these animals were brought to Adam to be named. God brought them or directed them to come to Adam so they could be introduced to each other and Adam could name them. It was a sign of authority over those who were named (Dan 1:7).

God put the man in the center of his dominion and brought the animals to him to be named as the first act of dominion over them. God gave names to everything else to show that he is the supreme

Lord of everything else, but he had Adam name the animals as their lord under God as God shared his authority with mankind.

Because of Mankind's dominion over the animals, they fell when mankind sinned and fell. And it is why the curse of the fall will be lifted from the creation when redeemed mankind is liberated from the bondage of sin (Rom 8:18-20).

As the animals passed before Adam, probably in pairs, it was clear that they had mates but he had no one suitable for him. Of all God's creatures, only he was without a mate (Gen 2:20). For the first time, something was found that was not good (Gen 2:18). Adam was alone and God was preparing him psychologically for Eve.

So the Lord God caused the man to fall into a deep sleep; and while he was sleeping, he took one of the man's ribs and closed up the place with flesh. Then the Lord God made a woman from the rib he had taken out of the man, and he brought her to the man (Gen 2:21-22).

"Rib" is from the Hebrew word that means simply "side." God took from his side both flesh and bone. When Adam awoke from his deep sleep, God brought the woman he had made to him, symbolizing the giving away of the bride to the groom.

And Adam said, "This is now bone of my bones and flesh of my flesh: she shall be called woman; for she was taken out of man." For this reason a man will leave his father and mother and be united to his wife, and they will become one flesh (Gen 2:23-24).

Adam called her woman. Adam was taken from the earth – "adamah" – so his name was Adam or man. She was taken from the man – so he called her woman.

Then we are given God's intended purpose and the nature of marriage. At a marriageable age, a man and woman were to leave their parents and be united with each other and the two were to become one. Permanence of marriage was God's intention. He was created as the head of the relationship and was to be honored and obeyed, but she was the precious gem, to be loved and cherished. This was God's intent and still is. God loved them both equally and gave them to each other as an expression of his love for them.

Now the man and his wife were both naked, and they felt no shame (Gen 2:25). Guilt and shame came after the Fall; men and women were then sinners and they pass on their sin-nature to their children, so sexual organs are now objects of shame.

CHAPTER THREE
Man's Fall and the Promise of the Coming One

Perhaps the most vexing question confronting a thinking person is: If God is a loving God why is there suffering and cruelty, sorrow, and pain in the world? The answer from Scripture is that these came into the world through man's sin. The next question is: If God knew this would happen, why did he allow it? All the suffering and death in the world that God had created to be very good could have been avoided if God had not allowed sin into his perfect creation. This is true. But man was created to be a morally responsible being and this is only possible if he has the freedom to choose.

Now the serpent was craftier than any of the wild animals the Lord God had made. He said to the woman, "Did God really say, 'you must not eat from any tree in the garden'?" (3:1). The devil asked this question as though he had heard this and couldn't believe that God would deceive them in such a way. The serpent's body was taken over by Lucifer, who had recently led the Angels in a revolt against God. He would now tempt God's human creation.

Jesus would later, during his earthly ministry, refer to this event when he said the devil was *a murderer and a liar from the beginning* (John 8:44). He snuck into the garden like a thief, and Jesus said, *"The thief comes only to steal, kill, and destroy"* (John 10:10). Satan seeks to pervert God's truth at every opportunity.

The woman said to the serpent, "We may eat from the trees of the garden, but God did say, 'You must not eat fruit from the tree that is in the middle of the garden, and you must not touch it, or you will die.'" "You shall not surely die," the serpent said to the woman. "For God knows when you eat of it your eyes will be opened and you will be like God, knowing good and evil" (Gen 3:2-5).

Sin always begins by questioning God's word or his goodness. This explains the Deceiver's methods: To get us to assert our own will based upon doubt of God's word. This is the foundation of all sin, that God is not trustworthy. The bitter spring of sin is doubt of God's goodness.

With these words, Satan got to the heart of the union between God and man, God's trustworthiness. Satan went for the jugular vein. The Lord had literally given them the whole world as well as each other. The Tempter promised that if she disobeyed God, she would be like God, knowing good and evil. They would be just like God and could decide for themselves what is right and what is wrong.

And the woman saw that the fruit of the tree was good for food and pleasing to the eye, and also desirable for gaining wisdom. She took some and ate it. She also gave some to her husband, who was with her, and he ate it. Then the eyes of both of them were opened, and they realized they were naked; so they sewed fig leaves together and made coverings for themselves (3:6-7).

The woman now saw what the tempter wanted her to see. The forbidden fruit was no better for food or pleasant to the sight than all the other trees. But what mostly appealed to her was that it would make her wise. Proverbs 3:5-6 exhorts: *Trust in the Lord will all you heart and lean not on your own understanding; in all your ways acknowledge Him, and He will make your paths straight.* She leaned on her own understanding rather than the words of God. She only saw what Satan wanted her to see; then her own lusts took over and each step became easier, so she took and she ate. And she gave some to Adam and he ate.

The tempter had won. They had taken control of their own lives and they had made themselves their own masters, which is the very essence of sin. They, not God, would write the unwritten history of the human race. Their own individual wills had replaced the will of God.

Then the man and his wife heard the sound of the Lord God as he was walking in the garden in the cool of the day, and they hid from the Lord among the trees of the garden. But the Lord God called to Adam and said to him, "Where are you?" He answered, "I heard you in the garden, and I was afraid because I was naked; so I hid" (Gen 3:8-10).

What a change! Having disobeyed God and partaken of the forbidden fruit, everything changed. Now instead of looking forward to their daily time with God, they ran from him. The serpent promised them great gain – he said they would gain wisdom and become like God. Satan's words were a lie and led to their destruction. As John R. Rice would say, "All Satan's apples have worms!" Because of his lies, they now experienced guilt and shame as they realized their nakedness. They were created for fellowship with God but now they ran from Him!

They heard the Lord God walking in the garden. This was a theophany of the Word of God, the pre-incarnate Christ, who often appeared as the Angel of the Lord. Up until then, they had not been aware of their nakedness. But now their sin had made them self-conscious instead of God conscious. The divine command had been for them to multiply and fill the earth. But now they knew that the source of life had been polluted by their sin. This awareness of guilt centered on their procreative organs. When God asked Adam, "Where are you?" it was a question filled with pain and sorrow. God knew exactly where they were. He was really asking why they were hiding from him: what happened to the fellowship they had?

Though covered with fig leaves, Adam knew that he was still naked before God. His love for God had now turned to fear. The fear that God wanted was not the sense of being afraid. God sought "reverence," a fear of offending or disappointing him because he is worthy of love and honor. As God had said, the day they disobeyed they would die spiritually and then begin to die physically. The principle of physical death took over their bodies. Now everything they did was tainted with sin. God had filled the world with life, now they had brought in death. *Who told you that you were naked? Have you eaten from the tree that I commanded you not to eat from?" The man said, "The woman you put here with me – she gave me some fruit from the tree and I ate it."*

Then the Lord said to the woman, "What have you done?" The woman said, "The serpent deceived me, and I ate" (Gen 3:11-13).

God was looking for confession and repentance but Adam blames God and Eve. *"The woman YOU gave me."* His emphasis was on "YOU." His sin had caused him to take refuge in half-truths and evasion. Once upright and loving God and his wife, he now blames them both for all his problems. Sin had caused an immediate division between them. Distrust had entered into their once blessed union. She had brought him forbidden fruit and he blamed her instead of trying to protect her.

Their love was tainted. The beautiful relationship of marriage that God had instituted was now a fleeting shadow of what once was. The fall had infected the entire human race. They had fallen and it was devastating to their relationship with God and with each other. In addition to spiritual death, which is separation from God, physical death came into the world and passed on to the race through Adam, its head and representative. The principle of sin and death is inherited from birth.

The apostle Paul said, *Therefore, just as sin entered the world through one man, and death came through sin, and in this way death came to all men, because all sinned* (Rom 5:12). As the representative man, when Adam sinned, sin entered the world and spread to everyone, for in Adam we all sinned. Adam's sin nature was passed to all men and leads to the practice of sin. All creation was put under the curse and death spread to everyone: *Against its will all creation was subject to God's curse* (Rom 8:20). Life became a struggle filled with grief and suffering in the world.

So the Lord God said to the serpent, "Because you have done this, cursed are you above all the livestock and all the wild animals. You will crawl on your belly, and you will eat dust all the days of your life, and I will put enmity between you and the woman, and between her seed and your seed. He will crush your head, and you will strike his heel."

To the woman God said, "I will greatly increase your pain in childbearing; with pain you will give birth to children. Your desire will be to your husband, and he shall rule over you." To Adam he said, "Because you listened to your wife and ate from the tree, about which I commanded you, 'you must not eat of it,' cursed is the ground because of you; through painful toil you will eat of it all the days of your life. It will produce thorns and thistles for you and you will eat the plants of the field. By the sweat of your brow you will eat your food until you return to the ground since from it you were taken; for dust you are and to dust you will return" (Gen 3:14-19).

The serpent was to be a perpetual reminder to mankind of the instrument of the fall and Satan's final doom. It may have stood erect and glided on its tail, but now it would crawl on its belly as an object of revulsion. It would eat dust and consume its prey in the dust. The implication here is that all animals were brought under the curse, but the serpent was cursed above them as a reminder to mankind of their fall and of their need to be restored to fellowship with God. Then in the midst of the sin and shame, the Creator gave a prophecy and a promise that he would not allow his creation to fail in its intended purpose of an intimate relationship with himself.

It was the beginning of the gospel message, the promise of a coming Redeemer who would become man through the *Offspring of the woman* – a virgin birth not connected with his fallen parents, not under sin's dominion, and not tainted by the fall. The phrase the "Offspring of the woman" is unique and occurs nowhere else as generation was through the male. This prophecy foretells the conflict of the ages. The primary Offspring of the woman is the Lord Jesus Christ. The primary offspring of the serpent is Satan. The conflict would involve the children of the kingdom and the children of the wicked one.

This began with Cain and Abel: *Do not be like Cain who belonged to the evil one and murdered his brother. And why did he murder him? Because his own actions were evil and his brother's were righteous* (1 John 3:12). This battle will continue to the end of the age: *Then the dragon was enraged at the woman and went off to make war against the rest of her offspring – those who obey God's commandments and hold to the testimony of Jesus* (Rev 12:17).

In Matthew 13:37-40 Jesus referred to this conflict: *He answered, "The one who sowed the good seed is the Son of Man. The field is the world, and the good seed stands for the sons of the kingdom. The weeds are the people who belong to the evil one, and the enemy who sows them is the devil. The harvest is the end of the age, and the harvesters are the angels. As the weeds are pulled up and burned in the fire, so it will be at the end of the age."*

The children of the kingdom are those who trust in Christ: *You are all the children of God through faith in Christ Jesus* (Gal 3:26). The children of the serpent are those who reject Christ – *"You brood of snakes"* (Matt 13:34). *"Snakes! Sons of vipers! How will you escape the judgment of hell?"* (Matt 23:33). *"For you are the children of your father the devil"* (John 8:44). In this struggle the seed of the woman would strike the serpent's head with a fatal blow and destroy the works of the devil. *But the Son of God came to destroy the works of the devil* (1 John 3:8).

God has an eternal plan for this world. This very earth will be the scene of the cosmic war where evil will be defeated. The Coming One, the Seed of the woman, would be another Adam, to lift humanity that the first Adam had brought down in the fall. As the first Adam brought death, the Last Adam would bring life. The Coming One would crush the serpent's head with his heel, but in the process he would have to expose his heel to the serpent's deadly fangs. Satan would be utterly defeated at the cross, but it would cost the Son of God great suffering and death, and ultimately Jesus will crush Satan under the feet of his people. *The*

God of peace will soon crush Satan under your feet (Rom 16:20). But He would have to give his life as a ransom to buy his people out of the marketplace of sin.

The Last Adam will restore fallen mankind and his lost paradise with a new redeemed mankind and restored paradise and renewed creation. The scriptures tell us: *The first man, Adam, became a living being, the Last Adam, a life-giving spirit. What comes first is the natural body, and then the spiritual body comes later. The spiritual did not come first, but the natural, and after that the spiritual. The first man was of the dust of the earth, the second man from heaven. As was the earthly man, so are those who are of the earth; and as is the man from heaven, so also are those who are of heaven. And just as we have born the likeness of the earthly man, so shall we bear the likeness of the man from heaven* (1 Cor 15:45-47).

Here we see that Christ and Adam are the heads of two distinct creations. One is the old fallen creation "in Adam." The other is the new creation "in Christ." One is from the earth and is earthly, while the other is from heaven and is heavenly.

Out of the ruins of the old creation "in Adam," God would build his new creation "in Christ." *For as in Adam all die, so in Christ all will be made alive* (1 Cor 15:22).

The woman's sorrow and pain in childbirth will be greatly multiplied. Children from then on will be born under the curse. Their entrance into the world would be a time of struggle and pain that would be a constant reminder that we are all sinners (Gen 3:16).

In Genesis 3:17-19 the curse is pronounced upon Adam as the head of all mankind and his whole realm, the whole creation; the "ground," literally the "earth," is cursed. The basic elements of creation were brought under the curse of decay (death), the very "dust" out of which man was formed. The ground would now produce thorns, weeds, and poisonous plants. The ground must now be cultivated through hard work and struggle.

God would remove his hand and allow the creation to gradually move toward disorder and death. Man's whole environment was now under the curse, confronting him with the tragedy of sin and his inability to reverse his journey toward death and judgment.

He would now have to fill his time with labor just to live, helping to hinder his tendency toward sin. He was no longer in control of nature and at home with his environment. The creation was now in conflict with him. His dominion was now one of cruelty, pain, suffering, and hardship. The whole creation would now groan under the burden of sin. All creation was frustrated with pain and suffering.

The universe came under the universal law of decay and death. All things that were made are being unmade: aging, wearing out, and finally dying. Disappointment and futility dominate the cosmos. Adam and Eve were told by Satan that they would know "good and evil." They knew good because God created everything good, but now they knew evil because they had made everything evil. The original goodness had been lost. Now God says, *There is no one righteous, not even one; there is no one who understands, no one who seeks God. All have turned away. They have together become worthless; there is no one who does good, not even one; there is no fear of God* (Rom 3:10-12,18). They thought they would become wise but they became fools. They exchanged the truth of God for a lie (Rom 1:22,25).

Satan lied; they gained nothing and lost everything. *Their thinking became futile and their foolish hearts were darkened ... since they did not think it worthwhile to retain the knowledge of God, he gave them over to a depraved mind* (Rom 1:21, 28). They would return to dust physically and face judgment. The world that God had filled with life was now filled with death. Sin had brought a division between the man and woman and they had lost peace with themselves. In their hearts, minds, and souls, they had only trouble and fear. Satan became the *prince of this world* (John 12:31; 14:30); and the *god of this age* (mindset) (2 Cor 4:4). The whole world is under his control (1 John 5:19). And he is the *spirit working in the children of disobedience* (Eph 2:2). He is the tempter (Matt 4:3). He is a *liar and the father of lies* (John 8:44); the deceiver *who leads the whole world astray* (Rev 12:9).

The price of their sin is incalculable. It was like a virus that affected everything in the whole creation. Mankind was never meant to die, but *the wages of sin is death* (Rom 6:23). Sin broke our relationship with God. Mankind became alienated from each other and a slave to sin. Jesus said, *"Everyone who sins is a slave to sin"* (John 8:34). We cannot even imagine what that original creation must have looked like: no sin, no death, no pain, no struggle – now in ruins. *The heart is deceitful above all things* (Jer 17:9). As the head of the race, Adam brought the fall to the whole creation. *Sin entered the world through one man* (Rom 5:12). *For all have sinned and come short of the glory of God*

(Rom 3:23). Man is a sinner because he rejected God as the ground of his existence and in his own mind took the place of God as self-existent. Instead of exalting God as the center of his universe, mankind took that position for himself and made everything revolve around himself. He challenged God's selfhood with his own. For him, God's selfhood ends where his begins. In this mankind followed the downward path of Lucifer. This is sin in its undiluted essence. Yet because man is born a sinner, he is unaware that he is one. He thinks that making himself center stage in his life is normal and natural. He declares that the source of his selfhood lies in himself, as he ascends the throne of his own life and declares: "I am God of my own life."

Adam named his wife Eve, because she would become the mother of all the living (Gen 3:20). Along with the curse, God announced grace and mercy through the coming Redeemer, the beginning of the gospel message. Adam and Eve now believed God and trusted in His word. Adam revealed his faith by giving his wife, whom he called "woman," a new name: he named her Eve (meaning "Life"), because through her would come the Redeemer who gives life. His message would be: *"I am the resurrection and the life; he who believes in me will live"* (John 11:25).

For Adam and his wife the Lord God made coats of skins and clothed them (3:21). Because of their faith in the promise, God clothed them with coats of animal skins. God would have had to slay two animals, probably in front of them. They would have been horrified! This is where God would teach them the need for substitutionary animal sacrifice as a type of the promised Coming One who must eventually shed his own blood to pay the actual atonement, of which all the others would be but types.

And the Lord God said, "The man has now become like one of us, knowing good and evil. He must not be allowed to reach out his hand and take also from the tree of life, and eat, and live forever. So the Lord God banished him from the Garden of Eden to work the ground from which he was taken. After he drove out the man, he placed at the east side of the Garden of Eden Cherubim and a flaming sword flashing back and forth to guard the way to the tree of life (Gen 3:22-24).

Verse 22 refers to the brief council of the persons of the Triune God as in 1:26. There it was recorded their decision to create man and now their decision to expel them from the garden. Mankind was not allowed to partake of the tree of life in their fallen, sinful state. So God banished them from the garden and they were evicted from God's presence.

The Hebrew word for "banished" in the NIV is also used for "divorce." Sin had brought about a divorce between God and mankind. Cherubs are beings of the angelic order and they have to do with God's holiness. Later in Israel's history, God's presence, symbolized by the Shekinah glory, hovered over the mercy seat in the holy of holies (Exod 25:17-22; Heb 9:3-5), and above the mercy seat were two golden cherubim representations who watched as the high priest sprinkled the sacrificial blood of atonement over the mercy seat. God is represented as sitting between the cherubim (Psa 80:1; 99:1).

The cherubim with the flaming sword were positioned to make the point that there was no way back apart from the coming Redeemer.

From now on mankind would seek for harmony and mastery of his world and himself, but would never succeed because he had lost his relationship with his Creator. God did not create mankind to succeed on their own. Deep in the heart of man is the awareness that his or her world is not what it should be, that his or her life is not what it should be. There is now conflict and insecurity instead of peace and wholeness. Life has become a burden as Augustine summed up, "O Lord, you have made us for yourself and our hearts are restless until they rest in you."

Adam was created in God's image, but that image was marred and barely recognizable, and now the malignant result would be passed on to the whole human race. Later Adam would have a son in his own image; their first son Cain became the first murderer, a stark reminder that something was very wrong with the creation that God had created "very good."

The human beings that God created "good" followed Satan to ruin. The only remedy was a new creation brought about by a New Head of the race, another representative of the race, to undo the tragedy of the first Adam. This was God's plan from the beginning. He would send his own Son to be the last Adam to undo the works of the devil.

The harmony of the universe was destroyed. What God had created to reveal his glory was now in discourse. In the heavenly realm, sin had entered in a fall that had taken place among the angels prior to the fall of Adam and Eve. The chief of the fallen angels tempted mankind to fall and man's sin has devastated the earthly realm. 1 John 5:19 tells us, *The whole world is under control of the evil one.* However, the day is set that only God knows when it will be said, . . . *The whole world has now become the kingdom of our Lord and of his Christ, and he will reign forever and ever* (Rev 11:15). *Then I heard what sounded like a great multitude, like the roar of rushing waters, and like loud peals of thunder, shouting: Hallelujah! For our Lord God Almighty reigns* (Rev 19:6).

But until then the earth stands under the shadow of death. Life will be a gradual dying, and birth will be the beginning of death. Angels fell individually but humans fell corporately. "in Adam" we all fell. Because Adam was the head or organic representative, death established itself on all his descendants as well. The fall was universal: *therefore just as sin entered the world through one man, and death through sin, and in this way death came to all men, because all sinned* (Rom 5:12). The root sickness of the human soul shows the poisoned condition or the entire organism and is known as "original sin." *There is no one that does good, not even one* (Psa 14:3).

Every member of the human race, through their mere birth, is inescapably a member of a fallen and corrupted race. The universality of sin and the all-inclusiveness of the fall necessitate the new birth of each individual and the incarnation of Christ as Savior and Redeemer. *For all have sinned and come short of the glory of God* (Rom 3:23). This is why Jesus declared, *"I tell you the truth. No one can see the kingdom of God unless they are born again"* (John 3:3). When Adam rejected God's Lordship over himself, he also shattered his own God-given lordship over creation.

L.M. Lehman expressed the heart of God when he penned these words in his hymn: *The Love of God.*

The love of God is greater far than tongue or pen can ever tell; it goes beyond the highest star and reaches to the lowest hell.

The guilty pair bowed down with care. God gave his son to win; His erring child he reconciled and pardoned from his sin.

When hoary time shall pass away and earthly thrones and kingdoms fall. When men refuse to pray, and on rocks and hills and mountains call; God's love so sure, still shall endure, all measureless and strong; redeeming grace to Adam's race; the saints' and angels' song.

Could we with ink the oceans fill and were the skies of parchment made; were every stalk on earth a quill and every man a scribe by trade, to write the love of God above, would drain the ocean dry; nor could the scroll contain the whole, though stretch from sky to sky.

Refrain
Oh the love of God, how rich and pure! How measureless and strong. It shall forever more endure – the saints' and angels' song.

The first creation "in Adam" has been ruined through sin and has come under condemnation through spiritual death. But "the Offspring of the woman," the virgin-born Redeemer, would come as the Last Adam. All who would believe in Him would be born again into a new creation by means of their connection to Christ – *For as in Adam all die, even so in Christ shall all be made alive* (1 Cor 15:22).

Being "in Adam" is the same as being in Satan, who tempted Adam to fall. *The whole world is under the control of the evil one* (1 John 5:19). *Therefore if anyone is "in Christ," he is a new creation; the old has gone, the new has come* (2 Cor 5:17)!

The believer "in Christ" is removed from his old sphere, "in Adam," the sphere of death, and placed "in Christ," the new creation, the sphere of life. As the Last Adam, *God placed all things under his feet and appointed him to be Head over everything to the church* (Eph 1:22).

As Adam and Eve left the garden, they went with God's gracious promise of the Coming One, a Savior who would one day be born of a virgin. As time went on, Satan would be very active in this world. "Satan" means "adversary." He is also called the "devil," which means "slanderer." He blinds the minds of unbelievers so they will not respond to the gospel (2 Cor 4:4).

However, God is very active in the world as well. His ultimate purpose is to bring all creation under the Lordship of Jesus Christ. God is working out His purpose on the earth, moving history toward that day when the curse will be lifted and He will dwell with his people. Mankind lives in the midst of this warfare, but God is in control. God is building His kingdom out of the ruins of this old ruined creation under Satan. *For he has rescued us from the dominion of darkness and brought us into the kingdom of the Son He loves* (Col.1:13). He restrains evil and transforms it for good. *And we know that in all things God works for the good of those who love him, who have been called according to his purpose* (Rom 8:28).

Throughout the Old Testament, the Messiah's coming would be proclaimed in types and shadows and prophecies. The Old Testament law and rituals pointed to Christ. They were a shadow thrown on the wall of the Old Testament pointing to the Coming One, as he approached and cast his shadow. Paul, referring to these laws and rituals, wrote in Colossians 2:17: *These are a shadow of things to come. The reality, however, is found in Christ.* As a shadow represented a person, these rituals represented Christ's Person and work.

Adam and Eve were expelled from the garden, and as they left paradise became a barren wilderness. They left with the comfort of God's promise of a coming Savior. They did not fully understand all that was involved, but God would leave a trail of evidence pointing to Him. As they walked through the gate, the sky became dark and lightning crashed into the trees of the garden. As they looked back they saw the Cherubim with the drawn sword standing in front of the tree of life, blocking the way with the sword of judgment, awaiting the day that the Son of God would come and clear the way by taking that sword into His own heart. They also noticed the trees that the lightning had struck. Two had fallen across each other forming a gigantic cross.

CHAPTER FOUR
Credentials of the Coming One

Since the promise of the coming Redeemer in Genesis 3:5, God kept his promise before the people throughout the Old Testament. The Redeemer is so clearly identified that when He arrived He could not be mistaken, and He could say: *"These are the words I spoke to you while I was still with you, that all things must be fulfilled which were written in the law of Moses and by the prophets and in the Psalms concerning Me"* (Luke 24:44). And those who wrote about Him could say repeatedly, "This was done that the Scripture might be fulfilled."

The fact that Abel brought a blood sacrifice to God (Gen 4:4) illustrates that the practice of approaching God through substitutionary sacrifice had been established since God had clothed Adam and Eve in animal skins in Genesis 3:21. This was based on God's promise of a coming Redeemer whose shed blood would be the price of redemption. In that great prophecy, God revealed the age-long conflict of the two seeds and their descendants. The history of this conflict was to begin with the sad story of Adam and Eve's first two sons, Cain and Abel (Gen 4:2-4; Heb 9:22; 1 John 3:12). The revelation of the coming Messiah in the Old Testament is very clear. It presents His humanity, His deity, His work, and His glory.

After the worldwide flood, God revealed that the Messianic line would come through Shem by Noah's prophecy about 2,300 B.C., *Blessed be the Lord, the God of Shem* (Gen 9:26). Then as humanity's corruption became worse and worse, God began to prepare a new nation that would be used by God to bring forth the Messiah according to the flesh. His revelation had to be given and His message of salvation had to reach the world.

God's revelation to the world would begin with Abraham, a descendant of Shem. God revealed to him that He would establish a new nation through him and all the nations of the earth would be blessed through the coming Messiah. About 1900 B.C. the Lord said to Abraham, *"Leave your country, your people, and your father's household and go to a land I will show you. I will make you into a great nation and I will bless you; I will make your name great, and you will be a blessing. I will bless those who bless you, and whoever curses you I will curse;*

and all the people will be blessed through you" (Gen 12:1-3). This blessing passed to Abraham's son Isaac: *"To you and your descendants will I give these lands and I will confirm the oath I swore to your father Abraham. I will make your descendants as numerous as the stars in the sky and I will give them all these lands, and through your offspring, all the nations of the earth will be blessed"* (Gen 26:3-4).

Then through Isaac's son Jacob: *Jacob left Beersheba and set out for Huran. When he reached a certain place, he stopped for the night because the sun had set. Taking one of the stones there, he put it under his head and lay down to sleep. He had a dream in which he saw a stairway resting on the earth with its top reaching heaven, and the angels of God were ascending and descending on it.*

There above it stood the Lord, and He said: "I am the Lord, the God of your father Abraham and the God of Isaac. I will give you and your descendants the land on which you are lying . . .. all the peoples of the earth will be blessed through your offspring" (Gen 28:13-14). Jacob's name was later changed to Israel (Gen 32:28).

In Genesis 49:10, Jacob prophesied concerning his son Judah: *"The scepter will not depart from Judah, nor the ruler's staff from between his feet, until he comes to whom it belongs and the obedience of the nations is his."*

The Messianic line would continue through King David: *A shoot will come up from the stump* (family tree) *of Jesse; from its roots a branch shall bear fruit* (Isa 11:1). *He will reign upon the throne of David forever, of the increase of His government and peace there shall be no end. He will reign on David's throne and over his kingdom, establishing and upholding it with justice and righteousness from that time on and forever. The zeal of the Almighty will accomplish this* (Isa 9:6-7).

SALVATION BY FAITH

Abraham believed the Lord and He credited it to him as righteousness (Gen 15:6). Abraham believed God concerning the promised Redeemer. Concerning this Jesus said, *"Your father Abraham rejoiced at the thought of seeing my day and saw it and was glad"* (John 8:56).

And Paul wrote, *Consider Abraham, he believed God, and it was credited to him as righteousness. The Scripture foresaw that God would justify the Gentiles by faith and announced the gospel in advance to Abraham: "all nations will be blessed through you. So those who have faith are blessed along with Abraham, the man of faith"* (Gal 3:6-9). *Brothers, let me take an example from everyday life. Just as no one can set aside or add to a human covenant that had been established, so it is in this case. The promises were spoken to Abraham and his seed. The Scripture does not say "and to seeds," meaning many people, but "to your seed," meaning one person, who is Christ. What I mean is this: the law introduced 430 years later, does not set aside the covenant previously established by God and thus do away with the promise. For if the inheritance depends on the law then it no longer depends on a promise; but God in His grace gave it to Abraham through a promise* (Gal 3:15-18).

In Romans 4 Paul develops his argument that justification is through faith alone. The new covenant was a continuation of the covenant with Abraham. This is why Abraham is the father of all those who believe in Christ. *So those who have faith are blessed along with Abraham, the man of faith* (Gal 3:9).

What does the Scripture say? "Abraham believed God and it was credited to him as righteousness." Now when a man works, his wages are not credited to him as a gift, but as an obligation. However, to the man who does not work but trusts God who justifies the wicked; his faith is credited as righteousness. David says the same thing when he speaks of the blessedness of the man to whom God credits righteousness apart from works: blessed are they whose transgressions are forgiven; whose sins are covered. Blessed is the man whose sins are covered. Blessed is the man whose sin the Lord will not count against him (Rom 4:3-10).

Although the work of salvation would not be accomplished until the actual crucifixion of the Messiah, people before this could share in the benefits of His work on the cross, by a faith that looked forward to Him. They *are justified freely by His grace through the redemption that came by Christ Jesus. God presented Him as a sacrifice of atonement, through faith in His blood. He did this to demonstrate His justice, because of His forbearance He had left the sins committed beforehand unpunished – He did it to demonstrate His justice at the present time, so as to be just and the one who justifies those who have faith in Jesus* (Rom 3:24-26).

Here Paul explains that the work of Jesus Christ on the cross reaches forward as well as backward. Those in the Old Testament were saved by a faith that looked forward to the cross just as we today look backward to the cross. Jesus' actual sacrifice on the cross demonstrated that God was not unrighteous when He passed over the sins of Old Testament believers.

The effects of His work were already present in that they were saved, so to speak, on credit, through the types, sacrifices, and promises that pointed to Him as the *Lamb slain from the foundation of the world*. The "credit tab" or "bill" would be picked up later on the cross – in actual human history. Infinite love meeting human need.

The law was added alongside of, not in place of, the covenant of grace to show the sinner that he cannot keep the law and must depend on grace through the coming one. *What then was the purpose of the law? It was added because of transgressions until the One the promise referred to had come . . . so the law was put in charge that we might be justified by faith* (Gal 3:19, 24).

Therefore no one will be declared righteous in His sight by observing the law; rather through the law we become conscious of sin (Rom 3:20). The purpose of the law was to show us our need of a Savior.

God chose Abraham for the purpose of establishing an elect nation. They would be a chosen people. *O descendants of Israel His servant, O sons of Jacob, His chosen ones* (1 Chron 16:13). *He has revealed His word to Jacob, His laws and decrees to Israel. He has done this for no other nation; they do not know His laws* (Psa 147:19-20). This is why Abraham was called. God was going to use him as a means of bringing salvation to all the nations. Israel was called to be a separate people to be used as a means to this end. But they failed. Instead of seeking to bring the truth to Gentiles, they thought they were too good to associate with them because they had the law even though they themselves were unable to keep it. *Is God the God of the Jews only? Is he not the God of the Gentiles too? Yes, of Gentiles too* (Rom 3:29).

God would use Israel as an example of the horrors of sin and the marvels of redemption. In Israel both sin and redemption were brought to a head. Israel's sin culminated in the rejection of Christ (Matt 23:25-28,32-39), and the destruction of Jerusalem and the temple. But not all Israel rejected Christ. The disciples and the early church were made up of Jews. Israel's blessing was the privilege of spreading the gospel to the whole world as prophesied in the Old Testament (Isa 42:6; 49:6) and referred to in the New Testament: *For this is what the Lord commanded us:*

"I have made you a light for the Gentiles, that you may bring salvation to the ends of the earth" (Acts 13:47).

Jesus said to them, "Go into all the world and preach the good news to all creation" (Mark 16:15). *"And this gospel of the kingdom will be preached in the whole world as a testimony to all nations"* (Matt 24:14).

God is not done with Israel. There are Messianic Jews today and Israel will be instrumental in proclaiming the gospel during the great tribulation period.

Christ is the theme of the Old Testament as He Himself said: *"You diligently study the Scriptures because you think by them you possess eternal life. These are the Scriptures that testify of me"* (John 5:39). *He said to them, "How foolish you are and slow of heart to believe all that the prophets have spoken! Did not the Christ have to suffer these things then enter His glory? And beginning with Moses and all the prophets, he explained to them what was said in all the Scriptures concerning Himself. He told them, "This is what is written: 'that Christ will suffer and rise from the dead on the third day'"* (Luke 24:44-46).

And Paul adds: *I am saying nothing beyond what the prophets and Moses said would happen – that Christ would suffer and, as the first to rise from the dead, would proclaim light to His own people and to the Gentiles* (Acts 26:22-23). Christ is the center of salvation in both the Old and New Testament. The Old Testament anticipates His coming. Abraham is the father of all believers. Before the law or any rites or ritual, he was "justified by faith."

It was not through the law that Abraham and his offspring received the promise that he would be the heir of the world, but through the righteousness that comes by faith (Rom 4:13). As Jesus said in John 8:56, *"Abraham saw my day and was glad."* God gave the law to Moses four hundred years later to show humanity their need for the coming Savior. *So the law was put in charge to lead us to Christ that we might be justified by faith* (Gal 3:24). So Christ is the one who was looked forward to in both the Abrahamic covenant and the Mosaic covenant.

The Old Testament worship found its meaning in Jesus Christ. The priesthood, the vessels and garments, the feasts, the Sabbaths, and the sacrificial offerings all pointed to Him and his work on the cross. The moral law, and our inability to keep it show the necessity of His saving work. He must come, otherwise all the types and symbols and prophecies have no meaning.

It was His glory Isaiah saw when he saw the throne of the Lord of hosts. *I saw the Lord seated on a throne, high and exalted* (Isa 6:1-3). *Isaiah said this because he saw Jesus' glory and spoke about Him* (John 12:41). The Tabernacle represented Him: As God incarnate He "tabernacled" (dwelt) among us (John 1:14). He represents the table of showbread or bread of life (John 6:44). He is the lampstand or light of the world (John 8:12). He is its offering (John 1:29; 6:53-57; Heb 10:14). He is the sacrifice and the Priest who offers up the sacrifice (Heb 7:27).

CHAPTER FIVE
Types of His suffering and death – the offering up of Isaac
(Genesis Chapter 22)

One day God tested Abraham when his son Isaac was about twenty-five years old. He was told to go to the region of Moriah and offer his son as a burnt offering on one of the mountains God would lead him to. He would have been stunned and confused because all of God promises were wrapped up in Isaac! Because of his advanced age, Abraham rode his donkey and when he had cut enough wood for his offering, he set out with Isaac and two servants for the mountains of Moriah. The trip took two full days and part of a third day, a distance of about fifty miles. Why would God direct him to this spot at such a distance? This was to become the site of Jerusalem where the temple would be built (2 Chron 3:1). This is where Israel's later sacrifices would be offered that pointed to the Coming One's sacrifice. They would point to the very spot where He would offer up the Great Sacrifice.

When Abraham saw the place from a distance, he got off his donkey and left it with his two servants and he put the wood on Isaac's back. The two of them walked on alone. Abraham told his servants that they were going on alone to worship and that they would both return. Abraham knew that all God's promises would come through Isaac, so he believed that God would raise Isaac from the dead.

Abraham's faith had been tested and proved once before concerning life from the dead (Gen 17:19) when God promised him and Sarah a son when Abraham was a hundred years old and Sarah was ninety years old. As we are told in Romans 4:19-21: *Without weakening in his faith, he faced the fact that his body was as good as dead – since he was about a hundred years old – and Sarah's womb was also dead. Yet he did not waver through unbelief regarding the promise of God but was strengthened in his faith and gave glory to God, being fully persuaded that God had power to do what He had promised.*

As Abraham and Isaac walked on, Isaac was puzzled about something. He said to Abraham, *"Father, the fire and the wood are here, but where is the lamb for the burnt offering?"* (Gen 22:7). As Abraham was tying Isaac to the altar, Isaac would have known the truth: that he was the sacrifice. But Isaac, who could have easily overpowered and escaped from his aged father, did not resist because he trusted his father and he trusted God.

Abraham said, "God himself will provide the lamb for the burnt offering, my son" (Gen 22:8). As Abraham lifted the knife to slay his son, the Angel of the Lord called to him telling him not to slay Isaac, *"For now I know that you fear God, because you have not withheld from me your son, your only son"* (Gen 22:12).

Many times in the Old Testament, the invisible God takes the form of the Angel of the Lord. This is made obvious by the description of this Being. Here He says that Abraham had not withheld Isaac from "Me." He is claiming to be the Lord Himself! In the Old Testament, the Second Person of the Trinity takes the form of an Angel to reveal the invisible God, while in the New Testament He became incarnate as a man to reveal himself to men. We cannot grasp God in His infinite essence. But in the FORM of an angel in the Old Testament and by His actually taking on humanity in Jesus Christ in the New Testament, we can grasp God in human language.

Here was the very One who would come through the "seed of Abraham" to bless the whole world. Then Abraham saw a ram caught in a thicket by his horns (Gen 22:13). God had promised to provide a lamb, but that day He provided a ram.

The true meaning must await the True Lamb of God. Another Lamb had been waiting from the foundation of the world of which the ram slain was but a foreshadow.

Years later in the same area, another Son, through whom the whole world would be blessed, would be led like a lamb to the slaughter (Isa 53:7). He, too, would carry the wood of the vertical cross-beam on His shoulder, as Isaac had carried the wood for the sacrifice, but He would not be spared.

Abraham believed that God would raise Isaac from the dead after he had offered him as a sacrifice. As the Book of Hebrew says: *By faith Abraham, when God tested him, offered Isaac as a sacrifice. He who had received the promises was about to sacrifice his one and only son, even though God had said to him, "It is through Isaac that your offspring will be reckoned." Abraham reasoned that God could raise the dead; and figuratively speaking, he did receive Isaac back from the dead* (Heb 11:17-19). Figuratively, Isaac was raised from the dead, pointing to the resurrection of the coming Redeemer after He offered Himself For the sin of the whole world.

In Genesis 22:14 Abraham named the place *God will provide.* To the day that Moses wrote this, it had been a common saying, *In the mount of the Lord it shall be seen,* a prophecy that in a coming day God would provide His Lamb on Mount Calvary for man's sin.

Mount Moriah is a ridge that travels through Jerusalem. Solomon's temple was built on one end on the southeast corner of the city. Part of the mountain was gouged and cut like a face of a skull looking down on the city. This was Golgotha or Calvary, where Jesus the Christ was crucified outside the gate near the city. Hebrews 13:12 tells us: *And so Jesus also suffered outside the city gate to make the people holy through His own blood.*

Abraham evidently understood the type of this event. Jesus said, *"Abraham, your father rejoiced at the thought of seeing my day, and he saw it and was glad"* (John 8:56). Isaac on Mount Moriah carrying the wood on his shoulder was a vivid picture of Christ carrying His cross to Calvary. Abraham looked forward to the Messiah's coming to fulfill the promises God made to him. As Isaac could have escaped, Jesus went willingly to the cross. Jesus said, *"The reason my Father loves me is that I lay down my life – only to take it up again. No one takes it from me, but I lay it down of my own accord. I have the authority to take it up again. This command I receive from my Father"* (John 10:17-18).

THE PASSOVER

The Passover event is found in Exodus 12:12-14. The children of Israel were to take a lamb without blemish and kill it at dusk and smear some of the blood on the doorposts at the entrance to their homes. *"On that same night I will pass through Egypt and strike down the firstborn . . . and I bring judgment on all the gods of Egypt. I am the Lord. The blood will be a sign for you on the houses where you are; and when I see the blood, I will pass over you. No destructive plague will touch you when I strike Egypt."* The essential truth of Passover was the slain lamb without blemish, which pointed to the Lamb of God whose precious blood was a propitiation (appeasement) for sin. When God sees the blood of His Lamb of God upon the hearts of His people through faith, His judgment for sin will "pass over" the believer.

THE PASSOVER LAMB
Exodus 12:3-13, 21-23

On the tenth day of the month of Nisan, each household was to choose a lamb without blemish. They were to separate it from the herd until the evening of the fourteenth day to observe it for flaws. They were then to kill it and sprinkle the blood on the doorpost and roast it. They were to eat the lamb with unleavened (without yeast) bread and bitter herbs. All leftovers were to be burned.

"Without blemish" pictures the perfection of Christ (1 Pet 1:19). Separating the lamb for observation from the tenth day to the fourteenth day pictures Christ entering Jerusalem four days before the Passover. After putting blood on the doorposts, they were to eat the lamb. By eating the lamb, they were identifying with the slain lamb by assimilating it. They were to eat the lamb with unleavened bread during the seven days after their flight from Egypt. Later on, the Passover observance included the seven days of unleavened bread. Just as the lamb pictures Christ as the great substitute for our sins, the bread points to Him as the Bread of Life, our spiritual food. Leaven is symbolic of corruption. But Christ was absolutely pure, holy, and undefiled, and to typify Christ the bread must be pure, without leaven (1 Cor 5:7).

THE MOSAIC SACRIFICE

In the temple God's throne rested upon the law, which had been broken by man. Thus, the throne of God was a throne of judgment. When the blood was applied to the broken law, God's throne of judgment became a throne of mercy. "Made atonement" (NIV), "propitiate" (KJV) means "mercy seated" God. The blood atonement mercy-seated God changing God's throne of judgment into a throne of mercy. Atonement, in pagan religions, refers to what the sinner could do to appease the offended deity. It was bribing God with some offering. But in the Biblical concept, it is God who takes the initiative. Christ was the SACRIFICE offered as well as the high priest who offered it up: *He offered Himself* (Heb 7:27). The gift was pleasing to the Lord because it displays His own glory in that He sacrificed His own life for the creatures of His love. This changed the whole nature of salvation. Amazingly, God is revealed as both the subject and the object of atonement or propitiation.

His wrath is removed because He did something, not us. His love would not let His beloved go, even though they were sinners. He chose us before we chose Him. *This is love, not that we loved God, but that He loved us, and sent His Son as an atoning sacrifice for our sins* (1 John 4:10). Atonement in the Old Testament simply meant "to cover." Animal blood only covered from God's view the sins of the people and held back judgment. In the ultimate sense, it only covered "on credit" until Christ could pick up the credit tabs and actually pay the bill in full, by offering up the perfect sacrifice on Calvary (Heb 9:25-26).

Eating the lamb and feeding on the showbread in the Old Covenant represented feeding on Christ: Christ "for us" must become Christ "in us." Christ must be appropriated to become Christ in us by faith. This is what the Lord meant when He said, *"Unless you eat the flesh of the Son of Man and drink His blood, you have no life in you. Whoever eats my flesh and drinks my blood has eternal life, and I will raise him up at the last day . . . The one who feeds on me will live because of Me"* (John. 6:53-57). This feeding is done by faith: not by eating a wafer or a piece of bread!

ISAIAH 7:14

God promised Eve that the Messiah would be of the Offspring of the woman. This was fulfilled in Jesus Christ, who was born of a virgin: *Therefore the Lord Himself shall give you a sign; a virgin shall conceive and bear a son and call his name Immanuel* (Isa 7:14). The Jewish Rabbis say that this refers to Hezekiah and that Matthew is wrong in applying it to the Messiah in Matthew 1:23. They say that the Hebrew word "Almah" does not refer to a virgin but rather to a young woman of marriageable age, not necessarily to a virgin.

Isaiah was written seven hundred and forty years before Jesus was born. The context of Isaiah 7:14 is that King Ahaz was the king of Judah and was under attack by the combined armies of Syria and Israel. Fearful of defeat, Ahaz decided to ask the aid of Assyria to save Judah's Davidic throne from being lost. Ahab realized that the cost of Assyria's help would be Judah's independence, but he felt he had no choice.

God sent the prophet Isaiah to Ahaz, who was a descendant of King David, with the message that he did not need Assyria's aid to save the Davidic line because it could not depart from Judah until Shiloh (Messiah) would come. God told Ahaz through Isaiah to ask for a sign so God could prove that He would enable Ahaz to win against his foes but Ahaz refused. He said, *"I will not ask, neither will I tempt the Lord"* (Isa 7:11-14). God said in effect, "If you will not ask for a sign, I will repeat the prophecy given to Eve and to Jacob. A virgin shall conceive and bear a son and call his name Immanuel and the scepter shall not depart until He comes" (Gen 49:10).

The Davidic line (the scepter) would not depart until Shiloh (Messiah) comes. They would know when the Davidic line would end: when the son of a virgin was born. Thus the Messiah would be the last king of the Davidic line. After Jesus' death, Jerusalem was destroyed and the Davidic line ended. Christ will take His rightful throne at His second coming as the King of Israel and of the world.

The "Offspring of the woman" and the Hebrew word "Almah" clearly imply a virgin birth to indicate the nature of the One who is to "crush" the serpent's head and who would be called Immanuel, "God with us." Of Jesus becoming incarnate as man, Isaiah tells us in 9:6-7: *For unto us a child is born, unto us a son is given: and the government shall be upon His shoulders; and His name shall be called Wonderful Counselor, Mighty God, Everlasting Father, Prince of Peace. Of the increase of His government and peace, there will be no end. He will reign on David's throne and over His kingdom, establishing and upholding it with justice and righteousness from that time on and forever. The zeal of the Lord will accomplish this.*

The word "Almah" occurs in six other places in the Old Testament (Gen 24:43; Exod 2:8; Song of Sol 1:3; 6:8; Psa 68:25; Prov 30:19), and each time it means virgin. The Septuagint, the Old Testament translation of the Hebrew into the Greek by the Jews themselves around 375 B.C., translated "Almah" as "Parthenos," the strongest Greek word for virgin. This version was used by the early Christians to prove to the Jews from their own Greek translation of the Old Testament that "Almah," translated "Parthenos," was a virgin in the strongest sense of the word. The virgin birth would be a wholly unique event in history.

ISAIAH 53

Looking down the centuries of time, Isaiah wrote this prophecy seven hundred years before Jesus' birth in Bethlehem: *Who has believed our message and to whom has the arm of the Lord been revealed? He grew up before Him as a tender shoot, and like a root out of dry ground. He had no beauty or majesty to attract us to Him, nothing in His appearance that we should desire Him* (1-2). The Messiah would rise as a tender plant, from lowly beginnings and littleness. The Messiah was thought (not from scriptures, but from popular expectations, by confusing His first coming with His second coming) to come with great fanfare and pomp and spectacle, but, rather, He was a poor carpenter. Born into a family very much like dry ground, out of which nothing green or great could grow. And He came from an insignificant town; in reality He was the root of David but did not appear so. *He is despised and rejected by men, a man of sorrows, and familiar with suffering. Like one from whom people hid their faces. He was despised, and we esteemed Him not* (v. 1).

It was common in ancient Israel to consider such sufferings as a sign of God's displeasure. Jesus' sufferings meant nothing to them and they looked the other way, having no concern for him. *Surely He took our infirmities and carried our sorrows, yet we considered Him stricken by God, smitten and afflicted. But was pierced for our transgressions, He was crushed for our iniquities, the punishment that brought us peace was upon Him, and by His wounds we are healed. We all, like sheep, have gone astray, each of us has turned to their own way; and the Lord has laid on Him the iniquity of us all* (4-6).

Jesus was suffering as God's sacrificial lamb for the sins of the whole world. He endured in our place the judgment that our sins deserve and mercy-seated God, that is, Jesus, turned God's throne of judgment into a throne of mercy and grace. God deals with us in grace. That is, He gives us the opposite of what we deserve. On the cross God dealt with Jesus as though he was the sinner and He treats the believing sinner as though he was His Son. Thus bringing about atonement, that is, at-one-ment, and thus ending the warfare and bringing about peace with God. Jesus bore "our sins" and was pierced for "our transgressions," and He was crushed for "our iniquities." This represents God's view.

Those who were observing His sufferings, however, looked upon them as judgment for His own sins and mocked Him. *He was oppressed and afflicted, yet he did not open his mouth; He was led like a lamb to the slaughter, and as a sheep before her shearers was silent, so he did not open his mouth. By oppression and judgment He was taken away. And who can speak of his descendants? For he was cut off from the land of the living; for the transgression of my people He was stricken* (7-8).

Jesus did not try to defend Himself from the false charges against Him. With no complaint, He voluntarily gave Himself over to be beaten, mocked, and crucified. His silence amazed Pilate, who could not understand how He could not plead His own defense when facing such a torturous and agonizing death. He was hurried from one place of judgment to another until pronounced guilty and crucified. *"He was assigned a grave with the wicked* and with the rich in His death, though He had done no violence, nor was any deceit in His mouth" (v. 9). Jesus was crucified between two criminals but then was placed in a rich man's tomb (Joseph of Arimathea). *Yet it was the Lord's will to crush Him and cause Him to suffer, and though the Lord will make a guilt offering, He will see His offspring and prolong His days, and the will of the Lord will prosper His hand* (v. 10).

It was not what man did to Him that made atonement and reconciliation but what He suffered at the hand of God, which led Him to cry out, *"My God, My God, why have you forsaken Me?"* He was forsaken that we might find acceptance. In His omniscience (all knowing) God knew who would believe, and God would raise Him from the dead (prolong His days) and make Him head of the new creation, comprised of all those who would trust in Him. *After the suffering of His soul, He would see the light of life and be satisfied. By His knowledge my righteous servant shall justify many and He will bear their iniquities. Therefore I will give Him a portion among the great, and He will divide the spoils with the strong, because He poured out His life unto death, and was numbered with the transgressors* (11-12).

The Messiah's sufferings were birth pangs. He travailed in His soul that many would be born to Him. "By His knowledge" has the meaning of "BY knowledge OF Him" shall My Righteous Servant justify many. Verse 12 pictures a conquering hero dividing the spoils with His army. He will greatly reward those who serve Him.

PSALM 22

There are two parts to this Psalm. Verses 1-21 cover the Messiah's suffering and verses 22-31 refer to His entering His glory. The first verses refer to His first coming: the second part refers to His Second Coming.

My God, My God, why have you forsaken me? Why are you so far from me, so far from the words of my groaning? O my God, I cry out by day, but you do not answer, by night and am not silent. Yet you are enthroned as the Holy One, you are the praise of Israel. In you our fathers put their trust; they trusted and you delivered them. They cried to you and were saved; in you they trusted and were not disappointed (1-5).

This is given from the point of view of the sufferer. Notice the contrast of helping others but not helping the sufferer here. They cried out and God answered, but when Jesus cried out, God is silent.

I am a worm, and not a man, scorned by men and despised by the people. All who see me mock me; they hurl insults, shaking their heads: He trusts in the Lord; Let the Lord rescue him. Let Him deliver him, since he delights in him (6-8)

In verse 16, *but I am a worm,* the emphasis is on "I" in contrast to the others whose prayers were heard by God. In verse 7, they mock me. In verse 8 His very trust in God was used to mock Him.

Lions tearing their prey open their mouth wide against me (12-13). The fierceness and aggressiveness of his persecutors is likened to that of wild bulls. Their mocking and shouting were like roaring lions.

I am poured out like water, and all my bones are out of joint. My heart is turned to wax; it has melted away in me. My strength is dried up like a potsherd, and my tongue sticks to the roof of my mouth; you lay me in the dust of death. Dogs have surrounded me; a band of evil men has encircled me, they have pierced my hands and feet. I can count all my bones; people stare and gloat over me. They divide my garments among them and cast lots for my clothing (14-18).

In verses 14-15 "poured out like water . . . heart like wax . . . strength is dried up" describe desperate exhaustion. "Tongue sticks to the roof of my mouth" describes the agonizing thirst during crucifixion. He is like a broken piece of pottery without any moisture, causing his tongue to stick to the roof of his mouth. Verse 14 describes all his bones being moved "out of joint" from the cross being lifted up, with the victim nailed to it, and then dropped into the stone socket, jarring every bone out of joint.

Verses 16-18 describe the piercing of His hands and feet as the victim is nailed to the cross. When David wrote this Psalm, crucifixion was unknown. The Phoenicians invented it and, five hundred years later, Rome perfected it.

Those standing around His cross are described as "dogs," these are not the tamed, loveable dogs we are accustomed to in the western world, but wild vicious dogs of the east, which ran in packs looking for food. Verse 18 tells of the soldiers casting lots for His garments.

But You, O Lord, be not far off; O my strength, come quickly to help me. Deliver my life from the sword, my precious life from the power of the dogs. Rescue me from the mouth of the lion; save me from the horns of the wild oxen (19-21).

CHAPTER SIX
The Angel of the Lord

No one has ever seen God, but God the One and Only, Who is at the Father's side, has made Him known (John 1:18). Here we are told that no one has seen God in His unveiled essence at any time. But God, veiled as the Angel of the Lord in the Old Testament and as incarnate (as Man) in the Person of Jesus Christ in the New Testament, has been seen by people. John 1:1 says, *In the beginning was the Word and the Word was with God and the Word was God.* The Greek term for "Word" is "Logos," and it means "manifestation" or "revelation." Jesus makes God known to His creation.

In the beginning, the Word was already there. He created all things for a specific reason, and that reason was so that He could make God known to His creation. He became flesh to show us the Father and redeem us back to God. This is why Jesus said, *"He that has seen me has seen the Father"* (John 14:9). What is the Father like? He is exactly like Jesus!

Throughout the Old Testament, we have this self-revelation of the Son of God: the "Angel of the Lord" (Gen 16:7; Isa 63:9; Exod 23:20-21). The word "angel" means "messenger." In the New Testament, Christ is called "Apostle," which also means "messenger" (Heb 3:1). The "Angel of the Lord" distinguishes this Personage from other mere angels, as is obvious from His descriptions.

In Genesis 16 Sarai, Abraham's wife, and Hagar, her Egyptian maidservant, have a falling out and Hagar runs away. The Angel of the Lord finds her by a fountain of water and tells her to return to Sarai and be submissive to her. Then in verse 13 we are told that Hagar *gave this name to the One who spoke to her: "You are the God who sees me." For she said, "I have now seen the One who sees me."*

So we soon see that this was no ordinary Angel; it is an appearance of God in angelic form and we are told that it has always been the pre-incarnate Christ who has always revealed the invisible God in the Old Testament, and incarnate as man in the New Testament. In Genesis 18 Abraham was visited by three men, but we are told in ten verses that One of them was the Lord! (1, 13, 17, 20, 26, 27, 30, 31, 32, 33). In Genesis 22 Abraham was told by

God to offer up Isaac. In verse 12, the Angel of the Lord stopped him: *"Do not lay a hand upon the boy. Do not do anything to him. Now I know that you fear God, because you have not withheld from me your son, your only son."* The Angel of the Lord identified himself as God.

In verse 15, *The Angel of the Lord called to Abraham from heaven a second time.* In verse 16 He says, "I *swear by Myself*," and He goes on to confirm His covenant with Abraham. In Genesis 32:24-30 Jacob wrestles with the Angel of the Lord. After the struggle is over and the Angel blesses him, he is told in verse 28, *"Your name will no longer be Jacob, but Israel, because you have struggled with God . . . .* And Jacob says in verse 30, "I *saw God face to face, and yet my life was spared."*

In Exodus 3:2 God speaks to Moses as the Angel of the Lord from within the burning bush. He says, *"Moses! Moses!"* And *Moses said, "Here am I." "Do not come any closer," God said. "Take off your sandals for the place where you are standing is holy ground."* Then He said, *"I am the God of your father, the God of Abraham, the God of Isaac and the God of Jacob." At this Moses hid his face, because he was afraid to look at God* (4-6).

Then Moses was sent to Egypt to deliver his people from bondage. Then in verse 13, *Moses said to God, "Suppose I go to the Israelites, and say to them, 'The God of your fathers has sent me to you,' and they ask me, 'What is his name?' Then what shall I tell them?"* In verse 14 *God said to Moses, "I Am Who I Am."* In verses 15 and 16, the Angel of the Lord Goes on to say that He is the God of Abraham, Isaac, and Jacob.

Joshua 15:13 has a man standing in front of Joshua with a drawn sword as Joshua nears Jericho. Joshua goes up to Him and asks *"Are you for us or for our enemies?* The man answers: *"Neither, but as Commander of the army of the Lord I have now come."* Then Joshua fell facedown to the ground in reverence, and asked him, "What message does my lord have for his servant?" He replied, "Take off your sandals, for the place where you are standing is holy," and Joshua did so.

In Judges 6:11-24 the Angel of the Lord appears to Gideon. Then, in verse 14 the Angel is referred to as God. Judges 13:15-22 tells of Manoah, the father of Samson, speaking to the Angel of the Lord, and he too is afraid he will die because he has seen God. In Genesis 48:15 Jacob refers to *"the God who has been my Shepherd all my life to this day, the Angel who has delivered me from all harm."*

THE GENEOLOGY LEADING TO THE MESSIAH

God told Abraham ". . .*and all peoples on earth will be blessed through you*" (Gen 12:3). The Messiah would come through the descendants of Abraham, and the whole world would be blessed through Him. Galatians 3:8-9 refers to this blessing: *The Scripture foresaw that God would bless the Gentiles by faith, and announced the Gospel in advance to Abraham: "All nations will be blessed through you."*

Galatians 3:14 tells us, *He redeemed us in order that the blessing given to Abraham might come to the Gentiles through Christ Jesus, so that by faith we might receive the promise of the Spirit.*

FULFILLMENT OF OLD TESTAMENT PROPHECIES
HE WOULD BE FROM THE TRIBE OF JUDAH

The scepter would not depart from Judah, nor the ruler's staff from between his feet, until He comes to whom it belongs (Shilo)*; and the obedience of the nations is His* (Gen 49:10). Here Jacob prophesied that out of Judah would come a line of kings (Davidic) until at last the Messiah would come. Shilo is a Messianic title. According to this prophecy, Shilo (Messiah) must have already come for the scepter or rule had long departed from Judah. There is no longer a tribal head, the Jewish people are scattered all over the world, and it is impossible to prove from which tribe they are descended. It is clear that the scepter, and along with it the authorized lawgiver or ruler, is no longer in Judah. Judah ruled over its own legal and religious systems from the time of Solomon until the destruction of the temple in 70 A.D.

Even during the Babylonian captivity, for seventy years they maintained their ability to rule their own courts and religious laws. This continued under the Persians and the Greeks into the early years of Roman authority over Judea. During the time of Jesus, Israel's Sanhedrin court lost its authority to judge capital cases. Augustus Caesar appointed a Roman to rule Judea directly as Procurator. This forced the Sanhedrin to bring Jesus to Pontius Pilate to give the death penalty (John 18:31).

HE WOULD BE OF THE HOUSE OF DAVID

Of the increase of His government and peace there shall be no end. He will reign on David's throne and over his kingdom, establishing and upholding it with justice and righteousness from that time on and forever. The zeal of the Lord Almighty will accomplish this (Isa 9:7).

HE WOULD BE A PROPHET LIKE MOSES

I will raise up for them a Prophet like you from among their brothers; I will put My words in His mouth, and He will tell them everything I command Him (Deut 18:18). *God spoke to Moses face to face* (Deut 34:10).

Jesus said: *"For I did not speak on my own, but the Father who sent me commanded me what to say and how to say it. I know that His command leads to eternal life. So whatever I say is just what the Father has told me to say"* (John 12:49-50).

Moses was the mediator of the covenant: *These are the terms of the covenant the Lord commanded Moses to make with the Israelites in Moab, in addition to the covenant He had made with them on Mount Horeb* (Deut 29:1).

Jesus is the Mediator of the New Covenant: *But the ministry Jesus has received is as superior to theirs as the covenant of which he is mediator is superior to the old one, and it is founded on better promises. For if there had been nothing wrong with that first covenant, no place would have been found for another* (Heb 8:6-7).

Moses was intercessor for his people. After the people had sinned and Moses broke the tablets of the Ten Commandments, he said: *"Then once again I fell prostrate before the Lord for forty days and forty nights; I ate no bread and drank no water, because of all the sin you had committed, doing what was evil in the Lord's sight and so provoking Him to anger"* (Deut 9:18).

Jesus is intercessor for his people. *Therefore He is able to save completely those who come to God through Him, because He always lives to intercede for them* (Heb 7:25)

Moses did miracles, the ten plagues, etc. *No prophet has risen in Israel like Moses, who the Lord knew face to face. Who did all those miraculous signs and wonders the Lord sent him to do in Egypt* (Deut 34:10-11).

Jesus did many miracles: *"The blind receive sight, the lame walk, those who have leprosy are cured, the deaf hear, the dead are raised, and the good news is preached to the poor"* (Matt 11:5).

Moses was lawgiver in Exodus 20 when the Lord gave him the Ten Commandments. Jesus gave us the Beatitudes (Matthew 5) and interpreted the Ten Commandments.

HE WOULD BE BORN OF A VIRGIN

Therefore the Lord Himself will give you a sign: the virgin will be with child and will give birth to a son, and will call His Immanuel (Isa 7:14).

All this took place to fulfill what the Lord had said through the prophet. "The virgin will be with child and will give birth to a son, and they will call him Immanuel – which means 'God with us'" (Matt 1:22-23).

HE WOULD BE BORN IN BETHLEHEM

But you, Bethlehem Ephrathah, though you are small among the clans of Judah, out of you will come for me One who will be ruler over Israel, whose origins are from of old, from ancient times (Micah 5:2). Micah was written in the eighth century B.C. Of all the towns available, he reveals the exact town. It was not the only Bethlehem in Israel. It was small among the clans of Judah. Ephrathah was a tribal district in which both Jerusalem and THIS Bethlehem was located.

HE WOULD HAVE A FORERUNNER

The voice of one calling in the desert prepare the way for the Lord: make straight in the wilderness a highway for our God. Every valley shall be raised up, every mountain and hill made low, the rough ground shall become level, the rugged places plain (Isa 40:3-5).

See, I will send my messenger, who will prepare the way before me. Then suddenly the Lord you are looking for will come to His temple, the messenger of the covenant, whom you will desire, will come says the Lord Almighty. (Mal. 3:1)

Many of the people of Israel he will bring back to the Lord their God. And He will go on before the Lord, in the spirit and power of Elijah, to turn the hearts of the fathers to their children, and the disobedient to the wisdom of the righteous – to make ready a people prepared for the Lord (Luke 1:16-17). This was fulfilled by John the Baptist. Matthew 3:1-3 says, *In those days John the Baptist came, preaching in the desert of Judea and saying, "Repent, for the kingdom of heaven is near." This is he who was spoken of through the prophet Isaiah: "A voice of one calling in the desert, prepare the way for the Lord, make straight paths for Him."*

The Old Testament points to the New Testament, and the New Testament looks back to the Old Testament. The last Messianic prophecy of Malachi 3:1 begins the New Testament and Luke 1:5-17 refers to John the Baptist.

HE WOULD BE FLOGGED AND SPIT UPON

I offered my back to those who beat me, my cheeks to those who pulled out my beard; I did not hide my face from the mocking and spitting (Isa 50:6).

But he had Jesus flogged (Matt 27:26). *Then they put a staff in his right hand and knelt in front of Him and mocked him, "Hail King of the Jews!" they said. They spit on him, and took the staff and struck him on the head again and again* (Matt 27:29-31).

HE WOULD BE GIVEN VINEGAR AND GALL

They put gall in my food and gave me vinegar for my thirst (Psa 69:21).

There they offered Jesus wine to drink, mixed with gall . . . (Matt 27:34).

THEY WOULD PIERCE HIS HANDS AND FEET

. . . A band of evil men has encircled me, they have pierced my hands and my feet (Psa 22:16).

And I will pour out on the house of David and the inhabitants of Jerusalem a spirit of grace and supplication. They will look on me, the one they have pierced, and they will mourn for Him as one mourns for an only child (Zech 12:10).

HIS GARMENTS WOULD BE TAKEN AND GAMBLED FOR

They divide my garments among them and cast lots for my clothing (Psa 22:18).

When the soldiers crucified Jesus, they took his clothes, dividing them into four shares, one for each of them with the undergarment remaining. This garment was seamless, woven in one piece from top to bottom. "Let's not tear it," they said one to another. "Let's decide by lot who will get it" (John 19:23-24).

HE WOULD BE MOCKED

All who see me mock me; they hurl insults, shaking their heads: "He trusts in the Lord; let the Lord rescue him, since he delights in him (Psa 22:7-8)

Those who passed by hurled insults at him, shaking their heads and saying, "You who are going to destroy the temple and build it in three days, save yourself! Come down from the cross, if you are the Son of God!" In the same way the chief priests and teachers of the law and the elders mocked him, "He saved others," they said, "but he can't save himself! He is the king of Israel! Let him come down now from the cross, and we will believe in Him. He trusts God. Let God rescue him now if He wants him, for he said, 'I am the Son of God'" (Matt 27:39-43).

HE WOULD THIRST

My strength is dried up like a potsherd, and my tongue sticks to the roof of my mouth; and you lay me in the dust of death (Psa 22:15).

Later, knowing that all was now completed, and so that the Scripture would be fulfilled, Jesus said, "I am thirsty" (John 19:28).

NONE OF HIS BONES WOULD BE BROKEN

He protects all His bones, not one of them is broken (Psa 34:20).

The soldiers therefore came and broke the legs of the first man who had been crucified with Jesus, and then those of the other. But when they came to Jesus and found that He was already dead, they did not break His legs (John 19:32-33).

HE WOULD BE BURIED WITH THE RICH

He was assigned a grave with the wicked, and with the rich in His death (Isa 53:9).

As evening approached there came a rich man from Arimathea, named Joseph who had himself become a disciple of Jesus. Going to Pilate, he asked for Jesus body and Pilate ordered that it be given to him. Joseph took the body, wrapped it in a clean linen cloth, and placed it in his own tomb that he had cut out of the rock. He rolled a big stone in front of the entrance to the tomb and went away (Matt 57:60).

HE WOULD BE RAISED FROM THE DEAD

Because you would not abandon me to the grave, nor will you let your Holy One see decay (Psa 16:10).

After the Sabbath, at dawn on the first day of the week, Mary Magdalene and the other Mary went to look at the tomb. There was a violent earthquake, for an angel of the Lord came down from heaven and going to the tomb, rolled back the stone and sat on it. His appearance was like lightning and his clothes were *white as snow. The guards were so afraid of him that they shook and became like dead men. The angel said to the women, "Do not be afraid, for I know you are looking for Jesus, who was crucified. He is not here; He has risen just as He said. Come and see the place where He lay. Go quickly and tell His disciples, 'He has risen from the dead and is going ahead of you into Galilee.' There you will see Him. Now I have told you"* (Matt 28:1-7).

CHAPTER SEVEN
The Time of His Coming

Daniel 9:24-26 tells us that the Messiah must come between 30 A.D. and 70 A.D:

Seventy sevens are decreed for your people and your holy city to finish transgressions and put an end to sin, to atone for wickedness, to bring in everlasting righteousness, to seal up the vision and prophecy and to anoint the Most Holy. Know and understand this: from the issuing of the decree to restore and rebuild Jerusalem until the Anointed One, the ruler, comes; there will be seven sevens, and sixty-two sevens. It will be built with streets and trench, but in times of trouble. After sixty-two sevens the Anointed One will be cut off and will have nothing. The people of the ruler who will come will destroy the city and the sanctuary. The end will come like a flood; war will continue until the end, and desolations have been decreed.

Here "Seventy sevens" or "seventy weeks" means seventy units. The Hebrew word is "Shabuim" and here it means years. This is made clear in Scripture. In Genesis 29:26-28 we read: *Laban replied, "It is not our custom here to give the younger daughter in marriage before the older one. Finish this daughter's bridal WEEK. Then we will give you the younger one also, in return for ANOTHER SEVEN YEARS of work." And Jacob did so. He finished the WEEK with Leah, and then Laban gave him his daughter Rachel to be his wife.*

Israel was very familiar with a "week of years" because of the concept of the SABBATICAL YEAR, which was based on THE SEVENTH YEAR AS A YEAR OF REST. Just as the SEVENTH DAY of the week of days was a day of rest (Lev 25; Deut 15). Israel had a calendar of a week of seven days: *Six days do your work, but on the seventh day do not work* (Exod 23:12). And also a WEEK OF SEVEN YEARS: *For six years sow your fields, and for six years prune your vineyards and gather your crops. But in the seventh year the land is to have a Sabbath of rest, a Sabbath to the Lord* (Lev.25:3-4).

The seventy-year captivity of Israel was the result of Israel's disobedience. They were to allow the land to remain idle every seventh year. But they disobeyed. After 490 years they had failed to keep 70 yearly Sabbaths, which led to 70 years of captivity: *The land enjoyed its Sabbath rests; all the time of its desolation it rested UNTIL THE SEVENTY YEARS were completed in fulfillment of the Word of the Lord spoken by Jeremiah* (2 Chron 36:21).

Daniel would have been familiar with the "week of years" because of the seventy years of captivity that Israel was going through at the time. Around 600 B.C. Daniel himself was taken as one of the captives to Babylon. Daniel would have understood when the angel Gabriel said it would be another period similar in length to the Babylonian exile. This is the context that led to the seventy-year captivity. Israel had not kept the yearly Sabbath for 490 years, which would equal 70 Sabbaths they had to make up for – thus the 70-year captivity.

The context of Daniel 9 makes these seventy-sevens to be seventy weeks of years – 70 times 7 weeks of years equaling 490 years were decreed for Daniel's people, Israel. It must be kept in mind that these years are Jewish in context and are 360 days each. Daniel 9:24 goes on to list six things that will be accomplished during this time period concerning God's program for Israel – ("For your people and your holy city").

1. Finish the transgression.
2. Make an end of sin.
3. Make reconciliation for iniquity.
4. Bring in everlasting righteousness.
5. Seal up vision and prophecy.
6. Anoint the Most Holy.

These last three will be fulfilled at Christ's second coming.

Verse 25 states that the total length of time from the command to rebuild Jerusalem, until Messiah's coming is 69 weeks, or 483 years. There was only one decree issued to rebuild Jerusalem. It was the one given by Artaxerxes Longimanus who reigned in Persia from 465 B.C. to 425 B.C. He had commissioned Ezra to return to Jerusalem in 457 B.C (Ezra 7:11-26). He commanded the rebuilding of Jerusalem in 445 B.C. This is based on the reference in Neh.2:1 saying that the decree was given in the 20th year of Artexerxes Longimanus. His reign began in 465 B.C. So twenty years later would make it the first of Nisan or March 14th 445 B.C.

Using the Jewish year of 360 days, we can determine the exact time of the "Messiah, the Anointed One. To determine the exact day, we must use the 360-day years in place of 365 days on our current calendars. We can therefore determine the total amount of days in 69 weeks. 69 weeks of years total 483 years. Then multiply this number by 360 days for each year. This totals exactly 173,880 days until the coming Anointed Messiah.

If we begin with the month Nisan, we come to Passover on April 6th 32 A.D. The day Jesus rode into Jerusalem on a donkey. Five hundred years before the birth of Christ, the prophet Zechariah wrote that the Messiah, the King would make Himself known to Israel by riding into Jerusalem on a donkey: *Rejoice greatly, O daughter of Zion! Shout, daughter of Jerusalem! See, your King comes to you riding on a donkey, on a colt, the foal of a donkey* (9:9).

Today this is known as Palm Sunday. *The disciples went and did as Jesus had instructed them. They brought the donkey and the colt, placed their cloaks on them, and Jesus sat on them. A very large crowd spread their cloaks on the road, while others cut branches from the trees and spread them on the road. The crowds that went ahead of Him and those that followed shouted, "Hosanna to the Son of David! Blessed is He who comes in the name of the Lord. Hosanna in the highest"* (Matt 21:6-9).

Hosanna means "save now," while the terms "Son of David" and "He who comes in the name of the Lord" were both strong Messianic terms. Only here did Jesus allow such public homage. This was a Jewish royal entry.

Donkeys were ridden by kings of Israel. The palm branches were used in victory celebrations. These were spread before Him along with their outer garments.

Jesus was publicly presenting Himself as the Messiah with full knowledge that it would lead Him to the cross.

Luke 19:41-44 tells us, *As He approached Jerusalem and saw the city, He wept over it and said, "If you, even you, had only known ON THIS DAY what would bring you peace – but now it is hid from your eyes. The days will come upon you when your enemies will build an embankment against you and encircle you and hem you in on every side. They will dash you to the ground, you and your children within your walls. They will not leave one stone upon another, because you did not recognize the time of God's coming to you."* Here "He" refers to the destruction of Jerusalem in 70 A.D, about 40 years after His crucifixion.

Daniel 9:26 states that after the 69 weeks, the Messiah would be "cut off" or killed. This ties in with the preceding part of the prophecy concerning the "making reconciliation for iniquity. That sin must be dealt with is the underlying reason of His being "cut off." He was cut off for the sins of the world: *Surely he took up our infirmities and carried our sorrows . . . but He was pierced for our transgressions. He was crushed for our iniquities; the punishment that brought us peace was upon Him and by His wounds we are healed. We all like sheep have gone astray; each one of us has turned to his own way; and the Lord has laid on Him the iniquity of us all* (Isa 53:5-6).

Then we are told in Daniel 9:26, . . . *The people of the ruler who will come will destroy the city and the sanctuary. . . .* This happened 43 years later when the Roman's destroyed Jerusalem and the temple in putting down the Jewish revolt in 70 A.D.

The Point of Daniel's prophecy is that 490 years were determined to deal with the question of sin by the Messiah, who would be "cut off" (killed violently), after which Jerusalem and the temple would be destroyed (70 A.D.).

The fact of His birth, life, death, and resurrection were given in vivid detail long before He actually appeared.

LEGAL AND SACRIFICIAL SYSTEMS

God began to teach the people of Israel that man could only be saved by substitution. Thus was instituted the sacrificial system as a reminder of the Coming One Who would be the true Lamb of God sacrificed for the sins of the whole world. The Legal system was instituted by God to show that we are sinners who could not keep the law and to highlight our need of the Coming Savior. The law was good and we should keep it. The problem is not with the law but with us – we cannot keep it.

What shall we say then? Is the law sin? Certainly not! Indeed I could not have known sin except through the law. For I would not have known what sin really was if the law had not said, "Do not covet," But sin seizing the opportunity afforded by the commandment, produced in me every kind of covetous desire. For apart from the law sin is dead. Once I was alive apart from law; but when the commandment came, sin sprang to life and I died. I found that the very commandment that was intended to bring life actually brought death. For sin seizing the opportunity afforded by the commandment, deceived me, and through the commandment put me to death. So then, the law is holy and the commandment is holy, righteous and good. In order that sin might be recognized as sin, it produced death in me through what was good, so that through the commandment sin might become utterly sinful (Rom 7:7-13).

Here we are told that Paul thought he was a pretty good person until he heard the law and realized that hidden sins, like coveting and envying, were made obvious by the law, and he knew that it condemned him, and therefore he needed a Savior. When the law was broken, an offering symbolizing the Coming One was to be made.

PREPARATION OF THE WORLD FOR THE MESSIAH

The Old Testament prepared the way for the coming Messiah by prophecies, types, and symbols. John the Baptist prepared His way by pointing Him out. And between the Old and New Testaments, His way was prepared by history and civilization.

Around 335 B.C. Alexander the great swept through the Middle East spreading Greek culture. The Pharisees rose to the forefront. They were a party of religious zealots. They fought to preserve their own culture against the influence of Greek culture. They sought to preserve the Mosaic Law by building a protective wall of additional laws around them. For instance: The Mosaic Law forbade working on the Sabbath, whereas protective laws forbid even carrying a mat! The problem was that these secondary laws became an authority of their own, taking on a greater authority than the Law of Moses itself. By their "traditions" they added to the Word of God.

Another party was known as the Sadducees. They EMBRACED the Greek culture. Though few in number, they had wealth and influence and consequently tended to control the High Priesthood, an office that had come to be bought and sold. They rejected much of the Old Testament, thus they took away from the Word of God. They were materialists and rationalists. They held to only the five books of Moses, thus they denied the afterlife, angels, and resurrection. The Scribes were another major social force. They copied the handwritten Word of God with extreme care.

About a hundred years later, the Romans ruled the Mediterranean with an iron fist. In 67 B.C. the Roman general Pompey took Jerusalem. Rome allowed the Jews to control their own religion so long as they paid their taxes and did not stir up rebellion.

Greek became the international language. While maintaining national languages and dialects, Greek was so well known in the world that it was called Koine Greek, and became the "common language." The early church's mission to preach the gospel to the whole world was greatly aided by eliminating a major difficulty of learning all the different languages.

Rome aided the spread of Christianity by building roads and bridges to even remote areas, and travel was aided by shipping. Pliny tells us that to travel from Spain to Ostia, Italy by ship took only four days: Africa to Rome was only two days. The Roman Empire was the center of a vast complex of peoples in every city. Many Jews settled in these cities and Rome allowed them to build Synagogues that served to teach the Old Testament and were the forerunners of Christian churches and schools. The Apostle Paul introduced the gospel in many cities through these simple places of prayer and Scripture reading. His evangelistic activities would have been inconceivable without these Jewish Synagogues. Jewish converts formed the foundation of the early church.

THE SEPTUAGINT

The Jews outside of Palestine soon lost contact with the Hebrew-Aramaic language because they lived in areas dominated by Hellenistic speech. This made a Greek translation of the Old Testament for use in Synagogues necessary. It was greatly used by God to further the proclamation of the gospel. Through it Gentiles became acquainted with the Old Testament, preparing them to hear the gospel. Christian preachers used it on their journeys. Almost all of the quotations of the Old Testament used by the New Testament writers came from it.

PEACE

For world evangelism, peace among nations was extremely important. Roman rule brought about the Roman peace (Pax Romana).

But when the fullness of the times was come, God sent forth His
Son . . . (Gal 4:4).

The "Fullness of the times" refers to the right time in world history.

CHAPTER EIGHT
The Incarnation

Jesus' coming had been prophesied thousands of years before, first in Eden, then in types and prophecies throughout the Old Testament. Abraham saw His coming as God's promised Lamb to be our substitute for sin. Israel symbolized it in the sacrificial system. From eternity He knew He would face the cross. He would take on humanity in order to represent us and die in our place as our substitute. He would suffer as no one had ever suffered. In John 1:1-5 we read of His coming from eternity: *In the beginning WAS* (eimi – eternally) *the Word, and the Word WAS* (eimi – eternally) *with God* (pros ton theon – Face to Face, meaning perfect equality and perfect love), *and the Word WAS* (eimi – eternally) *with God in the beginning.*

Through Him: He is the first cause and sustainer of all creation. *All things were made by Him* (v. 3). He is the source of all life, and the light of spiritual understanding: *All things were made by Him, without Him nothing was made that was made. In Him WAS* (eimi – eternally) *life, and that life WAS* (eimi – eternally) *the light of men. The light shines in the darkness, but the darkness has not understood it.*

Here the light shines in the darkness and the darkness has not understood it in the sense of knowing how to overcome the light to extinguish it. There is hostility between the light and the darkness but the darkness has not been able to overcome the light.

Then in verses 11-14, it continues: *He came to that which was His Own, but His Own did not receive Him. Yet to all who received Him, to those who believed in His name, He gave the right to become the children of God – children born not out of natural descent, nor of human decision or a husband's will, but born of God. The Word became flesh and made His dwelling among us. We have seen His glory, the glory of the one and Only, Who came from the Father, full of grace and truth.*

Then in verse 18: *No one has ever seen God, But God the One and Only, Who is at the Father's side, has made Him known.*

Here in verse 1, the veil is pulled aside to reveal a glimpse of eternity. *In the beginning was the Word.* The Greek word "WORD" is Logos and refers to that which reveals or communicates that which is in the mind or thought of God.

In Genesis 1 each new phase of creation begins *And God Said* (1, 9, 11, 14, 20, 24, 26, and 29). Why would God have to speak to create? Since the Word, Jesus, is the speech of God or means of revelation of the infinite God. When God spoke the command of creation, the Son went forth and revealed the intention of God and brought about creation.

For man's salvation, He took upon Himself humanity and revealed the infinite God. THIS IS THE HEART OF CHRISTIANITY. He was not merely God indwelling a man, but He was God taking upon Himself humanity, God and man in one person.

The Logos reveals the heart and mind of God. He expresses God's wisdom and love and His purpose for mankind. He did this in the Old Testament, as the Angel (Messenger) of the Lord, and in the New Testament as incarnate in the Person of Jesus Christ. He expresses the unseen and unapproachable God because He Himself is God. He can do this perfectly as Immanuel (God with us).

Isaiah is quoted in Matthew 1:22-23, *All this took place to fulfill what the Lord had said through the prophet: "The virgin shall be with child and will give birth to a son, and they will call Him Immanuel – which means God with us."* In John 14:9 Jesus said to Philip, *"Don't you know me, Philip, even after I have been among you for such a long time? Anyone who has seen me has seen the Father."* Jesus fully reveals God to mankind.

In Colossians.1:15 we see that Jesus is the *image of the invisible God, the Firstborn over all creation.*

Here we see that Jesus is the visible image of the invisible God, the exact representation. He is the Firstborn, not OF creation, but OVER creation. He has priority over creation. He is not a part of the creation, but the Creator Himself. This is why Colossians 1:16 tells us: *All things were created BY Him and FOR Him.*

The divine love found its perfect expression in the One who eternally abides at the Father's right hand, who receives and returns that love and who overflows that love to His creation. In verse 14 we see that He became flesh. He became one of us and one with us in our fallen state but without sin. By this I mean He shared in some of the effects of the fall but TOTALLY APART FROM SIN. In Romans 8:3 we read that Jesus came *in the LIKENESS of sinful man.* This means that there was no immunity to the physical infirmities: fatigue, hunger, thirst, and pain. But He had no sin nature.

God's plan to save sinners centered on the Second Person of the Trinity becoming a sinless Man to represent us as the last Adam and take the judgment for our sins. He became Man. He is as fully man as He is God. Forever He will remain God and Man. In Jesus Christ, God Himself entered into our human suffering. God has suffered WITH and FOR us. We can only marvel at His unfathomable love and how our sin and suffering caused Him to suffer. God is no far away and uncaring onlooker of our suffering. It pleased the Lord Jesus to identify with us so He could save the human race and forever bring us into union with Himself. It is truly said that the Son of God became the Son of Man, that the sons of men might become the sons of God. As the first Adam was the corporate head of the old creation, He is the corporate Head of the new creation, those who would believe in Him.

The designation "Son of man" is His identification with humanity, and is His title as the *Last Adam: Beyond all question, the mystery of Godliness is great: He appeared in a body, was vindicated by the Spirit, was seen by angels, was preached among the nations, was believed on in the world, and was taken up in glory* (1 Tim 3:16). As the "Son of Man," He was the seed of the woman of whom it was promised that He would *crush the serpent's head.* He was the *Seed of Abraham in whom all the nations shall be blessed* (Gen 3:15).

For as in Adam all die, so in Christ all will be made alive (1 Cor 15:22).

The Scriptures are very clear concerning Jesus' eternal existence and His taking on humanity to suffer and die on the cross for our sins:

Who, being in the very nature of God, did not consider equality with God something to be grasped, but made Himself nothing, taking the very nature of a servant, being made in human likeness. And being found in appearance as a man, He humbled Himself and became obedient to death – even death on a cross (Phil 2:6-8).

Here we are told that Jesus did not cling to His rightful position as God. But laid aside His inherent rights – the manifestations of His deity. He was truly God but He laid aside the outward appearance as such – His outward glory – and taking the form of a servant made in human likeness, He took on the appearance of a man, and humbled Himself to the point of death – even death on a cross.

When it says that Jesus was made in human "likeness," and took on the "appearance" of a man. It does not mean that Jesus merely took on the APPEARANCE of a man. Jesus truly became human, but the point here is that while He appeared to be ONLY a man He was much more. While He was Man, He was the God-Man. This does not mean He was half God and half man like the mythological Hercules. No, Jesus was FULLY God and FULLY man. As Man He could die, but not just die but die the humiliating death on a cross as a criminal.

Indeed as our representative, He took our sins upon Himself and was judged by God as though He had actually committed all the sins of all humanity.

Theirs are the patriarchs (referring to the Jews) *and from them is traced the human ancestry of Christ, Who is God over all, forever praised! Amen* (Rom 9:5).

Hebrews 1:6 tells us that when Jesus came to earth, the angels worshiped Him: *And again when God brings His Firstborn into the world, He says "Let all God's angels worship Him.*

And Hebrews 2:14-17 says: *Since the children have flesh and blood, He too shared in their humanity so that by His death He might destroy him who holds the power of death – that is, the devil – and free those who all their lives were held in slavery by their fear of death. For surely it is not angels he helps, but Abraham's descendants. For this reason He had to be made like His brothers in every way, in order that He might become a merciful and faithful High Priest in service to God and that He might make atonement for the sins of the people.*

Colossians.1:15 says: *He is the image of the invisible God, the Firstborn over all creation.* The Biblical use of the term "Firstborn" represents preeminent rights of rank and authority over the Father's possession. *Jesus knew that the Father had put all things under His power and that He had come from God and was returning to God* (John 13:3). This is based on His unique relationship with the Father. *"All things have been committed to me by My Father. No one knows the Son except the Father, and no one knows the Father except the Son and those to whom the Son chooses to reveal Him"* (Matt 11:27).

THE MESSIANIC LINE

Throughout the Old Testament, Jesus is considered the "Coming One," based upon the promise of God given about 4,200 years before Jesus' birth in Genesis 3:15, as the "Seed of the woman."

The Seed would come through Shem, the son of Noah (Gen 9:26) about 2,000 years B.C. and through Abraham (Gen 12:1-3) about 1900 B.C; then through Isaac (Gen 17:19-21); then through Jacob (who was renamed Israel by God) (Gen 26:1-4; 28:13-14); then through Judah (Gen 49:10), about 1,800 B.C; then through David around 1,000 B.C (1 Sam.7:16); then through Solomon to Joseph, Jesus' legal father (Matt 1:6, 16) and Eli, the father of Mary (Luke 3:23, 31) Jesus' actual mother.

THE VIRGIN BIRTH

A record of the genealogy of Jesus Christ the son of David, the son of Abraham (Matt 1:1).

As the son of David, Jesus is the King who is to rule in righteousness upon David's throne (Isa 9:6-7). As the son of Abraham, He is the promised seed in whom all the nations of the earth would be blessed (Gen 22:18). As Simeon said of the infant Jesus in Luke 2:30-32: *"For my eyes have seen your salvation, which you have prepared in the sight of all people, a light for revelation to the Gentiles and for glory to your people Israel."*

This is how the birth of Jesus Christ came about: his mother Mary was pledged to be married to Joseph, but before they came together, she was found to be with child through the Holy Spirit (Matt 1:18).

"For that which is conceived in her is from the Holy Spirit" (Matt 1:20). Thus while Jesus was BORN of a virgin mother, He was CONCEIVED by the Holy Spirit.

The PERSON who was taking on humanity already existed, a Divine Person entering into this new mode of existence. This creative miracle wrought by the Holy Spirit guaranteed His sinless humanity.

Because He was not born through a natural conception, He would not share in Adam's bloodline and his sin nature. The Coming Savior is the central theme of the Old Testament two thousand years before He came in the flesh. The virgin birth would mean that He would be free from the sin of Adam. It is through the Offspring of the woman that the fall would be conquered. He would be the new Adam of a renewed creation, the representative of a new race to inhabit a new Eden.

He is the promised seed of Abraham, David's greater son, the one greater than Moses. He is the suffering Servant who would bear the sins of the world. Conceived by the Holy Spirit, He would have the nature of God. Born of the virgin, He would be sinless Man; He is the God-Man who is the focal point of all history.

Way back in Genesis 3:15, God's answer to Adam's fall was to promise to send a redeemer who would be born of the *Offspring of the woman,* a reference to the virgin birth, as a child was always born of the seed of man. Thousands of years later, Isaiah continued this theme, prophesying that a special sign would be given to the house of David when *the virgin shall conceive and bear a son* (Isa 7:13-14).

The Hebrew word virgin is "almah" and refers to an unmarried girl, and unmarried Jewish girls under the Mosaic Law were virgins. Long before the writers of the New Testament, the translators of the Septuagint (the Greek translation of the Old Testament) in 285 B.C., who were much closer to the nuances of the original Hebrew language of the Old Testament, translated the Hebrew "almah" into the Greek "parthenos," which clearly refers to a virgin. The Jewish Bible scholars understood the prophecy to mean that the Messiah would be born of a virgin. Jesus Christ was born of the Virgin Mary in fulfillment of these two separate prophecies (Gen 3:15 and Isa 7:14).

All this took place to fulfill what the Lord had said through the prophet: "The virgin shall be with child and will give birth to a son, and they will call Him Immanuel, which means 'God with us'" (Matt 1:22-23).

God made a special human body for the incarnation of Christ, as we are told in Hebrews 10:5, *Therefore when Christ came into the world, He said: ". . . a body you prepared for me."* A biological, perfect body, unconnected to fallen parents, in embryonic form, was formed in the womb of the Virgin Mary who, with Joseph, would raise Him in a loving, Godly home.

He stands in contrast to all other men. God entered His creation as a Man in Jesus Christ. His teachings centered on Himself. Salvation is not attained by following certain rules, but by a personal relationship with Him. The Christian life also is lived in contact with Him for power and desire to do what is right. This is why Paul could say, *I know WHOM I have believed . . .* (2 Tim 1:12).

Joseph and Mary were betrothed, and as such they were considered married although they still lived with their parents. It may have been months before they were actually married. Any violation of the betrothal would be considered adultery, and the betrothal could only be dissolved, as in a marriage, by a regular divorce. After finding Mary with child, not knowing it was through the Holy Spirit, we read in Matthew 1:19, *Because Joseph her husband was a righteous man and did not want to expose her to public disgrace, he had in mind to divorce her quietly.*

Joseph determined to sever the betrothal by giving her a letter of divorce privately in the presence of two witnesses. Verses 20-25: *But after he had considered this, an angel of the Lord appeared to him in a dream and said, "Joseph son of David, do not be afraid to take Mary home as your wife, because what is conceived in her is from the Holy Spirit. She will give birth to a son, and you are to give Him the name Jesus, because He will save His people from their sins." All this took place to fulfill what the Lord said through the prophet: 'The virgin shall be with child and will give birth to a son, and they will call Him Immanuel – which means God with us.'" When Joseph woke up, he did what the angel of the Lord had commanded him and took Mary home as his wife, but he had no union with her until she gave birth to a son. And he gave Him the name Jesus.*

In chapter 2 we are told of the Magi from the east (v. 1). Babylon was east of Jerusalem across the Syrian Desert. These were not astrologers. They came to see the one born King of the Jews (v. 2). These Magi would have known of the Book of Daniel since Daniel wrote during the time he had lived among them during the Babylonian captivity of Israel (see Matt 1:11). At that time the prophet Micah lived, and wrote, in Palestine (Micah 1:1).

But these Magi would not have known of Micah's prophecy that He would be born in Bethlehem. From the Book of Daniel, they would have known that the Jews looked for a coming prince, a descendant of King David. They did know that the Messiah would have to come to Jerusalem eventually. The passage in Daniel that gave the Magi their expectation was Daniel 9:24-26, which he wrote while in Babylon. They had kept a careful record of the 483 years.

Apparently, they saw His star in the east and knew when to start their journey. They already knew that He was born "King of the Jews," and therefore they came expecting to find the "King," having been born in the capital city. The star would not have been needed to lead them to Jerusalem. When they left Jerusalem and started for Bethlehem, the star then would be needed to lead them to the very house of His birth (Matt 2:9-11). This was obviously a special star made for this purpose, as it would be impossible to follow a literal star anywhere on earth.

Verse 11 reads: *On coming to the house, they saw the child with His mother Mary and they bowed down and worshiped Him. Then they opened their treasures and presented Him with gifts of gold and of incense and of myrrh.* It is a clear foretaste from these representatives of the Gentile world, offering worship and gifts; that Jesus would be a light to the Gentiles: *Arise, shine, for your light has come, and the glory of the Lord rises upon you. See, darkness covers the earth and thick darkness is over the peoples, but the Lord rises upon you and His glory appears over you. Nations will come to your light, and kings to the brightness of your dawn* (Isa 60:1-3).

We are told in Jeremiah 22:30 concerning Jehoiachin: *This is what the Lord says, "Record this man as if childless, a man who will not prosper in his lifetime, for none of his offspring will prosper, none will sit on the throne of David or rule anymore in Judah."* Here we are told that no descendant of Jehoiachin would sit on the throne of David. Joseph was a descendant of Jehoiachin (Matt 1:11-16).

In Jeremiah 23:5-6 we read: *The days are coming declares the Lord when I will raise up to David a Righteous Branch, a King who will rule wisely and do what is just and right in the land. In His days Judah will be saved and Israel will live in safety. This is the name by which He will be called: The Lord our Righteousness.* None of Jehoiachin's descendants would reign on David's throne.

And yet Jesus will sit upon the throne of David. Jesus, therefore, could not be physically descended from Joseph and at the same time inherit the throne of David. The first prophecy of a virgin birth is given in Genesis 3:15, referring to the *Offspring of the woman* and then in Isaiah 7:14, *Therefore the Lord Himself will give you a sign: "The virgin shall be with child and will give birth to a son, and will call Him Immanuel."*

These prophecies give the solution to the problem, as we are told in Matthew 1:20-23: *But after He had considered this, an angel of the Lord appeared to him in a dream and said, "Joseph son of David, do not be afraid to take Mary home as your wife, because what is conceived in her is from the Holy Spirit. She will give birth to a son, and you will give him the name Jesus, because He will save his people from their sins." All this took place to fulfill what the Lord said through the prophet: 'The virgin shall be with child and will give birth to a son, and they will call Him Immanuel – which means 'God with us."*

Matthew gives the genealogy of Joseph in 1:12-16. Verse 16 reads, . . . *and Jacob the father of Joseph, the husband of Mary, of whom was born Jesus, who is called Christ.* The Scripture is very careful to show that Jesus was not the physical son of Joseph. The words "of whom" in the original Greek are feminine and refer to Mary.

Luke, who records Mary's genealogy in 1:32-33 reads: *He will be great and will be called the Son of the Most High. The Lord God will give him the throne of his father David, and He shall reign over the house of Jacob forever, His kingdom will never end.* Joseph was descended from David through Solomon (Matt 1:6) and Jesus was the LEGAL son of Joseph by adoption. The Kingship passed through the male line, while Mary was descended through Nathan, another son of David (Luke 3:31). Jesus was the literal descendant of David through Mary.

Jesus was born in Bethlehem, which was so crowded that they could only find a room in a stable. The Baby was laid in a manger, a feeding trough for cattle as His bed (Luke 2:7).

The shepherds were tending their sheep in nearby fields. Sheep from their flocks would be used in the Temple Sacrifices in Jerusalem a few miles from Bethlehem (Luke 2:8). While the Son of God, the True Lamb of God, was sleeping in a feeding trough, the shepherds were in the fields all night because it was the season when the lambs gave birth. The True Lamb of God, the fulfillment of the shadows and types, was born when the lambs were being born and He would die while they were being sacrificed for Passover. He would change everything.

HIS EARLY YEARS

The heart of the gospel record concerns the last three years of Jesus' ministry, which culminates in His death and resurrection. Very few details are given of His first thirty years. What are recorded are statements of the character of His life and the principles that are basic to an understanding of His growth and development. While Jesus was born of the kingly line as a remote ancestor of King David, by the time of His birth the Davidic line had lost its importance in the ancient world. He was born during the reign of Augustus Caesar, and Palestine was a little crossroad province of the powerful far-flung Roman Empire. Its people were conquered and were poor and despised. Jesus lived in a home that was also a carpenter's workshop.

He would have learned the family trade from Joseph (Matt 13:55; Mark 6:3). The Greek word for "carpenter" can be just as accurately translated as "craftsman" meaning in wood, stone, or metal, or in all of them. He would have worked hard helping His father, though little is known of this period. Jesus certainly attended a synagogue school. He learned to read and write and was taught the sacred Scriptures in the Torah. There would have been no further training because we know from John 7:15 that the Jews marveled at His teaching, saying, *"How did this man get such learning without having studied?"* They were referring to higher learning from the rabbis.

Luke 2:40 tells of His childhood: *And the child grew and became strong; He was filled with wisdom, and the grace of God was upon Him.* Of His youth we are told of His questioning the Rabbis in the Temple. We are also told that *He was subject to His parents* and that *He increased in wisdom and stature and in favor with God and man* (2:51).

Then nothing is said until His baptism by John the Baptist that began His public ministry. John was the forerunner of the Messiah prophesied in Isaiah 40:3-5: *The voice of one calling: In the desert prepare the way of the Lord; make straight in the wilderness a highway for our God. Every valley shall be raised up, every mountain and hill made low; the rough ground shall become level, the rugged places a plain. And the glory of the Lord will be revealed, and all mankind together will see it. For the mouth of the Lord has spoken.*

Luke 3:3-6a describes the ministry of John the Baptist; *He went into all the country around Jordan, preaching a baptism of repentance for the forgiveness of sin. As it is written in the words of Isaiah the prophet: "A voice of one calling in the desert, prepare the way of the Lord, make straight paths for Him. Every valley shall be filled in, every mountain and hill made low. The crooked roads shall become straight, the rough ways made smooth. And all mankind shall see God's salvation."*

In Luke 3:9 John goes on to say: *"The axe is already at the root of the trees, and every tree that does not produce good fruit will be cut down and thrown into the fire."* John's message was: *"Repent for the kingdom of heaven is near"* (Matt 3:2).

The One the Prophets spoke of was coming, and was even there already. This would have been startling to the Jewish mind:

the kingdom the prophets pointed to was at hand, as John the prophet confirmed. He, as King, would usher in the New Order of the kingdom of God. The axe is laid at the root of the Old Order, which would bring swift destruction; not a propping up of the Old Order. Not only Israel but also the whole world was faced with a crisis now approaching in the Person of the Promised One.

"I baptize you with water for repentance. But after me will come One who is more powerful than I, Whose sandals I am not worthy to carry. He will baptize you with the Holy Spirit and with fire. His winnowing fork is in His hand, and He will clear His threshing floor, gathering His wheat into the barn and burning up the chaff with unquenchable fire" (Matt 3:11-12). This sifting and separating would revolve around the Coming King. Those who believe in Him would be baptized with the Holy Spirit and those who reject Him will be baptized with fire.

The next day John saw Jesus coming toward him and said, "Look, the Lamb of God, who takes away the sin of the world!" (John 1:29). The emphasis is on the word "THE." Jesus was THE Lamb of God, to which all the others pointed. John continues in John 1:30-31: *"This is the One I meant when I said, 'A man who comes after me has surpassed me because He was before me.' I myself did not know Him, but the reason I came baptizing with water was that He might be revealed to Israel."* To the Jewish mind there was no other meaning to the phrase "Lamb of God," but sacrifice. Also, the Passover was nearing and the thought of sacrifice for sin was on everyone's mind. The first mention of "Lamb" in the Scriptures is concerning the offering up of Isaac. The question of Isaac from the past centuries, as he was being tied to the altar, still hung in the air, *"My father . . . behold the fire and the wood: but where is the lamb for the burnt offering?"*

Now the last of the Old Testament prophets cries out in answer, *"Look, the Lamb of God."* John's gospel continues in 1:32-34: *Then John gave this testimony: "I saw the Spirit come down from heaven as a dove and remain on Him. I would not have known Him except that the One Who sent me to baptize with water told me, 'The man on whom you see the Spirit come down and remain is He Who will baptize with the Holy Spirit.' I have seen and testify that this is the Son of God."*

Jesus, by being baptized, was identifying with His work on the cross and His resurrection. He identified Himself as the Coming One. When Jesus was baptized, it symbolized what He would do as our Savior. It symbolized His death and resurrection. It was His mission and by His baptism He had accepted it. At first John did not know that Jesus was the one until he baptized him and saw the Spirit descending and remaining on Him, as God had revealed to him.

Baptism, established by Jesus, signifies the believer's entrance into the Christian community and symbolizes the washing away of sins as the believer enters into Christ's death and resurrection. Here we see the King anointed for sacrifice.

The Levitical Law prescribed the lamb and the dove for sacrificial offerings, which is the primary thought here. Jesus would be the sacrifice for sin offered *through the eternal Spirit* (Heb 9:14). Matthew 17:5 tells of the voice from heaven: *"This is My beloved Son, in Whom I am well pleased."* This is God's approval of Jesus being anointed for sacrifice.

This ended Jesus private life. He was anointed for His ministry. The King is anointed to establish His Kingdom. John's ministry had reached its climax: He had pointed out the Promised One as the "Lamb of God" and before long he would say: *"This joy is mine, and it is now complete. He must become greater; I must become less."* John had the honor of declaring that the Kingdom of Heaven was at hand and he pointed out the King.

CHAPTER NINE
His Temptation – Matthew 4:1-11

Then Jesus was led by the Spirit into the desert to be tempted by the devil (Matt 4:1). As the Last Adam, Jesus would be tempted as the first Adam was. The title that Jesus typically used to refer to himself is the "Son of man" to clarify His position as the Last Adam; the head of redeemed humanity. Before beginning His public ministry, He went through a period of fasting for forty days (Matt 4:2). He would have to meet Satan and bind him as He said in Mark 3:27: *"No man can enter a strong man's house to carry off his possessions unless he first ties up the strong man. Then he can rob his house."* Jesus would have to succeed where the first Adam failed. The first Adam was tempted in a perfect world and had all the luxury of Paradise, while the Last Adam was weak from hunger. He would have to meet and overcome the one who had defeated the first Adam and became the prince of this world (John 12:31; 14:30; 16:11). However, Jesus could not restore Paradise from the curse of sin by the mere exercise of power.

He could only lift the curse off His creation by taking it on Himself and winning the human heart. Paradise could only be restored from suffering and death through HIS suffering and death. In the original temptation, Satan sought out the first Adam and defeated him and became the prince of this world. But he does not rule openly; he deceives man into thinking he is his own master and ruler. Behind the scenes, it is really Satan that rules: *As for you, you were dead in your transgressions and sins, in which you used to live when you followed the ways of the world and of the ruler of the kingdom of the air the spirit who is now at work in those who are disobedient* (Eph 2:1-2).

But now the Last Adam *was led by the Holy Spirit into the desert to be tempted by the devil* (Matt 4:1). Jesus was guided by the Holy Spirit to find the devil and compel him into a showdown. As the Last Adam, the Representative man, He did not face the devil in His deity, but by His perfect humanity empowered by the Holy Spirit. All His miracles were done by the power of the Holy Spirit. The first Adam was challenged and defeated by the devil, but the Last Adam challenged and defeated the devil. The first Adam brought defeat and ruin to the race he headed, while the last

Adam brought victory and life to the race He headed. *For as in Adam all die, so in Christ all will be made alive* (1 Cor 15:22).

Many times during His temptation, Satan's objective was to tempt Jesus to rely on His Deity rather than His humanity as the Last Adam. As the First Adam was defeated by doubting God's word, the Last Adam relied upon, "It is written." The first temptation set the pattern for each victory. *"If you are the Son of God, tell these stones to become bread"* spoken by Satan, was responded to with *"Man does not live on bread alone, but on every word that comes from the mouth of God"* (3-4) by the Last Adam. Jesus was saying, "I am here to represent humanity as the last Adam." The strength of His position as Representative Man was in His reply "It is written," representing His submission to the will of God. As the Last Adam, it was His desire to do the will of God rather than to use His Deity to turn stones into bread!

Then the devil took Him to the Holy City and had Him stand on the highest point of the temple. "If you are the Son of God," he said, "throw yourself down. For it is written: 'He will command His angels concerning you, and they will lift you up in their hands, so that you will not strike your foot against a stone" (5-6).

Jesus answered him, "It is also written: 'Do not put the Lord your God to the test" (v. 7). Jesus was saying that to jump off the highest point of the temple would be to put God to the test. Real trust consists of quiet confidence, not in going out of one's way to put God to the test to see if He will keep His word. This would not reveal trust but a lack of trust!

The third temptation: *Again the devil took Him to a very high mountain and showed Him all the kingdoms of the world and their splendor. "All this I will give you," he said, "if you will bow down and worship me."*

In this third temptation, the devil shows Him all the kingdoms of the world and their splendor and offers them to Jesus if He will worship him. But Jesus chose a Kingdom based on the cross, the Kingdom of a renewed creation that worships and serves God alone. Then we are told, *Then the devil left Him, and angels came and attended Him.* Luke adds that the devil only left Him until *an opportune time.* He would be back, but he had been defeated by the Last Adam. The final outcome was clear. From now on Jesus exercised His Kingly authority over a defeated foe.

Notice in verse 1 that the angels did not come during the conflict with the devil. As the Last Adam, He had to face the struggle alone, as He would at Gethsemane when again angels ministered to Him only after the victory had already been won. At the cross twelve legions of angels were waiting for His call, which never came. He had to drink the cup alone. But then after His resurrection, they were there. From now on the demons would cringe at His command and plead with Him not to torment them before their time (Matt 8:29).

JESUS AND NICODEMUS
JOHN 3:1-18

Now there was a man of the Pharisees named Nicodemus, a member of the Jewish ruling council. He came to Jesus at night and said, "Rabbi, we know you are a teacher who has come from God. For no one can perform the miraculous signs you are doing if God were not with him" (1-2).

Nicodemus was one of the 71 members of the Sanhedrin. He was a moral and religious man. He had a high reputation for learning in the Old Testament Scriptures. He had influence and power. We are told that he came to Jesus at night so as to have privacy from the Scribes and Pharisees. He later may have become a secret disciple, but at Jesus' crucifixion, he came openly to take the body down from the cross and helped in His burial.

In reply Jesus declared, "I tell you the truth, no one can see the Kingdom of God unless he is born again" (v. 3). As a Pharisee Nicodemus took for granted that he would enter the Kingdom of God in one of its chief positions. Nicodemus was going to continue, but Jesus interrupted him. It seems obvious that he was going to inquire of Jesus, whom he considered a prophet, about the Kingdom of God. Jesus said, in effect, "Nicodemus you do not need to inquire about the Kingdom of God because unless you are born again, you cannot see the Kingdom of God!"

These were startling words, for if anyone could earn his way to God's Kingdom by his goodness, it was people like Nicodemus. What Jesus literally said in the original Greek was "You must be born from above."

"How can a man be born when he is old?" Nicodemus asked. "Surely he cannot enter a second time into his mother's womb to be born?"

Jesus answered, "I tell you the truth, no one can enter the Kingdom of God unless they are born of the water and the Spirit. Flesh gives birth to flesh, but the Spirit gives birth to the spirit" (4-6).

Nicodemus said he could not understand how a man could be born when he is old. Jesus told him that he was not referring to a second natural birth because that which is born of the flesh would still be flesh. It is a spiritual birth from above that is required.

A common misunderstanding is to think that the water here refers to water baptism, but this is not scriptural, for we are told over and over again that the one who believes in Christ, in the Biblical sense, has, at that moment, everlasting life. Baptism comes after faith in Christ when the believer already HAS eternal life. We see this in many places in the Word of God.

Acts 10:44-48 tells us that when Peter was preaching, *The Holy Spirit came on all who heard the message. The Jewish believers who had come with Peter were astonished that the gift of the Holy Spirit had been poured out even on the Gentiles, for they had heard them speaking in tongues and praising God. Then Peter said, "Can anyone keep these people from being baptized with water? They have received the Holy Spirit just as we have." So he ordered that they be baptized in the name of Jesus Christ.*

Then in Acts 9 we read of a similar incident. Here we read of Saul's (Paul's) conversion on the road to Damascus. In verse 17, Ananias is sent by God to the blinded Saul. *Then Ananias went to the house and entered it, placing his hands on Saul, he said, "Brother Saul, the Lord Jesus who appeared to you on the road as you were coming here, has sent me so that you may see again and be filled with the Holy Spirit." Immediately, something like scales fell from Saul's eye, and he could see again. He got up and was baptized, and after taking some food, he regained some strength.*

Note in both these places that the Holy Spirit fell on them before they were baptized. The Holy Spirit can only fall on those who are saved. So it is obvious that they were saved before they were baptized. There is no place in the Bible where anyone was ever saved by water baptism. In 1 Corinthians 1:14 Paul says: *I am thankful that I did not baptize any of you except Crispus and Gaius.* That would be a very strange thing for Paul to say if baptism was essential to salvation. The driving force of Paul's life was to win people to Christ and yet he thanks God that he had only baptized two men! He adds *For Christ did not send me to baptize, but to preach the gospel . . ..*

Note how Paul distinguished between preaching the gospel and baptism. Baptism does not communicate life and is not essential to salvation. It is commanded by God as a picture of the believer's identification with the death and burial and resurrection of Jesus. It symbolizes what has already taken place before baptism. We must go to the Word of God to see what water here refers to. Nowhere does it symbolize baptism. But in many passages it refers to the word of God.

In Ephesians 5:26 we read of the *washing of Water through the word*. Notice the Word of God is associated with "washing" and "water." Then in James 1:18 we read: *He chose to give us birth through the Word of truth.* . . . And 1 Peter 1:23: *For you have been born again not of perishable seed but of imperishable through the living and enduring word of God*. These last two verses associate the Word of God with birth and being born again.

So we have seen that "water" is associated with the "Word of God" and with "birth."

"Spirit" of course refers to the Holy Spirit. The Holy Spirit uses His word to bring about the new birth: *He saved us through the washing of rebirth and renewal by the Holy Spirit* (Titus 3:5). Thus we see the meaning of the words, *"I tell you the truth, no one can see the kingdom of God unless they are born of water and the Spirit."* The Holy Spirit uses the word of God to bring about the new birth.

Romans 10:13-14 tells us, *For every one who calls upon the name of the Lord will be saved. How then can they call on the one they have not believed in? And how can they believe in the one whom they have not heard? And how can they hear without someone preaching to them?*

Paul continues in verse 17: *Consequently, faith comes from hearing the message, and the message is heard through the word of Christ.*

Here we see that we receive salvation through faith. But in order to believe, you must have something TO believe. Thus, when a person hears the gospel message concerning the Lord Jesus Christ and believes in Him, the Holy Spirit brings about the new birth – the imparting of eternal life. Thus, that person is born of water – the Word of God, the gospel message – and the Holy Spirit. Why is the new birth necessary? Because *that which is born of the flesh is flesh and that which is born of the Spirit is Spirit*. Here are two very different realms of life: the realm of the flesh, which we enter by physical birth, and the realm of the Spirit, which we enter by the new birth, from above. We are born physically with a sinful nature.

Surely I was sinful at birth, sinful from the time my mother conceived me. The sin nature of Adam passed on to him from his parents.

Through Adam (natural birth) we received a fallen, sinful nature which is hopelessly ruined and at war with God. This nature cannot be changed. The flesh nature can be religious; it can be baptized, tithe, attend church, give to the poor, pray, fast, and take communion – but it is still flesh! The New Birth is from God, just as our natural birth is from our natural parents. The two natures have nothing in common (Gal 5:17).

"You should not be surprised at my saying you must be born again. The wind blows wherever it pleases. You hear the sound, but you cannot tell where it comes from or where it is going. So it is with everyone born of the Spirit" (3:7-8). The word "MUST" is the Greek word "DEI," which means "a moral and spiritual necessity." Nicodemus was confused as to how this could be. Jesus, knowing this said, "Stop wondering, Nicodemus; you cannot understand it, but it is real; the new birth is a mystery like the wind."

"How can this be?" Nicodemus asked. "You are Israel's teacher," said Jesus, *"and you do not understand these things?"* (9-10).

The Old Testament Scriptures, in which Nicodemus was a "master," speaks of the need for the new birth: *I will pour out water on the thirsty land, and streams on the dry ground. I will pour out my Spirit on your offspring and my blessing on your descendants* (Isa 44:3).

Here we are told that those who are thirsty for God will find God pouring out the water of the Word and the power of the Holy Spirit to bring about the new birth.

"I tell you the truth, we speak of what we know, and we testify to what we have seen, but still you people do not accept our testimony. I have spoken to you of earthy things and you do not believe; how then will you believe if I speak of heavenly things? No one has ever gone into heaven except the One who came from heaven – the Son of Man" (11-13).

Here Jesus is saying that He and his disciples spoke of things that they knew. If Jesus told them of earthly things like the new birth, which is experienced on earth, and they don't understand, how could he expect to understand heavenly things that can only be grasped by those who have been born again.

Jesus tells him that if he did not believe his testimony then he could never know these things because no one has ascended to heaven to learn these things and returned to earth to tell them except he himself, who came to speak what he knew and to bear witness to what he had seen.

"Just as Moses lifted up the snake in the desert, so the Son of Man must be lifted up, that everyone who believes in him may have eternal life. For God so loved the world that He gave His One and Only Son, that whosoever believes in Him shall not perish but have eternal life" (14-16).

Here Jesus explains how a man can be born again. The incident of Moses lifting the serpent on a pole is found in Numbers 21:6-9: *The Lord sent venomous snakes among them; they bit the people and many died. The people came to Moses and said, "We have sinned when we spoke against the Lord and against you. Pray that the Lord will take the snakes away from us." So Moses prayed for the people. The Lord said to Moses, "Make a snake and put it on a pole." Then when anyone was bitten by a snake and looked at the bronze snake they lived.*

Here Jesus said that this incident was an illustration of His work on the cross. The Son was chosen as the Last Adam, to give His life as a sacrifice for the sins of the world, that all those who would believe in Him would become part of the new creation. Though we have forfeited every claim to God's love, He loved us still and sent His Son to redeem us. He loves the whole world. None are left out; He loves every one of us. He does not simply love us as the mass of humanity, but as individuals. He singles out each one of us. Nor does He divide His love among us. He loves each with the whole of His love.

He gave Jesus to be the sacrifice for our sin and to suffer the wrath that we deserve. John 3:17-18 says: *For God did not send His Son into the world to condemn the world, but to save the world through Him. Whoever believes in Him is not condemned, but whoever does not stands condemned already because he has not believed in the name of God's One and Only Son.*

Here Jesus says the same thing that we read in 1 Corinthians 15:22: *For as in Adam all die, so in Christ all will be made alive.* There are only two classes of people in the world: Those who believe in Christ and are "in Christ," and those who do not trust in Him and remain "in Adam."

JESUS GREATER THAN THE TEMPLE

"I tell you one greater than the temple is here" (Matt 12:6). In John 2:13-22 Jesus had entered the temple in the court of the Gentiles and found them selling animals for sacrifice as a convenience for the worshippers, especially for those who had to travel great distances and bring animals with them. So it was arranged for them to purchase an animal at the temple, as well as pay the annual temple tax as a convenience for those who had not paid it on time at their residence, after which it had to be paid at the temple. It was required to be paid in a specific coin. Therefore moneychangers were there to provide the proper coins and a charge was made for this service. It quickly became a business for profit. Exorbitant charges were made for sacrifices and money changes. The profit went to the providers of these services rather than into the Temple treasury.

Because Annas, a former High Priest who still held great influence, and his sons ran this business, it was called "the Bazaars of Annas." Jesus made a scourge of small cords of rope (v. 15) and drove all from the temple area and overturned their tables, and scattered the coins of the money changers, saying, *"How dare you turn My Father's house into a market!"* (v. 16).

This was prophesied in Malachi 3:1: *See, I will send my messenger, who will prepare the way before me. Then suddenly the Lord you are seeking will come to His temple: "The messenger of the covenant, who you desire, will come," says the Lord Almighty*. Then His disciples recalled the Scripture of Psalm 69, the Messianic Psalm, verse 9: *The zeal of your house will consume me.*

Then the Jews demanded of Him, "What miraculous sign can you show us to prove your authority to do all this?" Jesus answered them, "Destroy this temple and I will raise it up again in three days" (John 2:18-19).

Here Jesus used the Greek word "naos" for "temple," which referred to the Holy of Holies (the area of the temple where the Shekinah Glory, representing the presence of God, dwelt). In John 1:14 we are told concerning Christ, *The Word became flesh and made his dwelling among us*. Here the word for "dwelling" is literally "tabernacle." He made his tabernacle among us. Jesus was comparing Himself to the Temple.

The Jews replied, *"It has taken forty-six years to build this temple, and you are going to raised it in three days?" But the temple he had spoken of was his body. After He was raised from* the dead, his disciples recalled what he had said. Then they believed the Scripture and the words Jesus had spoken (John 2:20-22).

When He drove the money changers out of the temple, He referred to it as "MY House" in Matt 21:13: *"It is written," he said to them, 'MY HOUSE will be called a house of prayer,' but you are making it a den of robbers."* In Matt 23:38, when it became clear that they were going to reject Him, He pronounced seven "woes" on the Scribes and Pharisees. He said to them, *"Look YOUR house is left to you desolate."*

They had rejected the God of the Temple and all that was left was an empty Temple. He would be killed and rise from the dead three days later, then the center of worship would not be the temple but Jesus Himself. Jesus purposely compared Himself to the earthly Temple to illustrate that the earthly Temple was about to be set aside because Yahweh now tabernacled among them in the flesh Jesus declared: *"One greater than the temple is here"* (Matt 12:6).

Christ the True Passover Lamb (1 Cor 5:7) to which all the types and symbols pointed rendered the sacrifice of the Temple meaningless. Now the worship of God in Spirit and Truth made the Temple in Jerusalem or the Samaritan Temple obsolete. To the Samaritan woman at the well, *Jesus declared, "Believe me, woman, a time is coming when you will worship the Father neither on this mountain nor in Jerusalem. You Samaritans worship what you do not know; we worship what we do know, for salvation is from the Jews. Yet a time is coming and has now come when the true worshippers will worship the Father in Spirit and truth, for they are the kind of worshippers the Father seeks. God is Spirit, and His worshipers must worship in Spirit and truth"* (John 4:21-24).

The earthly Temple would be destroyed when Jerusalem was destroyed in 70 A.D.: *As he was leaving the temple, one of his disciples said to him, "Look, Teacher! What massive stones! What magnificent buildings!" "Do you see all these great buildings?" replied Jesus. "Not one stone here will be left on another; every one will be thrown down"* (Mark 13:1-2).

The Temple Mount covered an area of about 30 football fields and was the largest site like it in the world. Its walls were about ten stories in height. One of its stones weighed 400 tons. How little they had understood its meaning. Everything in the Temple spoke of Him and His work of redemption. Yet when He came and walked among them, they did not know Him.

When the Shekinah glory (The visible cloud representing the presence of the Lord) departed the Temple in the Old Testament, God said to them, *"I will go back to my place until they admit their guilt. And they will seek my face; in their misery they will earnestly seek me"* (Hos. 5:15). Before departing, He promised restoration to the remnant of faithful believers. Then from the midst of Jerusalem, the Shekinah glory went out to the Mount of Olives and lingered until finally ascending into heaven.

In the New Testament, the Lord Jesus said, *"For I tell you, you will not see me again until you say, 'Blessed is he who comes in the name of the Lord,'"* He was crucified and then rose from the dead, and went to the Mount of Olives and ascended into heaven and will return to it (Acts chapter 1; Zech 14:4). The destruction of Jerusalem and the Temple showed that everything pointing to the Coming One was fulfilled.

When John the Baptist said Jesus was the *Lamb of God who takes away the sin of the world* (John 1:29), he was saying that Jesus was the final sacrifice as well as the King who would bring in the Kingdom of God. We are told in Hebrews 7:27: *Unlike the other High Priests, he does not need to offer sacrifices day after day, first for his own sins, and then for the sins of the people. He sacrificed for their sins once for all when HE OFFERED HIMSELF.*

Here we see that Jesus was both the Sacrifice and the High PRIEST who offered it up; *He offered Himself.*

God's dwelling place is now in His people as His LIVING TEMPLES. As 1 Peter 2:5 tells us: *You also, like living stones are being built into a spiritual house to be a holy priesthood, offering spiritual sacrifices acceptable to God through Jesus Christ.* And 1 Peter 2:9 says: *But you are a chosen people, a royal priesthood, a holy nation, a people belonging to God, that you may declare the praises of Him who called you out of darkness into His wonderful light.*

Christ is the fulfillment of the types and shadows of the Old Testament, of the temple, the High Priest, and the sacrifice. He is the PERFECT OFFERING and the PERFECT HIGH PRIEST WHO OFFERED HIMSELF. Hebrews 10:29 says that to go back to the old sacrificial system is to trample the Son of God under foot and they have treated the blood of the covenant as if it were common and unholy. Such people have insulted the Holy Spirit who brings God's mercy to His people.

Christ is now the center of God's program and we look forward to the New Jerusalem of which Christ is the King of Kings and Lord of Lords (Rev 19:6; 21:22-27).

THE LORD OF THE SABBATH
(Matt 12:1-8)

Matthew 12:1-6 tells of a controversy about the Sabbath: *At that time Jesus went through the grain fields on the Sabbath, His disciples were hungry and began to pick some heads of grain and eat them. When the Pharisees saw this, they said to him, "Look! Your disciples are doing what is unlawful on the Sabbath." He answered, "Haven't you read what David did when he and his companions were hungry? He entered the house of God, and he and his companions ate the consecrated bread – which was not lawful for them to do, but only for the priests. Or haven't you read in the law that on the Sabbath the priests in the temple desecrate the day and yet are innocent. I tell you that One greater than the temple is here."* Then in verse 8 Jesus said, *"For the Son of Man is Lord of the Sabbath."*

God the Creator was Lord of the Sabbath. It was given by Yahweh and belonged to Him. What the disciples were doing was perfectly legal; to pluck a few heads of grain was allowed, and rubbing it in their hands was hardly work. But these religious leaders considered pulling off the heads of grain as reaping. They considered the rubbing of the grain as threshing. What was considered unlawful was that it was done on the Sabbath.

The Pharisees divided the commandments into sections and then subdivided these into hundreds of subdivisions and prohibitions, many of which were downright silly! They debated such questions as, "Should one remove a speck from one's eye on the Sabbath. It was work to remove it, but it was also work to keep blinking because of the speck!

Jesus was claiming to be the God of the Sabbath as Creator, and since He gave the Sabbath and it points to Him as our Sabbath or rest from self-effort to attain salvation, He could do with it what He wanted. He did not weaken it but He reclaimed it from the Scribes and Pharisees who were degrading it by making it an unnecessary burden. Jesus restored dignity and sense to the commandment. He said in Mark 2:27: *"The Sabbath was made for man, not man for the Sabbath."* The purpose of the Sabbath was blessing, not burden.

MIRACLES AND HEALINGS

The Old Testament gives us a remarkable portrait of the coming Messiah. In Isaiah 35:5-6 we read: *Then will the eyes of the blind be open and the ears of the deaf unstopped. Then will the lame leap like a deer, and the mute tongue shout for joy.*

This is a description of the Messianic Kingdom. Jesus said that His miracles testified of Him. He claimed to be the fulfillment of the Old Testament types and prophecies. In Luke 4:16-21 we read: *He went to Nazareth where He had been brought up, and on the Sabbath day He went into the synagogue, as was His custom. And He stood up to read. The scroll of the prophet Isaiah was handed to Him. Unrolling it, He found the place where it was written: "The Spirit of the Lord is on me, because He has anointed me to preach the good news to the poor, to release the oppressed, to proclaim the year of the Lord's favor." Then he rolled up the scroll, gave it back to the attendant and sat down. The eyes of everyone in the synagogue was fastened on him, and he began by saying to them, "Today this Scripture is fulfilled in your hearing."*

In Luke 10:23-24 we read: *Then he turned to His disciples and said privately, "Blessed are the eyes that see what you see. For I tell you that many prophets and kings wanted to see what you see but did not see it, and to hear what you hear but did not hear it."* They were actually seeing and hearing what the Old Testament prophets had longed to see and hear themselves, but did not. The disciples lived in the days of the fulfillment of what the prophets could only anticipate. All the prophecies converged and met in Jesus.

These fulfilled prophecies were His credentials. *"I have a testimony weightier than that of John. For the very work that my Father has given me, and which I am doing, testifies that the Father has sent me"* (John 5:36). Healings and miracles were essential to the Messiah's mission. We read in Luke 7:7-22: *This news about Jesus spread throughout Judea and the surrounding country. John's disciples told him about all these things. Calling two of them, he sent them to the Lord to ask, "Are you the One who was to come, or should we expect someone else" At that very time Jesus cured many who had diseases, sickness and evil spirits, and gave sight to many who were blind. So he replied to the messengers, "Go back and report to John what you have seen and heard. The blind receive sight, the lame walk, those who have leprosy are cured, the deaf hear, the dead are raised, and the good news is preached to the poor."*

These miracles were called "signs" or credentials that He was the Coming One – proofs of His mission. They showed the goal of His mission. He came as the Last Adam, whose final goal was the eternal restoration of creation from Adam's fall. He is the Life giver of the physically dead as well as the spiritually dead. His miracles proved that He has supreme authority over nature as well as man's soul and body – all human disorders, spiritual and mental. His work is a cosmic work as He destroys the works of the devil (1 John 3:8).

These were signs that the deliverer was here. His miracles symbolized the coming Kingdom of God. This refers to the whole creation won back from Satan by the Last Adam. Paradise lost through Adam would become Paradise regained through Christ. At His death on the cross, the earthquake represented the birth pangs of the new age. The old, fallen universe will perish. *But the day of the Lord will come like a thief. The heavens will disappear with a roar; the elements will be destroyed by fire, and the earth and everything in it will be laid bare* (2 Pet 3:10). It will give birth to the new creation: *And I heard a loud voice from the throne saying, now the dwelling of God is with men, and He will live with them. They will be His people, and God himself will be with them and be their God. He will wipe away every tear from their eyes. There will be no more death or mourning or crying or pain, for the old order of things has passed away. He who was seated on the throne said, "I am making everything new!"* (Rev 21:3-5).

There will be a new glorified earth and a glorified humanity. The glorification of humanity depends on the glorification of Christ, while the glorification of creation depends on the glorification of mankind, as we are told in Romans 8:18-19: *I consider that our present sufferings are not worth comparing to the glory that will be revealed in us. The creation waits in eager expectation for the sons of God to be revealed.*

As the Son of Man, the last Adam, He has accomplished what the Father gave Him to do. As man he wore the crown of thorns representing the curse that He took upon himself and destroyed the works of the devil, and someday as man, the Head of redeemed humanity, He will rule over this redeemed earth through His redeemed people. *And God placed all things under his feet and appointed him to be Head over everything for the church, which is his body, the fullness of Him who fills everything in every way* (Eph 1:22-23).

His own suffering will ultimately end suffering. By His death He will ultimately bring death to sin, and the curse upon creation, including death itself. *Since the children have flesh and blood, He too shared in their humanity so that by his death he might destroy him who holds the power of death – that is, the devil– and free those who all their lives were held in slavery by their fear of death* (Heb 2:14-15).

His resurrection life is now imparted spiritually to all who trust in Him and they are removed from being "in Adam" to being "in Christ." And the Lord of Life will renew and glorify His creation with the greatest glory of all: He himself will dwell with them.

His healing ministry was a foretaste of that coming day. The healings were so many that in many places the Biblical writers were forced to use generalizations. For instance: *Healing every disease and sickness among the people . . . All who were ill with various diseases, those suffering severe pain, the demon possessed, those having seizures, and the paralyzed, and He healed them* (Matt 4:23-24).

Healed all their sick (Matt 8:16). *Healed all their sick* (Matt 12:15). *Healing every disease and sickness* (Matt 9:35). *Large crowds followed Him, and He healed them there* (Matt 19:2). *The blind and the lame came to Him . . .and he healed them* (Matt 21:14). *And all who touched Him were healed* (Mark 6:56).

All who had various kinds of sickness, and laying His hands on each one, He healed them (Luke 4:40).

As the Last Adam, Jesus showed that He was the One through whom the creation itself will be set free from the curse of the fall. His miracles and healings were a demonstration of this. His healing ministry was an earnest or down payment of what will come when He will wipe away every tear from their eyes. There will be no more death or mourning or crying or pain, for the old order of things has passed away (Rev 21:4). Death will be swallowed up by everlasting life (1 Cor 15:54; 2 Cor 5:4). All nature will be restored to the perfection of the Garden of Eden (Rom 8:18-21).

AUTHORITY OVER DEMONS

As the last Adam, He has been shown to be the Victor over Satan and his demons, a foretaste of the final destruction of the kingdom of darkness and the establishment of Christ's own kingdom: *"What do you want with us, Son of God? Have you come here to torture us before the appointed time?"* (Matt 8:29). Recognizing Jesus as their final judge, the demons ask Him if He is going to send them to the place of torment before the designated last judgment. They knew that their time was limited. James 2:19 tells us, *The demons believe and tremble.* They know that their grip on mankind and the fallen creation is limited.

After casting a demon out of a deaf and dumb man, we are told: *All the people were astonished and said, "Could this be the Son of David?" But when the Pharisees heard this, they said, "It is only by Beelzebub the prince of the demons that this fellow drives out demons." And Jesus knew their thoughts, and said to them, "Every kingdom divided against itself will be ruined, and every city or household divided against itself cannot stand, if Satan drives out Satan, he is divided against himself, how then can it stand?"* (Matt 12:23-26).

Then in verse 28 He says, *"But if I drive out demons by the Spirit of God, then the Kingdom of God has come upon you."* This is exactly what was happening. This is one of the credentials of the Messiah. It showed that He was the Coming One, the Last Adam Who would overthrow Satan's kingdom and replace it with His Own.

RAISING THE DEAD

The most revealing and informative raising from the dead was the raising of Lazarus in John 11. Jesus and His disciples received word that Lazarus was sick and we are told that Jesus deliberately delayed two days before going and then said to them, *"Let us go back to Judea again."* His disciples reminded Him that recently in Judea they sought to stone Him. Jesus knew that Lazarus was really dead and said that He was going there to "awaken" him. They misunderstood and said that since he was sick it would do him good to sleep.

Then Jesus told them plainly that Lazarus was already dead and that He was glad for them that He was not there to prevent his death so that their faith in Him would be confirmed. Then Thomas, very pessimistic about returning to Judea, but loving Jesus, said: *"Let us also go that we might die with him"* (v. 16). When Jesus arrived Lazarus had already been dead for four days (v. 17). Martha met Him and Jesus told her, *"Your brother will rise again.*" Martha answered that she knew he would rise again at the resurrection at the last day.

Jesus told her that they did not have to wait until then because standing before her was the very One who would raise the dead on the last day. *"I am the resurrection and the life."* In the Greek He literally said, "I and I alone, am the resurrection and the life" (John 11:25). He went on the say, *"He who believes in me will live, even though he dies; and whoever believes in me will never die. Do you believe this?"* (25-26).

Here in verse 25, *"He who believes in me will live, even though he dies"* refers to the resurrection of the body. In verse 26, *"Whoever lives and believes in me will never die"* refers to spiritual life.

"Yes Lord," she told Him, I believe that you are the Christ, the Son of God, who was to come into the world" (v. 27). Then Martha went and called for Mary. Verse 32 states: *When Mary reached the place what Jesus was and saw Him, she fell at His feet and said, "Lord, if you had been here, my brother would not have died." When Jesus saw her weeping, He was deeply moved and troubled. "Where have you laid Him?" He asked. They said to Him, "Lord, come and see"* (32-34). *Then Jesus wept* (v. 35).

In verse 38 we read: *Jesus, once more deeply moved, came to the tomb. It was a cave with a stone laid across the entrance. "Take away the stone," He said.*

Then Martha said: "By this time there is a bad odor, for He has been there four days." Then Jesus said, "Did I not tell you that if you believed, you would see the glory of God?" So they took away the stone.

The Son of Man, the Last Adam, stands in front of the grave of Lazarus and is face to face with the rotting results of the fall. *Then Jesus looked up and said, "Father, I thank you that you have heard me. I knew that you always hear me, but I said this for the benefit of the people standing here, that they may believe that you sent me."*

When He had said this, Jesus called in a loud voice, "Lazarus come out!" The dead man came out, his hands and feet wrapped in strips of linen, and a cloth around his face. Jesus said to them, "Take off the grave cloths and let him go" (39-44). This "loud voice" of the Lord is the same as the "loud command" in 1 Thessalonians 4:16: *For the Lord Himself will come down from heaven with a loud command, with the voice of the archangel and with the trumpet of God, and the dead in Christ will rise first.* Here Jesus gave a sample of that coming great day!

STILLING THE STORM

Mark 4:35-41: *That day when evening came He said to His disciples, "Let's go over to the other side." Leaving the crowd behind, they took Him along, just as He was, in the boat. There were also other boats with Him. A furious squall came up, and the waves broke over the boat, so that it was nearly swamped. Jesus was in the stern, sleeping on a cushion. The disciples woke Him and said to Him. "Teacher don't you care if we drown?"*

He got up and rebuked the wind and said to the waves "quiet! Be still!" Then the wind died down and it was completely calm. He said to His disciples, "Why are you so afraid? Do you still have no faith?" They were terrified and asked each other, "Who is this? Even the wind and waves obey Him?"

That day when evening came refers to the evening of the day begun in chapter 3. It was a long and busy day. Jesus would have been very tired. He wanted to go to the other side of Lake Gennesaret (Sea of Galilee) (v. 35). After sending away the crowd, the disciples took Jesus in a fishing boat. Mark mentions: *Other boats followed them* (v. 36). Jesus could not avoid the crowds; they followed Him everywhere but turned back probably because of the approaching storm. Then we are told, *A furious squall came up* as suddenly an unexpectedly a violent wind swept down.

This area was 680 feet below sea level and the hot air pulled the storm system down from the area of Mount Herman, making it seem like a violent earthquake that made the waters roll and churn as in a furious hurricane. A fisherman's worst fears became a reality. They were in the middle of the lake and violent waves tossed the boat. They frantically tried to row and bail water until bailing became impossible. The waves filled the boat faster than they could bail the water out.

But an exhausted Jesus slept through it all! He had curled up with the cushion provided for the steersman, as a pillow. He was so tired and in need of sleep that He slept through the violent storm. They woke Jesus up and He rebuked the wind and there was silence. Psalms 89:9 referring to Yahweh says, *You rule over the surging sea; when its waves mount up, you still them.* As the hostile forces against mankind, they are rebuked by the greater authority of the Son of Man, the Last Adam.

After His rebuke of the great storm, there was a great calm. The disorders of mankind of sickness and death and the disharmony of nature are overcome by Christ and one day all disorders and disharmony will be restored by Him who *appeared to destroy the works of the devil* (1 John 3:8).

He said to them, "Why are you so afraid? Do you still not have faith in me?" They were terrified and asked each other, "Who is this? Even the wind and waves obey Him!" (40-41). They were terrified by the wind and the sea, but they were even more awed by the One who rebuked the wind and the sea – and they obeyed!

THE TRANSFIGURATION

After six days Jesus took Peter, James and John with Him and led them up a high mountain where they were all alone. There He was transfigured before them. His clothes became dazzling white, whiter than anyone in the world could bleach them. And there appeared before them Elijah and Moses, who were talking with Jesus. Peter said to Jesus, "Rabbi, it is good for us to be here. Let us put up three shelters – one for you, one for Moses and one for Elijah" (He did not know what to say, they were so frightened).

Then a cloud appeared and enveloped them, and a voice came from the cloud: "This is My Son, whom I love, listen to Him! Suddenly, when they looked around, they no longer saw anyone with them except Jesus. As they were coming down the mountain, Jesus gave them orders not to tell anyone what they had seen until the Son of Man had risen from the dead. They kept the matter to themselves, discussing what "the rising from the dead" meant (Mark 9:2-10).

To fully understand the transfiguration, we must begin with Mark 8:31-33, for the background. *Then He began to teach them that the Son of Man must suffer many things and be rejected by the elders, chief priests and teachers of the law, and that He must be killed and after three days rise again. He spoke plainly about this, and Peter took Him aside and began to rebuke Him. But when Jesus turned and looked at His disciples, He rebuked Peter, "Get behind Me, Satan." He said, "You do not have in mind the things of God, but the things of men."*

They just could not accept that He had come to die. This shows the misunderstanding that Jesus' disciples had regarding His coming crucifixion. Six months remained for instruction before

His actual death on the cross. They were men of their age. Their concept of Messiah was of a military leader, which was far from the truth; they would need to proclaim Him as the Savior of the world. Jesus met this lack of understanding by taking the three leading disciples up a mountain to teach them a crucial lesson.

In Mark 9:2 the verb "Was Transfigured" in the Greek is "metamorphoo," from which we get our word "Metamorphosis," meaning "showing outwardly one's inward character." The transcendent glory of Christ's deity showed through the veil of His humanity like the sun bursting forth from behind a cloud. The three disciples saw the outward expression of His inner nature.

When Moses came down from Mount Sinai after receiving the Law from God in Exodus 34, his face shown from a reflected glory of God so that the people could not look at him (29-34). The glory of the Lord Jesus Christ was not a reflected glory of God but the inner glory of His own person shining through until His clothing became dazzling white (Mark 9:3). The Greek word for "Dazzling" is "Stilbonta," which means a "glistening," shining as snow in the bright sunshine. Matthew 17:2 says, *His face shown like the sun.*

In verse 4 Moses and Elijah appeared and talked with Him. These two men represent the Law and the Prophets of the Old Testament, which bears witness to Christ's coming and His atoning death and resurrection. They were discussing His redemptive work soon to take place. Luke 9:31 tells us that they spoke of His *departure which He was about to bring to fulfillment at Jerusalem.*

Peter had rebuked Jesus for speaking of His death, but here before Peter, James, and John, Moses and Elijah discuss it with Jesus as witnesses to the fulfilling of the Old Order of types and foreshadows, and the incoming "New Order" or "Testament" of substance or fulfillment through Christ.

His death was not an accident or a misfortune but a fulfillment of Scripture for salvation and renewing of all creation. OUR physical deaths are natural and normal as a consequence of our being sinners, but Christ's death is the FULFILLMENT of God's redemptive plan.

In 9:5-6 we read that Peter asks if they can make three shelters or tabernacles for Jesus, Moses, and Elijah, as it was near the time of the feast of tabernacles. He said this because he did not know what to say concerning what he was seeing. Overwhelmed, he was afraid and did not know what to say. The cloud that overshadowed them in verse 7 was the "shekinah," the visible presence of God that dwelled over the tabernacle in the Old Testament (Exod 33:9; 1 Kings 8:10). Now it appeared here in fulfillment of the Old Testament type or foreshadow: God in human flesh now dwelling with men in human form. As is brought out in John 1:14 where we read, *The Word was made flesh and made His dwelling* (literally "Tabernacled") *among us.*

And the voice of the Father came out of the cloud saying, *This is My Son, Whom I love, listen to Him.* There was no need to detain Moses and Elisha, for everything centered in the Son. Then it suddenly ended. Only Jesus alone remained. In verse 9, as they came down the mountain, they were solemnly told by Jesus to tell no one what they had seen until He was raised from the dead. The experience was to prepare them for the trying, dark days ahead of them, which would not be fully understood by them until after His resurrection and the coming of the Holy Spirit. Verse 10 shows that they still could not comprehend His death and resurrection, and would not fully until the resurrected Christ explains it in Acts 1:2-8.

FORGAVE SIN
MARK 2:1-12

A few days later, when Jesus again entered Capernaum, the people heard that He had come home. So many gathered that there was no room left, not even outside the door, and He preached the Word to them. Some men came bringing to Him a paralytic, carried by four of them. Since they could not get him to Jesus because of the crowd, they made an opening in the roof above Jesus, and after digging through it, lowered the mat, the paralyzed man was laying on. When Jesus saw their faith, He said to the paralytic, "Son, your sins are forgiven." Some of the teachers of the law were sitting there, thinking to themselves, "Why does this fellow talk like that? He's blaspheming! Who can forgive sins but God alone?" Immediately Jesus knew in His spirit that this is what they were thinking in their hearts, and He said to them, "Why are you thinking these things? Which is easier: to say to the paralytic, 'Your sins are forgiven' or to say, 'Get up, take your mat and walk? But that you may know that the Son of Man has authority on earth to forgive sins . . . ." He said to the paralytic, "I tell you get up, take your mat and go home." He got up, took his mat, and walked out in full view of them all. This amazed everyone and they praised God, saying, "We have never seen anything like this."

Jesus' fame for healing was well known throughout that area. As He was proclaiming the Kingdom, He often showed some of the blessing of that coming time. The news of His return produced large crowds who pressed to see Him to the point that the house was filled and a crowd waited outside, blocking the door so that no one could enter. A paralytic man lying on a mat was being carried by four of his friends. When they could not get near Him through the door they brought him to the roof of the house, which was flat, and could be reached by stairs outside the house. The roofs were made of twigs mixed with sand and mud. When they made a large enough hole, they lowered the men down with ropes.

The Scribes were probably there to spy on Jesus and report back to the Sanhedrin. When Jesus saw the faith of the five men, He said that the paralytic's sins were forgiven. The teachers of the Law who were sitting there said that only God can forgive sin. Knowing their thoughts Jesus asks which is easier, to say to the man that his sins are forgiven or to tell the man to walk? Jesus was saying that no one could actually see the man's sins being forgiven, but could see the man take up his bed and walk. Since both would take Divine power, He could show that He could forgive sin by making him walk. An imposter could say his sins were forgiven and no one could prove him wrong, but could not make the man walk.

FORGAVE SIN
LUKE 7:36-50

Now one of the Pharisees invited Jesus to have dinner with him, so He went to the Pharisee's house and reclined at the table. When a woman who had lived a sinful life in that town learned that Jesus was eating at the Pharisees house, she brought an alabaster jar of perfume, and as she stood behind Him at His feet weeping; she began to wet His feet with her tears. Then she wiped them with her hair, kissed them and poured perfume on them.

When the Pharisee who had invited Him saw this, he said to himself, "If this man were a prophet he would know who was touching him and what kind of woman she is – that she is a sinner." Jesus answered him, "Simon, I have something to tell you."

"Tell me, teacher," he said.

"Two men owed money to a certain moneylender; one owed him five hundred denarii, and the other fifty. Neither of them had

the money to pay him back, so he cancelled the debt of both. Now which one of them will love him more?"

Simon replied, "I suppose the one who had the bigger debt cancelled." "You have judged correctly," Jesus said.

Then He turned to the woman and said to Simon, "Do you see this woman? I came into your house, you did not give me any water for my feet. But she wet my feet with her tears and wiped them with her hair. You did not give me a kiss, but this woman, from the time I entered, has not stopped kissing my feet. You did not put oil on my head, but she has poured perfume on my feet. Therefore I tell you, her many sins have been forgiven – for she loved much. But he who has been forgiven little, loves little."

Then Jesus said to her, "Your sins are forgiven!" The other guests began to say among themselves, "Who is this who even forgives sins." Jesus said to the woman, "Your faith has saved you, go in peace."

Here one of the Pharisees asked Jesus to come to his house for a meal, and Jesus accepted the invitation. He was probably invited out of curiosity and was not extended the common courtesies of the culture. Houses were often built around a courtyard in that climate. Formal meals were served in the open courtyard, with guests reclining on couches around a low U-shaped table. They lay on their left side, heads propped up with their left hand and they used their right hand to eat.

Their feet were bare, with knees bent with feet outward, so that servants could easily wash their feet, which was furthest from the table. Usually there were uninvited guests standing about observing. With a guest of honor, it was open to the public and cushions were provided around the border of the courtyard for visitors. From among these visitors came a woman with an alabaster jar of very expensive perfume on a thin rope around her neck as jewelry.

In verse 38 we see that she could easily approach Jesus, intending to anoint Him with the perfume. But as she saw His dusty, unwashed feet, as the common courtesy had not been given to Him, she could not control her emotions and her tears fell on His feet. Unconcerned about public opinion, she wiped them with her hair. It was a shame for a Jewish woman to let her hair down in public. She literally kept continuously wiping His feet with her hair, "her adornment."

Then, in her deep devotion, she kept kissing His feet and anointing them with perfume. Normally the perfume would have been poured on the head, but she poured it on His feet as a sign of humility and devotion. To attend to the feet was a lowly task only assigned to the lowest slaves, and to use such costly perfume in such a way was considered extremely improper.

At some point this woman trusted in Jesus and turned from her sinful ways and she was expressing her love and gratitude. When the host saw what was happening and who the woman was he said to himself, *"If this man were a prophet, he would know who was touching him and what kind of woman she is – that she is a sinner."* In verse 39 her act of devotion was interrupted and criticized by the host's thoughts, which were known to Jesus.

The Pharisee would not even mention Jesus by name, a sign of contempt. Then Jesus spoke up and answered his thoughts. Jesus told the Pharisee that there were two men who owed money to a certain moneychanger. One owed him five hundred denarii, and the other fifty. A denarius was about a day's wages. Neither of them could pay him back, so both debts were cancelled. Then Jesus asked who of the two would be the most grateful? Simon answered the one who owed the most. Then Jesus applied the teaching. The Pharisee had no concept of his own sin and pride and assumed that Jesus was no prophet because He tolerated this show of emotion from such a woman. Jesus showed that He did know what kind of woman she was but also what kind of person he was. He did not extend the ordinary courtesy of offering water to wash the dust and dirt off a guest's feet after walking the dusty roads in sandals.

It was customary to kiss a guest on both cheeks. It was also a common courtesy to provide some olive oil to sooth and moisturize the head and face after walking in the hot sun in that dry climate. These were humiliating words for Simon to hear in front of his guests, as these courtesies were strictly held in the Middle Eastern societies. Then Jesus turned to the woman and said to Simon, *"When I entered your home you did not give me water to wash my feet, but she has washed them with her tears and wiped them with her hair. You did not give me a kiss of greeting, but she has kissed my feet repeatedly. You neglected the courtesy of oil to anoint my head, but she has anointed my feet with perfume. I tell you, her sins have been forgiven, so she has shown me much love."* Then He said to the woman, *"Your sins have been forgiven, your faith has saved you, go in peace."*

Lack of faith in Him left the Pharisee in his sins, but the harlot entered the kingdom, as He had said to the Pharisees in Matthew

21:31: *"The Publicans and harlots go into the Kingdom of God before you."*

RECEIVED WORSHIP

In Matthew 4:10, after Satan told Jesus that he would give him all the kingdoms of the world if he would worship him, Jesus quoted from the first commandment: *"Away from me, Satan! For it is written: 'Worship the Lord your God, and serve Him only.'"*

Worship was rejected by angels: In Revelation 19:10 John falls down to worship an angel: *At this I fell at his feet to worship him, but he said to me, "Do not do it. I am a fellow servant with you and your brothers who hold to the testimony of Jesus: Worship God."* And again in Revelation 22:8-9: *And 1 John saw these things and heard them. And when I heard and saw: I fell down to worship at the feet of the angel who had been showing them to me. But he said to me, "Don't do it! I am a fellow servant with you and with your brothers the Prophets and to all who keep the words of this book. Worship God."*

Worship was also rejected by the best of men. Peter in Acts 10:25-26: *As Peter entered the house, Cornelius met him and fell at his feet in reverence. But Peter made him get up. "Stand up,"* he said. *"I am only a man myself."* And when Paul and Barnabas were in Lystra, after Paul had healed a man who was crippled in his feet, the priest of Zeus attempted to offer sacrifices to them. We are told: *When the apostles Barnabas and Paul heard of this, they tore their clothes and rushed out into the crowd, shouting: "Men why are you doing this? We too are only men, human, like you . . .* (Acts 14:8-15). But worship was freely received by Jesus Christ.

Matthew 2:11 concerning the Magi says, *And coming to the house, they saw the child with his mother, and they bowed down and worshipped him.*

Matthew 14:33: *Then those who were in the boat worshipped Him, saying, "Truly you are the Son of God."*

In Matthew 28:9 we read: *Suddenly Jesus met them, "Greetings," He said. They came to Him, clasped His feet and worshipped him.*

Luke 24:52: *Then they worshipped Him and returned to Jerusalem with great joy.*

John 9:38: *Then the man said, "Lord, I believe," and he worshipped Him.*

In John 20:28 worship is not mentioned specifically but is clearly and unmistakably implied by the words of Thomas, *"My Lord and my God."*

THE GOOD SHEPHERD
JOHN 10:1-18

"I tell you the truth, the man who does not enter the sheep pen by the gate, but climbs in by some other way, is a thief and a robber. The man who enters by the gate is the shepherd of the sheep. The watchman opens the gate for him, and the sheep listen for his voice. He calls his own sheep by name and leads them out. When he has brought out all his own, he goes on ahead of them, and his sheep follow him because they know his voice. But they will never follow a stranger; in fact they will run away from him because they do not recognize a stranger's voice. I tell you the truth; I am the gate for the sheep. All who ever came before me were thieves and robbers, but the sheep did not listen to them.

"I am the gate; whoever enters through me will be saved. He will come in and go out, and find pasture. The thief comes only to steal and kill and destroy; I am come that they might have life, and have it to the full. I am the good Shepherd. The good Shepherd lays down His life for the sheep. The hired hand is not the shepherd who owns the sheep. So when he sees the wolf coming, he abandons the sheep and runs away. Then the wolf attacks the flock and scatters it. The man runs away because he is a hired hand and cares nothing for the sheep.

"I am the Good shepherd; I know my sheep and my sheep know me, just as the Father knows me and I know the Father – and lay down my life for the sheep. I have other sheep that are not of this sheep pen. I must bring them also. They too will listen to my voice, and there will be one flock and one shepherd. The reason My Father loves me is that I lay down my life – only to take it up again. No one takes it from me, but I lay it down of my own accord. I have authority to lay it down and authority to take it up again. This commandment I received from my Father" (John 10:1-18).

The flocks were normally kept in the open field. Shepherds were skilled with the sling and rod or club to protect them from robbers and wild animals. But the shepherd would have to build a sheepfold to protect them at night. It would be made of low stone walls, with thorny branches on top. He had a shepherd's staff to count the sheep to make sure that none were missing, and to guide them and protect them (Psa 23:4).

Different shepherds would bring their flocks together in the evening into the large pen. The pen had one gate. A gatekeeper, hired by the shepherd, would open the gate in the morning for the shepherds who cared for the sheep. Obviously if anyone was caught climbing over the wall instead of going to the gatekeeper and entering through the gate, he would be a thief and a robber. A thief would steal, and a robber would steal violently. Psalm 23 presents God Himself as Israel's Shepherd, as does Psalm 80:1, *Hear us, O Shepherd of Israel, you who lead Joseph like a flock.*

Isaiah 40:11 refers to the Messiah: *He tends His flock like a shepherd: He gathers His lambs in His arms and carries them close to His heart: He gently leads those who have young.*

John 10:2: There were others before who claimed to be the Messiah, or to represent God, but only Christ came through the prescribed door of Scripture that give many pointers to the Messiah so He could be clearly identified when He came. And God raised up John the Baptist to announce His coming and to open the gate.

John 10:3: There is a personal and intimate relationship between Christ and His own. A true shepherd gives names to his sheep and calls them individually and leads them out to pasture. Our names are written in the *Lamb's book of life* (Rev 21:27). Psalms 23:1-2 says: *The Lord is my shepherd: I shall not be in want. He makes me lie down in green pasture. He leads me beside quiet waters.*

Sheep lie down in contentment after being led to lush green pastures and quiet waters. Sheep are afraid to drink from moving water. The shepherd must produce "quiet" waters by blocking the flow.

John 10:4-5: The shepherd goes ahead of his sheep and leads them. Psalms 23:3 says the Lord restores his soul and leads him in paths of righteousness. Sheep are very attached to their shepherd. They must be led, not driven. They follow. Often several flocks would be put in the same fold for the night. But the shepherd knows his own sheep and they know him. They follow him because they trust the shepherd and know his voice and the name he has given them. They love and trust their shepherd.

So in the morning the shepherd would give a certain sound when He was ready to lead them out. Only his sheep would follow him. They would not follow another. If two shepherds met, the flocks would mix together. But when they were ready to part from each other, they would simply call their sheep and they would know the voice of their shepherd and follow him.

In 2 Samuel 12:1-6 Nathan told King David of a man who had one little ewe lamb who slept in his arms, ate his food and drank from his cup, and was like a daughter to him. So the affection between a sheep and its master is very close. So, too, a believer who is born again has an inward draw toward Christ.

In verse 1 Jesus said He was the True Shepherd who entered through the gate to the sheep. In verse 7 He changes the metaphors to show different sides of the truth. Now He is the door itself. When the shepherd was alone he himself would be the gate. He would make a pen and make his sheep comfortable for the night. Then in the entrance the shepherd would lay on his side and no wild animal could enter and no sheep would go over his body.

All who came before Him were false Messiahs or false prophets or leaders, like the Scribes and Pharisees, seeking to mislead the sheep. But the sheep would not follow these thieves and robbers. But Jesus protects them and makes them safe and leads them to food and water. The thief comes only to make merchandise of the sheep. The robber comes not only to steal, but to destroy and kill. They care nothing for the sheep. But Jesus came in order for them to have life to the fullest. His coming was in contrast to all others. They TAKE, He GIVES, they KILL, He gives LIFE.

John 10:11. As the Good Shepherd He leads His sheep to food and water, protects them from danger, and *He lays down His life for the sheep.* In His words "FOR the sheep," the word "FOR" in the Greek is "HUPER" and literally means "OVER" the sheep, and implies that as harm is to fall on the sheep, He throws His body over the sheep and takes the harm intended for them. He will die protecting His sheep.

His hearers knew that He was applying to Himself what refers to God in the Old Testament. Ezekiel 34:10-12 says, *This is what the Sovereign Lord says, "I am against the shepherds and will hold them accountable for my flock. I will remove them from attending the flock so that the shepherds can no longer feed themselves. I will rescue my flock from their mouths, and it will no longer be food for them." For this is what the Sovereign Lord says: "I myself will search for my sheep and look after them. As a shepherd looks after his scattered flock when he is with them, so I will look after my sheep. I will rescue them from all the places where they were scattered on a day of clouds and darkness."*

John 10:12-13 speaks of the "hired hand" who works for wages. This one works for pay and does not really care for the sheep and will desert them in a crisis. He forsakes the sheep when the wolf approaches. The wolf catches some and scatters the rest as he wreaks havoc on the abandoned flock. The hired hand does not have the commitment of a true shepherd. Like the Pharisees who pose as shepherds and as many professional ministers and religious workers do, who care more for their salaries and prestige.

But Jesus knows His sheep and they know Him. They have experiential knowledge of each other and THIS is the secret of their mutual love and loyalty.

He knows our struggles and trials and disappointments. There was a man whose wife died and he was left with a little six-year-old boy who was blind. At night in bed the little boy would ask his father: "Daddy, are you looking at me?" He meant was his father facing him while he was sleeping. He wanted his father facing him, and then he could sleep. Psalms 121:3 says: *He who watches over you will not slumber.* His face is always toward us.

In John 10:15 Jesus says: *"Just as the Father knows me and I know the Father – and I lay down my life for the sheep."* Here "knowing" means "trusting" or "having confidence." The Father knows or has confidence in the Son to lay down His life for the sheep, and the Son knows or has confidence in the Father's will for Him to lay down His life for the sheep. This is why we are told in Psalms 23:4: *Even though I walk through the valley of the shadow of death, I will fear no evil, for you are with me.* Those who are His sheep do not face death, but merely the shadow of death. The substance of death – its sting – has been removed by the Shepherd, and now they have mere shadows to face.

One day a small boy was being chased by a bee. He ran into the house to his mother, crying. His mother placed her apron over him, hiding him. A few moments later she said, "You can come out now." He peeked out from behind her apron and watched as the bee slowly crawled down her arm. "See, its harmless now," she said. "It stung mommy and its stinger is in mommy's arm and now it cannot hurt you; its harmless." This is what Christ has done for His people. At the cross he removed death's sting by taking the sting Himself.

Verse 16 refers to the Gentiles, who were also included in God's plan of salvation, and would be brought into the same fold as the Jewish believers. The Old Testament has many references to the universal nature of Jesus' mission (Gen 18:18; 26:4; 28:14). These refer to all nations being blessed through Abraham's seed (Christ). Then there will be one flock and One Shepherd, referring to all believers without distinction.

In John 10:18 Christ says that He lays down His own life while John 3:16 says God gave His only begotten Son. The Father sent the Son and the Son came willingly. The Father gave the Son, and the Son wanted to be given. God not only gave the Son FOR the sheep but TO the sheep. It was not the nails that held Him on the cross. No nails could have held Him; it was love that held Him there, love for the Father and love for us. This is why in Psalms 23:5 we are said to feast at the table HE prepares for US and He will make sure that our cup of joy will not only not run dry, but will overflow.

The point is that it is God who takes the initiative. He sought His fallen creatures before they sought Him. The Divine Shepherd goes into the wilderness to find His lost sheep. It is His very nature to go after the lost. He is *not willing that any should perish*. The message of the cross is that God is the One who takes the initiative. He is the Divine Shepherd whose very nature is to protect His sheep at His own expense. In order to crush the serpent's head, He must expose His heel to its deadly fangs.

CHAPTER TEN
The Kingdom of God at Hand

The present condition of the human race and the world is not the result of an evolutionary progressive growth upward, but of a devastating fall downward, with catastrophic consequences for all creation. It brought down the whole human race and the whole creation that was put under its dominion. The marvelous creation that God had declared "very good" was defiled by sin. Nothing escaped the corrosive and degrading results of the fall. The whole creation groans under its effects while suffering and death reign over all.

Romans 8:20-22 says that the creation was made subject to "Frustration" and the "bondage of decay." God's solution was to appoint Jesus Christ to be our Redeemer as the Last Adam to undo all that the first Adam had done. God gave Christ to die for us and all who believe enter into the new creation through a relationship with Christ. As we entered the first creation through the first Adam, we now have the offer from God Himself to trust in Christ, the Last Adam, and enter into the new creation through Him. As the first Adam brought ruin, the Last Adam, Jesus Christ, brings salvation and restoration to the creation.

We all share in the effects of the fall because of our relationship with the first Adam, who brought sin and death and ruin to all of God's creation. Christ came to redeem the ruined creation and offer us a new relationship with God. The Kingdom of God is a central theme of Scripture. It is the redemption of all that was ruined. *The reason the Son of God appeared was to destroy the devil's work* (1 John 3:8). The coming of Christ was the fulfillment of the Old Testament prophecies of redemption through the Offspring of the woman. *For as in Adam all die, so in Christ will all be made alive.*

Jesus not only proclaimed the Kingdom of God but also demonstrated its coming by the restoration of creation. After casting a demon out of a man, He said to the Pharisees: *"But if I drive out demons by the Spirit of God, then the Kingdom of God has come upon you"* (Luke 11:20). His healings demonstrated His authority to destroy the works of the devil. When John the Baptist sent messengers to ask if Jesus was the Promised One who was to come, He said His works were the proof that He was. *"Go back* and report to John what you hear and see: *The blind receive sight, the lame walk, those who have leprosy are cured, the deaf hear, the dead are raised, and the good news is preached to the poor"* (Matt 11:4-5).

At His first coming, He established a beachhead that would guarantee victory through His death and resurrection. At His second coming, He will take control and set up His Kingdom. In the meantime His followers are to share the gospel and win recruits for Him in anticipation of the renewal of all creation. *Jesus said to them, "I tell you the truth, at the renewal of all things, when the Son of Man sits on His glorious throne, you who have followed me will sit on twelve thrones, judging the twelve tribes of Israel. And everyone who has left houses or brothers or sisters or father or mother or children or fields for my sake will receive a hundred times as much and will inherit eternal life. But many who are first will be last and many who are last will be first"* (Matt 19:28).

We are now in a spiritual war to win souls for Christ. 2 Corinthians 10:3-4 states: *For though we live in the world, we do not wage war as the world does. The weapons we fight with are not the weapons of the world. On the contrary, they have divine power to demolish strongholds.* We must not allow the world to weaken our effectiveness for Christ. *See to it that no one takes you captive through hollow and deceptive philosophy which depends on human tradition and the basic principles of this world rather than on Christ* (Col 2:8).

The redemption brought by Jesus Christ is universal and involves the whole creation. Just as the fall through Adam, as head of the old creation, brought down the whole creation, so too the redemption accomplished by Jesus Christ, the Head of the new creation, involves the whole creation. As the resurrected victor over sin and death, Christ now has all power in heaven and earth. *Then Jesus came to them and said, "All authority in heaven and on earth has been given to me. Therefore go and make disciples of all nations . . ."* (Matt 28:18).

As Son of God, Jesus always has all authority in heaven and earth. But the point here is that as the victorious Son of Man, the Last Adam, the God who became man, He now has, in this capacity, as representative of the New Humanity and on the throne of heaven with the Father sitting at His right hand, all power in heaven and earth has been given to Him by the Father.

As Head of the church, He gives his followers their marching orders to preach the gospel to every creature. He has been given power and authority to restore all creation. But He is now waiting for the completion of the gospel age, the period we now live in, during which time He is calling out a people for His name.

He has called for His followers to proclaim the gospel to bring others into the Kingdom before He comes back to set up His Kingdom. So there are three parts to the Kingdom of God:

1. Christ's work of redemption
2. The proclamation of the gospel worldwide
3. The return of the King to set up His Kingdom

We are now in the second part of this and waiting for the third part to come. The Kingdom of God will bring a return to the original perfect creation before sin ruined it. The Kingdom will be the union of Heaven and earth and the King will be God incarnate in the Man Jesus Christ. The word "redemption" brings this out. Redeemed means to buy or purchase.

Because of the first Adam, we have been sold into slavery to the bondage of sin and death. Christ paid our ransom by His own suffering and death. God does not abandon His old creation. He recreates the original fallen creation. He builds the new out of the ruins of the old. He takes the old sinner and remakes him anew in Christ, and he will take the old, fallen, cursed creation and renew or regenerate it.

The Kingdom is the Kingly rule of God, through the Messiah on the new earth. The new earth is based on Christ's redemption and will be established upon the old earth. The old earth will continue eternally in the new earth. This was foretold by the prophets, and the Kingdom will come in power at the second coming of Christ and will be given to His "little flock": *"Do not be afraid, little flock, for your Father has been pleased to give you the kingdom"* (Luke 12:32).

The kingdom of God begins with salvation; it is the reign of God in the hearts of men, and this transforms their lives. When Christ returns we will actually enter the kingdom in literal form. This is why the Kingdom of God is presented in Scripture as a present possession through the new birth as in Colossians 1:13: *For He has rescued us from the dominion of darkness and brought us into the kingdom of the Son He loves.* Sometimes the Kingdom is referred to as a future possession as in Acts 14:22: *Strengthening the disciples and encouraging them to remain true* to the faith. *We must go through many hardships to enter the kingdom of God.*

In Luke 19:11-27, Jesus gives a parable about a nobleman who goes off to a far country to receive a kingdom. He entrusts to his servants his treasures and when he returns he settles his accounts with his servant. Those who are faithful to him are given positions of authority in his kingdom. We are left here on earth to carry on Jesus' business and look after His interests. After His resurrection He went back to heaven to receive His kingdom and He will return to reward those who faithfully devote their lives to carrying out His business of the Great Commission given in Matthew 28:18: *"All authority in heaven and earth has been given to me. Therefore go and make disciples of all nations, baptizing them in the name of the Father and of the Son and of the Holy Spirit, and teaching them to obey everything I have commanded you. And surely I am with you always, to the very end of the age."* These were Jesus' last words before ascending back into Heaven. The treasure He left us is the gospel and our business is to share the good news that Jesus died and rose again from the dead and offers a free salvation to all who will come to Him. He did this to open the door to Heaven and we are doorkeepers in our everyday lives to reach those in our sphere of influence. When He returns He will settle accounts by giving those who are faithful positions of authority in His Kingdom.

In Revelation 21:1-5 God's final goal has come. There is a new creation: a new heaven and a new earth. John sees the holy city, the New Jerusalem, descending out of Heaven. He hears a voice saying that the dwelling place of God is with mankind and He will live with them. He will wipe all tears from their eyes and there will be no more death or mourning or crying or pain. All these things will have passed away. He who sits on the throne said: *"I am making everything new!"*

The heavenly Jerusalem descends to become the capital city of earth. The Divine Redeemer came to earth and took upon Himself humanity so that the earth would become the dwelling place of God. His throne will be moved to earth; the place where Christ, as the Last Adam, won back what the first Adam had lost.

Hebrews 12:22-24 refers to that city: *But you have come to Mount Zion, to the Heavenly Jerusalem, the city of the living God. You have come to thousands upon thousands of angels in joyful assembly, to the church of the Firstborn, whose names are written in heaven. You have come to God, the Judge of all men, to the spirits of just men made perfect, to Jesus the Mediator of a new covenant, and to the sprinkled blood that speaks a better word than the blood of Abel.*

This is the city that Abraham looked for: *by faith Abraham, when called to go to a place he would later receive as his inheritance, obeyed and went, even though he did not know where he was going. By faith he made his home in the promised land like a stranger in a foreign country; he lived in tents, as did Isaac and Jacob who were heirs with him of the same promise. For he was looking forward to the city with foundations, whose architect and builder is God* (Heb 11:8-10).

This present life is a pilgrimage, as was illustrated by his living in tents. He did not put down roots in this world because he knew that the only foundation was in that heavenly city because it was built by God. Nothing in this world lasts except what we do for Christ. We have no foundation in this world. But all those who belong to Christ have an *inheritance that can never perish, spoil or fade – kept in heaven for you* (1 Pet 1:4).

Luke 10:1-20 tells about how Jesus sent out 70 disciples to preach and He gave them power over demons. When they returned they were filled with joy that even the demons were submissive to them when they used Jesus' name. Jesus reminds them in verse 20: *"However, do not rejoice that the spirits submit to you, but rejoice that your names are written in Heaven."* It is a very unique Kingdom, whose King died for His people. All His people were once enemies and now they reign with Him!

JESUS FORETELLS HIS DEATH

From that time on Jesus began to explain to His disciples that He must go to Jerusalem and suffer many things at the hands of the elders, chief priests and teachers of the law, and that he must be killed and on the third day be raised to life (Matt 16:21). What Jesus had spoken of before in veiled language, His coming death and resurrection, He now speaks of clearly in plain language. His disciples must be ready to face this event.

Earlier He had said that if the temple of His body were destroyed, He would raise it again in three days (John 2:18-22). Then the Jews demanded of Him, *"What miraculous sign can you show us to prove your authority to do this?" Jesus answered them, "Destroy this temple and I will raise it again." The Jews replied, "It has taken forty-six years to build this temple, and you are going to raise it in three days?" But the temple he had spoken of was his body. After he was raised from the dead, his disciples had recalled what he said. Then they believed the Scripture and the words Jesus had spoken.*

And Jesus had told Nicodemus that He must be lifted up like Moses lifted up the serpent in the wilderness (John 3:14-15). He had also said that as Jonah spent three days and nights in the belly of the whale He would be three days and nights in the heart of the earth (Matt 12:38-41).

But now He is clear: *"The Son of Man shall be delivered up to the chief priests and to the Scribes, and they shall condemn Him to death, and shall deliver Him up to the Gentiles: They shall mock Him and shall scourge Him and shall spit upon Him and shall kill Him. Three days later He will rise"* (Mark 10:33-34).

And, *"The Son of man must suffer many things and be rejected by the elders and chief priests and teachers of the law, and he must be killed and on the third day be raised to life"* (Luke 9:22).

And, *Jesus took the twelve aside and told them, "We are going up to Jerusalem, and everything that is written by the prophets about the Son of Man will be fulfilled. He will be handed over to the Gentiles. They will mock Him, insult Him, spit on Him, flog Him and kill Him. On the third day He will rise again"* (Luke 18:31-33).

But this did not fit well with their expectations of the Messiah, nor what they wanted to hear about Jesus. *But they did not understand what He meant and were afraid to ask Him about it* (Mark 9:32).

The disciples did not understand any of this. Its meaning was hid from them, and they did not know what He was talking about (Luke 18:34).

Matthew 26:2-5: Jesus said, *"As you know, the Passover is two days away – and the Son of Man will be handed over to be crucified." Then the chief priests and the elders of the people assembled in the palace of the high priest, whose name was Caiaphas and they plotted to arrest Jesus in some sly way and to kill Him. "But not during the Passover feast," they said, "or there may be a riot among the people."*

Here Jesus shows that He is really in control of what was going to happen. He tells His disciples that He will be betrayed and crucified on the *Feast of the Passover,* while the very ones who would carry this out were deciding that it would NOT take place on the Feast of Passover! And of course it did.

But few understood. Mary had understood His words about His death. Mary and Martha served a dinner in Jesus honor. During the dinner *Mary took about a pint of pure nard, an expensive perfume. She poured it on Jesus' feet and wiped His feet with her hair. And the house was filled with the fragrance of the perfume* (John 12:3). According to Matthew 26:7, she poured some of it on His head too. It was worth a fortune, a year's wages; probably her life's savings. The guests would have been speechless when Mary let her hair down and used it as a towel to dry His feet. Adult women did not allow their long hair to be seen in public, and the cost of the perfume was considered extremely excessive to be used in this way. Also, only the lowest servants attended the feet.

Judas rebuked her, asking why the ointment had not been sold for three hundred pence (a normal year's wages) and given to the poor. He said this because he held the moneybag and he loved money. *"Leave her alone," Jesus replied. "It was intended that she should save this perfume for the day of my burial. You will always have the poor among you, but you will not always have me"* (John 12:7-8).

PASSOVER

When Israel was in bondage in Egypt for four hundred years, God sent Moses to Pharaoh to demand the release of his people. Pharaoh refused repeated demands. When Pharaoh was set in his refusal, God sent ten plagues; finally in the last plague, God said He would slay the firstborn of Egypt (Exodus chapter 11). God told the Jews to kill a lamb and take its blood and smear it around the doorpost of each house so when the Death Angel saw the blood, it would be "a sign" and he would PASS OVER the house and spare their firstborn (Exod 12:1-3). Then they were to get ready to leave Egypt. The lamb pointed to the Messiah and His blood that would be shed on Calvary, as John the Baptist would later point out.

God had established a yearly memorial to commemorate this event, followed by a seven-day feast of unleavened bread on the 15th to 21st of Nisan, making it an eight-day feast during which no work was to be done (By the first century, Passover and the Feast of Unleavened Bread had been combined into one event). The first and last days of the feast were holy convocations (Sabbaths that fall on holy days. And special sacrifices were offered at the temple.).

Everything was set up before sunset. On a low table, elements symbolizing the Passover night were meticulously positioned: The roasted lamb, unleavened bread, four cups of wine, bitter herbs, and other condiments. It began at sunset with a candlelight search of the house for any leaven, which was symbolic of evil, and any found was removed.

Then they reclined at the table. Hands were washed ceremonially and the story of the first Passover was told. Then they sang a portion of the Hallel from the Psalms (113-118). Reclining at the table Jesus said: *"I have looked forward to this hour with deep longing, anxious to eat this Passover meal with you before my suffering begins. For I tell you now that I won't eat it again until it finds fulfillment in the Kingdom of God"* (Luke 22:14-16).

As they began to eat, Jesus took a loaf of unleavened bread and said the Hebrew blessing over it: "Blessed art thou, O Lord our God, King of the universe, who brings forth bread from the earth." Then He broke the pieces and passed them to the disciples. Then He added the now traditional Christian words: *"Take, eat. This is My body which is broken for you: do this in remembrance of me."*

The meal continued until it was time to pass the first large cup around for everyone to drink from, adding the words: *"This cup is the New Testament in my blood. Do this often, as you drink of it, do it in remembrance of me.* Thus Jesus gave the celebration its true meaning, pointing to Him as the True Lamb of God who would be slain that very day, as the judgment would fall on Him and would "PASSOVER" all those who would believe in Him.

WHO IS THE GREATEST?

Also a dispute arose among them as to which of them was considered to be the greatest (Luke 22:24). This had come up before, the question of who would be the greatest in the Kingdom: *Then the mother of Zebedee's sons came to Jesus with her sons and, kneeling down, asked a favor of Him. "What is it you want?" he asked. She said, "Grant that one of these two sons of mine may sit at your right and the other at your left in your Kingdom"* (Matt 20:20-21). In verse 24 we read: *When the ten heard about this, they were indignant with the two brothers!* They wanted those positions.

After they had arrived in Capernaum, and Jesus and His disciples had settled in the house where they would be staying, Jesus asked them, *"What were you arguing about on the road?"*

But they kept quiet because on the way they had argued about who was the greatest. Sitting down Jesus called the twelve and said, "If anyone wants to be first, he must be the very last, and the servant of all" (Mark 9:33-35).

Before the Passover Feast, Jesus decided He would teach them by example in such a way that they could not forget. They had no servant to wash their feet and, evidently, they were determined that they were not going to lower themselves to wash the other's feet. Then we are told: *It was just before the Passover Feast. Jesus knew that the time had come for him to leave this world and go to the Father. Having loved his own who were in the world, He now showed them the full extent of His love. The evening meal was being served, and the devil had already prompted Judas Iscariot, son of Simon, to betray Jesus. Jesus knew that the Father had put all things under His power and that He had come from God and was returning to God* (John 13:1-3).

The meal referred to here was the preliminary meal the night before the Passover itself. Knowing that His time was limited, that Judas would betray Him, that the Father had given all things into His hands, and that He came from God and was about to return to God, Jesus' heart was drawn out toward His Own. His concern was for those who would be left behind. If they were to carry on His work, it was vital that they stop struggling for superiority and learn that they must serve to be great in His Kingdom.

So He got up from the meal, took off His outer clothing, and wrapped a towel around His waist. After that he poured water into a basin and began to wash his disciple's feet, drying them with the towel that was wrapped around him (4-5). It must have caused them great bewilderment as He removed His upper garment, wrapped a towel around His waist, and poured water into a basin, like a slave. This would shine a light on their pride and shame them as nothing else could.

He came to Simon Peter, who said to Him, "Lord, are you going to wash my feet?" Jesus replied, "You do not realize now what I am doing, but later you will understand."

'No,' said Peter, 'you shall never wash my feet!" Jesus answered, "Unless I wash you, you have no part with me" (6-8).

In verse 6 Peter's words are emphatic, "DO YOU wash MY feet?" Jesus says that Peter does not understand now what he is doing but later he would. But Peter is unyielding and says that he would NEVER allow Jesus to wash his feet. Jesus is just as emphatic. He says that unless Peter allows him to wash his feet he will have no part with Him.

"Then, Lord," Simon Peter replied, "not just my feet but my hands and my head as well." Jesus answered, "A person who has had a bath needs only to wash his feet; his whole body is clean. And you are clean, though not every one of you" (9-10). When invited to a feast, guests would bathe before coming, leaving only the feet needing washing after walking to the feast in their sandals. The spiritual meaning here was that those who are saved have been bathed, but daily they would still need cleansing from the defilement of the world. Peter, who was bathed (saved), would understand better later, after denying Jesus and needing his fellowship restored.

They were clean, but not all, *for Jesus knew who would betray him* (v. 11). He was referring to Judas who was not saved. *When He had finished washing their feet He put on His clothes and returned to his place. "Do you understand what I have done for you?" He asked them. "You call me teacher and Lord, and rightly so, for that is what I am. Now that I, your Lord and Teacher, have washed your feet, you also should wash one another's feet; I have set you an example to do what I have done for you"* (12-15). Jesus left us an example. Of course He does not refer to literally washing feet, but to humble service. Willingness to do the most menial tasks for each other, especially restoring an erring brother to fellowship.

Peter was bathed (saved) and would later need to be restored to fellowship (have his feet washed). As believers in Christ, we have been bathed by the *washing of regeneration* (Titus 3:5). We need our feet washed from walking in a dirty world. Peter would need to be cleansed and restored to fellowship. Judas, however, was never bathed or saved to begin with. Jesus referred to this fact in John 6:70: *"Have I not chosen you, the twelve, yet one of you is a devil."* So while Peter needed restoration to fellowship, there was no place for Judas to be restored to.

"I am not referring to all of you: I know those I have chosen. But this is to fulfill the Scripture: 'He who shares my bread has lifted up his heel against me.' I am telling you now before it happens, so that when it does happen you will believe that I am He" (18-19). The word "he" is not in the Greek. Jesus wants them to know that He is the I Am (Exod 3:13-14).

Verses 21-30: *After he had said this, Jesus was troubled in spirit and testified, "I tell you the truth, one of you is going to betray me." His disciples stared at one another at a loss to know which of them he meant. One of them, the disciple whom Jesus loved, was reclining next to him. Simon Peter motioned to this disciple and said, "Ask Him which one He means." Leaning back against Jesus, John asked Him, "Lord, who is it?" Jesus answered, "It is the one to whom I give this piece of bread when I have dipped it in the dish." Then, dipping the piece of bread, he gave it to Judas Iscariot, son of Simon. As soon as Judas took the bread, Satan entered into him.*

"What you are about to do, do quickly," Jesus told him, but no one at the meal understood why Jesus said this to him. Since Judas had charge of the money, some thought Jesus was telling him to buy what was needed for the feast, or to give something to the poor. As soon as Judas had taken the bread, he went out. And it was night.

Jesus was very troubled and saddened that one of His disciples would betray Him. The disciples were bewildered, looking about the table speechless. In the synoptic Gospels, each disciple begins asking, *"Lord is it I?"* (Matt 26:22), until finally Judas, so as not to look conspicuous, asked, *"Rabbi, is it I?"* (Matt 25:26). He didn't say "Lord," as the others did, but simply "Rabbi."

John, the human author of this gospel, never refers to himself by name. At the table, Jesus had the first place of honor. Reclining on his left side, the next place of honor was John. He was the youngest and was leaning back on Jesus chest. Close enough for conversation with Jesus without being overheard by the others (v. 23).

Peter beckons to John (v. 24) to ask whom Jesus was referring to. John asks who it is. Jesus said the one to whom He will give the bread He had dipped in the dish (v. 26). This was a special act of honor the host shows to his guests. Jesus did not point him out openly because the others may have reacted violently. After Judas had received the dipped bread, Satan entered into him. Jesus wanted him to get on with his betrayal and said, *"What you are about to do, do quickly"* (v. 27).

The others did not understand what Jesus meant by saying this. They had no idea of Judas' intention, and because he carried the moneybag, they thought that Jesus had told him to go out and buy food for the next eight days of the feast, or to give something to the poor (28-29). Judas then went out into the night.

When he was gone, Jesus said, *"Now is the Son of Man glorified and God is glorified in Him, God will glorify the Son in*

Himself, and will glorify Him at once. My children, I will be with you only a little while longer. You will look for me, and just as I told the Jews, so I tell you now. Where I am going, you cannot come. A new command I give you: Love one another. As I have loved you, so you must love one another" (John 13:31-35).

Judas' leaving would lead to Jesus' crucifixion in a few hours. The Son would be glorified, and the Father would be glorified in Him. God would glorify Him "at once." It is at hand, first in the cross, then in His resurrection and ascension. God would glorify Him with His own Self with the eternal glory He had with the Father before the world began.

Soon He would be taken from them. Because the world hated Him, it would also hate those who belong to Him who would be left behind. They would have to depend on each other in a hostile world. The measure of love they were to have for each other was to be Christ's love for them.

Simon Peter asked Him, "Lord, where are you going?" Jesus replied, "Where I am going, you cannot follow now, but you will follow later." Peter asked, "Lord why can't I follow you now? I will lay down my life for you." Then Jesus answered, "Will you really lay down your life for Me? I tell you the truth, before the rooster crows, you will disown Me three times" (36-38).

Peter's mind was still on Jesus' words in verse 33, that He was leaving and they could not come with Him. So Peter asks the question they were all thinking, "Lord where are you going." Peter did seem to understand the drift of Jesus' words about leaving. Jesus said Peter could not follow Him now, but would later. He is referring to Peter's own death by crucifixion later on. Peter pleads, *"Lord, why can I not follow you now? I will lay down my life for you."*

Peter was sincere and meant what he said, and later that night he did risk his life by taking his sword and swinging at the high priest's servant. Aiming at his neck or head but missing and cutting off his ear as the servant turned his head to avoid the blow. He was willing to fight until he learned that Jesus was not going to resist. He was willing to die in battle but not to stand and face the accusers with Jesus.

Jesus knew Peter's strengths and weaknesses and said: *"Will you really lay down your life for me? I tell you the truth, before the rooster crows, you will disown me three times."* But Peter was not alone in his claims to be willing to die for Jesus. In Matthew 26:35 we are told: *All the other disciples said the same.* And we know that only a little while before this they were all arguing who was the greatest. Jesus would say to them a little later that they would all run off and leave Him that night (John 16:32). And they did just that.

JOHN CHAPTER 14

"Do not let your hearts be troubled. Trust in God: trust also in me. In My Father's house are many rooms; if it were not so, I would have told you. I am going there to prepare a place for you. And if I go and prepare a place for you, I will come back and take you to be with me, that you also may be where I am. You know the way to the place where I am going." Thomas said to Him, *"Lord we do not know where you are going, so how can we know the way?"*

Jesus answered, "I am the way and the truth and the life. No one comes to the Father except through me. If you really knew me, you would know My Father as well. From now on you do know Him and have seen Him." Philip said, *"Lord show us the Father and that we be enough for us."* Jesus answered: *"Don't you know Me, Philip, even after I have been among you such a long time? Anyone who has seen me has seen the Father. How can you say, 'Show us the Father?' Don't you believe that I am in the Father, and that the Father is in me?*

"The words I say to you are not just my own. Rather, it is the Father, living in Me who is doing his work. Believe me when I say I am in the Father and the Father is in me; or at least believe on the evidence of the miracles themselves. I tell you the truth, anyone who has faith in me will do what I have been doing. He will do even greater things than these, because I am going to the Father" (John 14:1-12).

The disciples finally began to grasp what was going to happen. The talk about Jesus leaving and the symbolism of the memorial supper had made it clear to them and greatly saddened them, and they needed reassurance. He told them of His coming death, that one of them would betray Him, and the rest would abandon Him. They would all face grave danger.

Could they continue to trust Him in light of what was soon going to take place? They were not to be troubled but continue to trust God and in Jesus' mission. It would all work for good and His glory. He literally said, "Keep on believing in God and in Me." They were to remain steadfast in their trust and commitment. For what was about to happen was the will of God, and out of the darkest night would come the greatest expression of His love and purpose for them.

Here we are told that there is really only one mansion in Heaven and that is the Father's house, Heaven itself, and as children of God we have dwelling places or rooms in our Father's house. Jesus' picture of Heaven is that of home. Home is the sweetest place on earth. In Heaven with the Father and Jesus and the Holy Spirit, we will finally be at home. Jesus was going to leave them and they would face persecution and death. However, they were not to be troubled for they have a home in Heaven with the love and security that only God can give. It is our relationship to God that makes Heaven our home.

Heaven is a vast Kingdom of unimaginable glory and it is our home! *"I am going there to prepare a place for you, I will come back to take you to be with me, that you also may be where I am"* (John 14:2-3). It is natural for us to want to be with Him but here we are told the He longs for us to be with Him.

When children are born, the parents joyfully prepare a place in the home for them. Jesus went ahead to prepare a place for those who would be born again as children of God. Another analogy is of a Jewish wedding. In which case the couple is engaged and the dowry has been paid. The engagement is as binding as the wedding itself and could only be broken by a divorce, even though they still lived with their parents. The believer is engaged to Christ. The dowry was the purchase price of our salvation, and the Holy Spirit has been given as an earnest, or down payment, of our inheritance: *Do you not know that your body is a temple of the Holy Spirit, who is in you, whom you have received from God? You are not your own; you were bought at a price. Therefore honor God with your body* (1 Cor 6:19-20).

Then at the proper time, the groom would go to the Father's house to add rooms for his bride and then he would return to get his bride and take her to his father's house that he had prepared for her and they would be married. This takes place at the Lord's return.

"And you know the way to the place where I am going and how to get there." "No, we don't know, lord, said Thomas. "We don't know where you are going, so how can we know the way?" Jesus said, "I am the way, the truth, and the life, no one can come to the Father except through me" (4-6).

Jesus is the way to God, the only way; the absolute eternal TRUTH; and the fullness of true LIFE. Here the "I" is emphatic. "I and no other always am" the way the truth, and the life. There is no salvation apart from Christ, neither in the Old or New Testaments. It is through the types and shadows of the Old Testament that point to Jesus as The Coming One that Abraham's faith was counted to him as righteousness.

"If you really knew me you would know My Father as well. From now on, you do know Him and have seen Him" (v. 7). Though they loved Jesus, they had not known Him in the fullest sense. He had been revealing Himself more and more fully until now. To know Him is to know the Father. The Father is just like Jesus. If we believe in Jesus, we believe in the Father. *"I and My Father are One"* (John 10:30). We are told this in many Scriptures. In John 3:36 he says: *"Whoever believes in the Son has eternal life. . . ."* Then in John 5:24 we read: *". . . Whoever hears my word and believes Him who sent me has eternal life."*

Hebrews 1:1-3 tells us: *In the past God spoke to our forefathers through the prophets at many times and in various ways, but in these last days He has spoken to us by His Son Whom He appointed heir of all things, and through whom He made the universe. The Son is the radiance of God's glory and the exact representation of His being, sustaining all things by His powerful word. After He had provided purification for our sins, He sat down at the right hand of the majesty in Heaven.* Here we see that Christ is the expression of the being or essence of God.

Philip (not grasping what Jesus had just said) said, *"Lord, show us the Father and that will be enough for us."* Philip had asked to see the Father with his physical eyes. Jesus told him that throughout Philip's acquaintance with Jesus, he HAD seen the Father! Jesus is in the Father and the Father is in Him. What Jesus says and does, the Father says and does. The union of the Father and Son is indissoluble. Everything Jesus does He does in fellowship with the Father. This is what He meant when He said in John 5:19-23: *"I tell you the truth, the Son can do nothing by Himself. He can do only what He sees the Father doing, because whatever the Father does the Son also does. For the Father loves the Son and shows Him all He does.*

"Yes, to your amazement He will show Him even greater things than these. For just as the Father raises the dead and gives them life, even so the son gives life to whom He is pleased to give it. Moreover the Father judges no one, but has entrusted all judgment to the Son, that all may honor the Son just as they honor the Father. He who does not honor the Son does not honor

the Father, Who sent Him." It is impossible that the members of the Trinity would do anything that is not in perfect harmony with the others.

In verse 12 He says that those who believe in Him enter into the work of God in getting the gospel out. 1 Corinthians 3:9 says: *For we are God's fellow workers . . .* Jesus would say to the Father: *"As you sent Me into the world; I have sent them into the world"* (John 17:18). In John 20:21 Jesus said to His disciples, *"Peace be with you, as My Father has sent Me, I am sending you."* Believers may do greater works in getting the gospel out. Only Jesus could pay for our sins, which we can never enter into. However, as far as spreading the gospel, they may do greater works than Jesus did in His limited ministry.

Peter at Pentecost won three thousand souls, and think of Paul's missionary journeys, winning converts all over the known world. Also consider the ministries of George Whitefield, John Wesley, and the circuit riders: Finney, Spurgeon, Moody, William Booth, Billy Sunday, Billy Graham, John R. Rice, Jack Van Impe, and many others. Jesus gives the reason for this winning of converts by others: *"Because I go to My Father."*

Jesus spent three and a half years centered in Israel preparing His disciples while bringing in many believers, forming a nucleus to send out the gospel to the whole world after Pentecost, when He would send the Holy Spirit to empower them.

"And I will do whatever you ask in my name, so that the Son may bring glory to the Father. You may ask me for anything in my name, and I will do it" (13-14). For this purpose He gives us the privilege of praying in His name, and with His authority. This means to ask according to His WILL and PURPOSE as His representatives who He sent out to do His work.

2 Corinthians 5:17 says that all believers are sent on the same mission. Some are sent as missionaries, ministers, evangelists, etc. and are given certain gifts, but ALL believers are called to witness for Christ. Here we are told: *Therefore if anyone is in Christ, he is a new creation; the old has gone, the new has come! All this is from God, who reconciled us to Himself through Christ and gave us the ministry of reconciliation. That God was reconciling the world to Himself in Christ, not counting men's sins against them. And He has committed to us the message of reconciliation. We are therefore Christ's ambassadors, as though God were making His appeal through us. We implore you on Christ's behalf: be*

reconciled to God. God had made Him who knew no sin to be sin for us, so that in Him we might become the righteousness of God.

Here we are told that all those who are "IN CHRIST" are new creatures with a new relationship to God. Things concerning the believer's old life before he was saved are passed away. All his old relationships to the First Adam and the world are now gone as all things are made new and all these relationships are now from God, who has reconciled us to Himself by Jesus Christ.

Part of these new things is a NEW PURPOSE IN LIFE – It is the ministry of reconciliation. And our message is that God was in Christ reconciling the world to Himself, and that God is not counting the trespasses of those who believe in Christ against them. As ambassadors for Christ, we speak for God and plead with people to be reconciled to God. We plead this on the basis that Christ, who knew no sin was made to be sin for us so that we could be made the righteousness of God through Him.

The reason the Holy Spirit empowers believers and Christ gives us the authority to pray in His name is so that *"the Father may be glorified in the Son."* Jesus was about to complete His mission of redemption and would send the Holy Spirit to empower believers and send them out to proclaim His accomplished redemption so that God can be glorified in His Son. We carry on His mission in Jesus' name and glorify the Father though the Son.

"If you love me, you will obey what I command. And I will ask the Father, and he will give you another counselor to be with you forever – the Spirit of truth. The world cannot accept him, because it neither sees him nor knows him. But you know him, for he lives with you and will be in you" (15-17).

Love is not mere sentimentalism or merely emotionalism. There is no real love that does not desire to please God. True love will lead to obedience to his commandments. All believers have the Holy Spirit's indwelling. All love and obey him in varying degrees; to the degree of their obedience, the Holy Spirit's power will be realized in their lives. The Holy Spirit has been in the world since the beginning. Many Old Testament saints had the Holy Spirit's power come UPON them. However after Jesus resurrection, he came in a special way to INDWELL all believers so he could continue what Jesus had begun.

The word "Counselor" in verse 16 means Helper. The word "another" is "Allos" and means "just like." The Holy Spirit is another Divine Helper "just like" Jesus, even as Jesus was "just like" the Father. The Divine Helper stands for and with the believer. Through the Holy Spirit, the life of Christ is manifested in his people. Therefore the believer has Christ to plead his case to the Father and the Holy Spirit to plead the Father's case with us.

His disciples were heartsick because Jesus was going away, but He promised them that, instead of being with them, now through the Holy Spirit, He would live IN them and never leave them again. Jesus is the Truth and the Holy Spirit is identified with Him as the Spirit of Truth. Because the world does not believe in Jesus it cannot receive the Holy Spirit, for it neither sees Him nor knows Him. Today when one is indwelt by the Holy Spirit He seals the believer as belonging to God and is the earnest or guarantee that God will complete His promised salvation and bring it to its completion at the resurrection.

In 1 Corinthians 6:19 we read of the Spirit's indwelling: *Do you not know that your body is a temple of the Holy Spirit, who is in you, whom you have received from God? You are not your own; you are bought at a price. Therefore honor God with your body.*

The word for temple here is "NAOS." This was the Holy of Holies in the temple at Jerusalem where God dwelt. Now He dwells in each believer. He indwells the believer's spirit that indwells his body.

"I will not leave you as orphans; I will come to you" (v. 18). Jesus was going away but He would not leave them as orphans, or helpless. He would come to them through the Holy Spirit.

"Before long, the world will not see me anymore, but you will see me, because I live you also will live. On that day you will realize that I am in my Father, and you are in me, and I am in you. Whoever has my commands and obeys them, he is the one who loves me. He who loves me will be loved by my Father, and I too will love him and show myself to him." (19-21). Jesus said the world would see Him no more, and after His body was laid in the tomb, He was never again seen by an unbeliever. However, believers would see Him again. "YOU" will see me again is emphatic, in contrast to the unbelieving world. Because He lived so would those who believe in Him. Because He would live eternally, they would too. Jesus' eternal living is our guarantee of eternal life.

As the Last Adam, the risen Christ is the guarantee of a better covenant (Heb 7:22). After His resurrection and the coming of the Holy Spirit (John 14:20), His people have an abiding fellowship with the Father through Him by the indwelling of the Holy Spirit.

The MANIFESTATION of God's fellowship and blessing will depend on our love for Him. There is no sincerity in a love that does not want to please Him.

Nevertheless, if we honestly and earnestly seek to do God's will, then the Holy Spirit will make the Father and the Son real and there will be continuous fellowship with the Triune God.

Then Judas (not Iscariot) said, "But Lord why do you intend to show yourself to us and not to the world?" Jesus replied, "If anyone loves me he will obey my teaching. My Father will love him, and we will come to him. He who does not love me will not obey my teaching. These words you hear are not my own; they belong to my father who sent me" (22-24).

Judas Iscariot had left. This Judas was also known as Thaddaeus or Lebbaeus (Mark 3:17; Matt 10:3). He wanted to know why Jesus was going to show Himself to believers and not to the unbelieving world. If they truly love and obey Him, He and His Father would make their home with them. The Holy Spirit makes their heart His temple and a fit dwelling place for the Father and the Son. But the unbelieving world would never have this fellowship.

"All this I have spoken while still with you. But the Counselor, the Holy Spirit whom the Father will send in my name will teach you all things and will remind you of everything I have said to you" (24-26). These words were spoken to them while He was still with them to give them comfort and reassure them after He left them. The Holy Spirit would teach them all things pertaining to spiritual truth and He would bring them to mind.

Through the Spirit's illumination, they would be able to relate Jesus' life to the gospel message, including its relation to the old Testament Scriptures. Here we have the explanation of the inspiration of the New Testament: *Holy men of God spoke as they were carried along by the Holy Spirit* (2 Pet 1:21).

"Peace I leave with you; my peace I give you. I do not give to you as the world gives. Do not let your heart be troubled and do not be afraid" (John 14:27). It is a peace that only He can give. Therefore they were not to be fearful at His leaving and the coming events that were soon to take place.

"You have heard Me say, I am going away and I am coming back to you. If you loved me you would be glad that I am going back to the Father, for the Father is greater than I. I have told you now before it happens, so that when it does happen you will believe. I will not speak to you much longer, for the prince of this

world is coming. He has no part in me, but the world must know that I love the Father and that I do exactly what the Father has commanded me. Come let us leave." (28-31)

They should rejoice for Him because the One they loved so much was returning home to the Father. He said the Father was greater than Him. He does not refer to His essence or nature concerning which He said, *"I and my Father are One"* (John 10:30). It refers to Him becoming a man and coming as a servant to do the will of the Father. He came in subjection to the Father.

As we are told in Philippians 2:6-8 concerning Jesus: *Who, being in very nature God, did not consider equality with God something to be grasped, but made himself nothing. Taking on the very nature of a servant, being made in human likeness. And being found in appearance as a man, He humbled himself and became obedient to death – even death on a cross!*

Jesus willingly took the place of subjection to the Father. As a father and son are equal in essence, but the father is greater in authority, this is what Jesus meant.

In verse 29 He says He is telling them these things before they happen so their faith would be strengthened. He would not have much time to talk with them because even now the prince of this world was on his way through Judas Iscariot, along with those who hated Him. However, he has no power over Jesus. But so that all would know the love He has for the Father and that He obeys His will, He would submit Himself into the hands of evil men to offer Himself up for the sins of the whole world. Finally He says, *"Come now; let us leave."* At this point they arose and walked out into the night and finished the talk on the way to Gethsemane; and from there, to Calvary.

JOHN 15

"I am the True Vine, and my Father is the Gardener. He cuts off every branch in Me that bears no fruit, while every branch that does bear fruit He prunes so that it will be even more fruitful" (1-2). Here the "I" is emphatic – "I and no one else, am the True Vine."

The nation of Israel was called the "vine" in Isaiah 80:8: *You brought a vine out of Egypt: You drove out the nations and planted it.* Israel was set apart by God to be a witness to the rest of the world. The nation was established to bear fruit for God among the Gentile nations of the world. Isaiah 5:7 says, *The vineyard of the Almighty is the house of Israel.* Eventually we are told in

Hosea 10:1: *Israel is an empty vine; he brought forth fruit for himself.* All the types and symbols of Israel's institutions and rituals pointed to Christ for their fulfillment. Jesus is the True Vine and His Father is the Vinedresser.

In Matthew 21:33-46 Jesus gives us the parable of the tenants: *"Listen to another parable: There was a landholder who planted a vineyard. He put a wall around it, dug a winepress in it and built a watchtower. Then he rented the vineyard to some farmers and went away on a journey. When the harvest time approached, he sent his servants to the tenants to collect his fruit.*

The tenants seized his servants, they beat one, killed another, and stoned a third. Then he sent other servants to them, more than the first time, and the tenants treated them the same way. Last of all, he sent his son to them. 'They will respect my son,' he said. But when the tenants saw the son, they said to each other, 'This is the heir. Come, let's kill him and take his inheritance.'

"Therefore, they took him, threw him out of the vineyard, and killed him. Therefore, when the owner of the vineyard comes, what will he do to those tenants?" "He will bring those wretches to a wretched end," they replied. "And he will give the vineyard to other tenants, who will give him his share of the crops at harvest time." Jesus said to them, "Have you never read in the scriptures: 'The stone the builders rejected has become the capstone; and the Lord has done this, and it is marvelous in our eyes?'

"Therefore I tell you that the kingdom of God will be taken from you and given to a people who will produce fruit. He who falls on this stone will be broken to pieces, but he on whom it falls will be crushed." When the chief priests and Pharisees heard Jesus' parables, they knew he was talking about them. They looked for a way to arrest Him, but they were afraid of the crowd because the people held that he was a prophet.

1 Peter 2:5-9 tells us who it is that will bring forth fruit for God: *You also, like living stones, are being built into a spiritual house to be a holy priesthood, offering spiritual sacrifices acceptable to God through Jesus Christ. For the Scripture says: 'See, I lay a stone in Zion, a chosen and precious Cornerstone; in addition, the one who trusts in Him will never be put to shame.*

Now to you who believe, this stone is precious. But to those who do not believe, the stone the builders rejected has become the Cornerstone, and, a stone that causes men to stumble and a rock that makes them fall. They stumble because they disobey the message – which is also what they were destined for. But you are a chosen people, a royal priesthood, a holy nation, a people belonging to God, that you may declare the praises of Him who called you out of darkness into His wonderful light.

This new nation would be the church, the "called out ones who believe in Christ," both Jews and Gentiles. Christ is the True Vine, and all those who are His are branches in the Vine, drawing life from Him, and will bear fruit for God.

John 15:2: *"He cuts off every branch in me that bears no fruit, while every branch that does bear fruit he prunes so that it will be even more fruitful."*

This verse describes two kinds of connections to the vine. One is in appearance only, with no sap or life flowing through it; the other is vital and receives life through the sap that is in the vine. Judas was the first kind of branch: in appearance only, as we are told in John 6:70-71: *Then Jesus replied, "Have I not chosen you, the twelve? Yet one of you is a devil." (He meant Judas, the son of Simon Iscariot, who, though he was one of the twelve, was later to betray Him).*

Judas was a dead branch with no life (the Holy Spirit) flowing into it. He had already been broken off. The other kind of branches, with life flowing through them, were the remaining eleven disciples. Nevertheless, even the true branches needed pruning to remove dead twigs (things in our lives that hinder the Holy Spirit) to increase their ability to produce more and better fruit. Otherwise the flow of life-giving sap will be blocked and there will be no fruit. In John 14:20 Jesus said: *"On that day you will realize that I am in my Father and you are in me, and I am in you."* Believers are "in Him" as branches and His life flow is in them. The Bible speaks of fruit bearing in two ways: One is the Fruit of the Spirit in Galatians 5:22-23: *Love, joy, peace, patience, kindness, goodness, faithfulness, and self-control.* This refers to Christian character that the Holy Spirit produces in the believer. The other fruit is referred to in in Proverbs 11:30: *The fruit of the righteous is a tree of life, and he who wins souls is wise.* Here believers are to be trees of life giving out the gospel and producing other trees of life.

"You are already clean because of the word I have spoken to you" (15:3). The eleven were already clean because they believed His word or teaching. They were clean with *the washing of water by the word* of Ephesians 5:26, and Titus 3:5: *He saved us through the washing of rebirth and renewal by the Holy Spirit.*

This refers to the cleansing of the believer in a legal sense. Legally his record of sins is blotted out through his faith in Christ.

This is positional. The believer is legally clean forever based on his position in Christ. But he personally needs cleansing daily. He still walks in a dirty world, and daily gets his feet dirty, and needs daily cleansing through confession and repentance (1 John 1:8-9).

This is what Jesus meant when He said in John 13:10-11: *"A person who has had a bath needs only to wash his feet; his whole body is clean, though not every one of you." For he knew who was going to betray him, and that is why he said, "Not all of you are clean."*

The eleven were bathed (saved) but they still needed daily cleansing to maintain fellowship with God. Peter, though saved, denied Jesus and needed cleansing. Judas, however, was not clean (bathed = saved) to begin with and he had no relationship with God to restore.

"Remain in me, and I will remain in you. No branch can bear fruit by itself; it must remain in the vine. Neither can you bear fruit unless you remain in me. I am the vine; you are the branches. If a man remains in me and I in him, he will bear much fruit; apart from me you can do nothing. If anyone does not remain in me, they are like a branch that is thrown away and withers; such branches are picked up and thrown into the fire and burned" (4-6).

"Remaining in Christ' means maintaining fellowship. The only way to be a fruitful believer is by maintaining an obedient fellowship with the vine. Fruit-bearing is not a matter of talent, or being gifted or natural ability. It is a matter of staying close to Jesus so that the Holy Spirit's enablement flows through us. We must sow seeds of course, but without the Holy Spirit's power it is impossible to bear fruit.

When Jesus said, *"I am the vine, you are the branches"* in verse 5, both "I" and "you" are emphatic in the Greek, "I, and no one else, am the vine; you and no others, are the branches." Only believers can bear fruit, and they can only do this as they stay in fellowship with Jesus.

In verse 6 Jesus refers to a common scene in Israel of a vineyard to emphasize the difference between living and nominal relationships to Christ. Believers have a vital union with Christ, but they must maintain communion or fellowship in their daily lives in order to bear meaningful fruit. They must keep the life-giving power from being blocked by sin, which will allow our love to cool and our lives will be like dead branches. If a believer has no burden for what God wants and his priorities are confused, as far as his fruit-bearing is concerned, he is set aside and withers as a dead branch.

Paul speaks of the danger of blocking the flow of the Holy Spirit's power into our lives in 1 Corinthians 9:26-27: *Therefore I do not run like a man beating the air. No, I beat my body and make it my slave so that after I have preached to others, I myself will not be disqualified for the prize.*

Paul did not want his life to be disqualified from bringing fruit to God as a dead branch. Vine branches had only two uses. They were useless as building material and as food. They were good only for bearing fruit or for fuel to heat the oven for baking. This is what people did with fruitless vines: they pruned them off and burned them.

"If you remain in me and my words remain in you, ask whatever you wish, and it will be given you. This is my Fathers glory, that you bear much fruit, showing yourselves to be my disciples" (7-8).

Those who truly abide in Christ will constantly draw from Him the ability to bear fruit.

If our delight is in the Lord, we will want and ask only for things He wants us to have for His glory. We may want to please God but if we do not occupy ourselves with His word, our desires will have no direction. When we pray we must be sure of God's will and be willing to change our prayer according to His will. We see this in Paul's life in 2 Corinthians 12:7-10: *To keep me from becoming conceited because of these surpassing revelations, there was given to me a thorn in the flesh, a messenger of Satan, to torment me. Three times I pleaded with the Lord to take it away from me. But He said, "My grace is sufficient for you, for my power is made perfect in weakness." Therefore will I boast all the more gladly about my weaknesses, in insults and hardships, in persecutions, and in difficulties, for when I am weak, then I am strong.*

Paul is told that he would be a better servant if God left the thorn because Paul would have to depend on God in his weakness. Paul changed his prayer according to God's will. We are not told what Paul's thorn was so we can all identify it with our own weakness.

Verse 8 literally says: "So that you will keep on bearing much fruit." The Father is glorified if we KEEP ON bearing more and more fruit. This will show that we are truly His disciples.

"As the Father has loved me, so have I loved you, now remain in my love. If you obey my commands you will remain in my love, just as I have obeyed my Father's commands and remain in His love" (John 15:9-10). Here Jesus says He loves us just as the Father loves Him. In John 17:23 He says: *"May they be brought to complete unity to let the world know that you sent me and have loved them even as you have loved me."* From the Father through the Son, God's love is revealed in and through His people.

"I have told you this so that My joy may be in you and that your joy may be complete" (John 15:11). If we maintain fellowship with Jesus and are occupied with bringing Him glory, He will share His joy with us and this joy will be complete or full. Our faithful service will add to His joy and to ours.

"My command is this: Love each other as I have loved you. Greater love has no one than this, that he lay down his life for his friends" (12-13). Self-sacrifice is the essence of true love. Soon Jesus would demonstrate this, as we are told in 1 John 3:16: *This is how we know what true love is: Jesus Christ laid down His life for us. And we ought to lay down our lives for our brothers.*

"You are my friends if you do what I command. I no longer call you servants, because a servant does not know his master's business. Instead I have called you friends, for everything I have learned from my Father, I have made known to you.

"You did not choose me, but I chose you and appointed you to go and bear fruit – fruit that will last. Then the Father will give you whatever you ask in my name (14-16).

We do not become Christians by works but by faith in Christ. After putting our faith in Christ, we become His friend by obeying Him. Verse 14 literally reads: "If you keep on doing what I command you" – not merely occasional obedience. Jesus was going to lay down His life for them to show His love for them. In turn, they were to show their love for Him by following in His service.

He would take their place in judgment on the cross, and they were to take His place in the world. In John 5:9 Jesus said: *"While I am in the world, I am the light of the world."* As long as He remained in the world, He was the light of the world, but the time would come when He would leave and THEY would become the light of the world.

In verse 16 the word "appointed" shows a permanent state into which they were to enter. He has entrusted to us HIS PURPOSE AND PLAN that He had heard from His Father. We are literally to CONTINUOUSLY be bearing fruit through CONTINUOUSLY remaining in Christ.

This privilege also carries great responsibilities. Concerning salvation God takes the initiative, but we must respond to it. God also elects us to service. In Ephesians 1:3-14 Paul stresses that God's election is "IN CHRIST." In this passage this phrase or its equivalent – "in Him," "in the beloved," "in Whom" – is used eleven times in twelve verses.

God has sovereignly elected all those who are "in Christ," but as free moral agents we must choose to be in Christ and accept the terms of our Sovereign God. Mankind is free to choose, but is responsible for their choice. This is also true concerning service; if we refuse to serve, we will lose our present joy and future rewards. If one is obedient, they are promised the authority of His name, so we can bear fruit that will LAST.

The believer will meet his fruitfulness or lack of it at the Judgment Seat of Christ. Therefore, He wants us to be in intimate touch with Him to maintain His Life-force flowing through us to produce fruit. This relationship is so personal and intimate that we may pray for things in Jesus' name. Using His name means praying with His authority and for His glory. But if we are living selfish lives, we do not have His authority.

"This is my command: Love each other" (v. 17). Jesus repeats this command from 13:34 and 15:12 to emphasize the importance of loving each other because they would be rejected and hated by the world. They would need to depend on each other all the more since Jesus was soon to be taken from them.

"If the world hates you, keep in mind that it hated me first. If you belonged to the world it would love you as its own. As it is, you do not belong to the world, but I have chosen you out of the world. That is why they hate you. Remember the words I spoke to you: no servant is greater than his master. If they persecuted me, they will persecute you also. If they obeyed my teaching, they will obey yours also. They will treat you this way because of my name, for they do not know the One who sent me" (18-21).

We live in enemy territory and should expect to be treated as the enemy in this world with its mind set against God. We are not of this world but belong to the Kingdom of Heaven. We belong to Christ whom they hate. The servant is not greater than his lord.

Jesus' enemies would be the enemies of His servants. Those who accept His teachings would accept theirs. They would fellowship with His rejection and with His acceptance.

In Matthew 5:10-12, we are encouraged: *"Blessed are those who are persecuted because of righteousness, for theirs is the Kingdom of Heaven. Blessed are you when people insult you, persecute you falsely and say all kinds of evil against you because of me. Rejoice and be glad, because great is your reward in Heaven, for in the same way they persecuted the prophets who were before you."*

"If I had not come and spoken to them, they would not be guilty of sin. Now, however, they have no excuse for their sin. He who hates me hates my Father as well. If I had not done among them what no one else did, they would not be guilty of sin. Now they have seen these miracles, and yet they have hated both my Father and me. However, this is to fulfill what is written in their law: They hated me without reason" (John 15:22-25).

They hated Him because he revealed their sin. They could no longer hide behind a cloak of ignorance and self-righteousness. They who hated Him also hated His Father because He reveals His Father. He came in love and did only good.

However, this was expected because the Scripture said, *They hated me without a cause* (Psa 35:19; 69:4).

"When the counselor comes, whom I will send to you from the Father, the Spirit of truth, who goes out from the Father, He will testify about me. And you also must testify, for you have been with me from the beginning" (26-27).

The counselor, the Holy Spirit, will counsel and direct them in the truth concerning Jesus Christ. The disciples would be the instruments and the Holy Spirit the source, providing the words and the power, as Jesus said in John 14:26: *"But the Counselor, the Holy Spirit, whom the Father will send in my name, will teach you all things and will remind you of everything I have said to you."*

JOHN 16

"All this I have told you so that you will not go astray. They will put you out of the synagogue; in fact, a time is coming when anyone who kills you will think he is doing a service to God. They will do such things because they have not known the Father or me. I have told you this so that when the time comes you will

remember I warned you. I did not tell you this at first because I was with you" (John 16:1-4).

Jesus spoke these things so that when trials and persecution came, they would not have doubts, or be discouraged, or unprepared. The religious leaders would drive them out of the synagogues and they would be outcasts and considered enemies of God, so that killing them would be considered a service to God.

One of these would be Saul of Tarsus, who would later become the Apostle Paul. We read in Acts 8:3: *As for Saul, he made havoc of the church, entering into every house and hauling men and women off to prison.*

They would do this because they did not know the Father or the Son. He told them these things to prepare them for what was ahead of them. It is common to think when trials come that we are not doing God's will and to become discouraged. Nevertheless, those who are doing God's will are the very ones who can expect opposition from Satan.

We are called to suffer for Christ. From jail Paul wrote to Timothy: *So do not be ashamed to testify about our Lord, or ashamed of me his prisoner. But join me in suffering for the gospel* (2 Tim 1:8). And 1 Peter 1:21 tells us: *To this you were called, because Christ suffered for you, leaving you an example that you should follow in His steps.* He did not tell them these things at first while He was still with them to encourage them and to bear the brunt of the attack.

"Now I am going to Him who sent me, yet none of you asks me where are you going. Because I have said these things, you are filled with grief. But I tell you the truth: it is for your good that I am going away. Unless I go away the Counselor will not come to you: but if I go, I will send him to you. When he comes he will convict the world of guilt in regard to sin and righteousness and judgment. In regard to sin, because men do not believe in me; In regard to righteousness because I am going to the Father, where you can see me no longer; And in regard to judgment, because the prince of this world now stands condemned" (John 16:5-11).

They were no longer asking where He was going because now they understood and were filled with sorrow. Their sorrow was such that they could not see how they could go on without him, on whom they depended so much. However, despite their sorrow it was expedient for them that he go away because of what it means for the Holy Spirit to come as our Helper.

He has always been in the world with God's people, but now He will live in His people in intimate union and fellowship to represent Christ to us and to the world.

He would reveal to the world the real nature of sin, of righteousness, and the coming judgment.

In 1 John 2:1 Jesus is said to be our Representative or Defense Attorney with the Father, pleading on our behalf what He provided for us on the cross: *My dear children I write this to you so that you will not sin. But if anybody does sin, we have One who speaks to the Father in our defense – Jesus Christ, the Righteous One.*

So while Christ presents our case to the Father, the Holy Spirit presents the Father's case to the unbelieving world. Pleading against their sins and their need of Christ. The sin of all sins is the rejection of Christ. His resurrection proves that His work on the cross was accepted by God.

"I have much more to say to you, more than you can now bear. But when He, the Spirit of truth, comes, he will guide you into all truth. He will not speak on his own; He will speak only what he hears, and he will tell you what is yet to come. He will bring glory to me by taking from what is mine. This is why I said the Spirit will take from what is mine and make it known to you. In a little while you will see me no more, and then after a little while you will see me" (12-16).

After teaching them for over three years, He still had many things He wanted to teach them, but they were not ready for them. The Holy Spirit would guide them into all truth concerning Christ, who is the Truth. He will continue the teaching of Jesus, as Jesus would have done. He will continue Jesus' work. He will not speak of Himself. As Jesus spoke what the Father said to Him (John 14:10), so the Spirit will continue this and show them things to come concerning God's purpose in Christ. Not merely an outline of coming future events, but the doctrines concerning Christ and salvation.

He will guide us into all truth. The Holy Spirit will explain the things of Christ. There is such a Oneness within the Trinity that the Holy Spirit takes Christ's place, not in the sense of replacing Him, but of continuing Christ's presence. The Spirit speaks what He hears the Father say and He opens to the believer the riches he has in Christ.

Some of his disciples said to one another, "What does He mean by saying, 'In a little while you will see me no more, and then after a little while you will see me,' and 'because I am going to the Father?' They kept asking, "What does He mean by a 'little while'? We don't understand what he is saying." Jesus saw that they wanted to ask Him about this, so he said to them, "Are you asking one another what I meant when I said, 'In a little while you will see me no more, and then after a little while you will see me?' I tell you the truth; you will weep and mourn while the world rejoices. You will grieve but your grief will be turned to joy. A woman giving birth to a child has pain because the time has come; but when her baby is born, she forgets her anguish because of her joy that a child is born into the world. So it is with you; now is your time of grief, but I will see you again and you will rejoice, and no one will take away your joy" (17-22).

In verse 16 Jesus reassures them that His leaving them would be for a little while between His death and resurrection – three days. In verse 17, uncomfortable to interrupt Him, they spoke among themselves. They think there is a contradiction between what He says now and what He says in chapter 14 about going to the Father's house and sending the Holy Spirit.

They were concerned about His saying that in a little while they would not see Him, and then in a little while they would see Him again. They kept asking, *"What does he mean by a 'little while? We don't understand what he is saying."*

Jesus saw that they wanted to ask Him about this. He explains to them that soon they would weep bitterly while the world rejoiced to be rid of Him. However, this would be short-lived and soon their sorrow would be turned to joy, for they would see Him again. Their sorrow would be intense but of short duration, as a woman in labor; it gives way to great joy when a child is born. They would see Him again, after His resurrection, and rejoice. Unlike their sorrow, their joy would be permanent, as they would share in His victory over sin and death.

"In that day you will no longer ask me anything. I tell you the truth; my Father will give you whatever you ask in my name. Ask and you will receive, and your joy will be complete. Though I have been speaking figuratively, the time is coming when I will no longer use this kind of language but will tell you plainly about my Father. In that day you will ask in my name. I am not saying that I will ask the Father on your behalf. No, the Father Himself will love you because you have loved me and have believed that I came from God. I came from the Father and entered the world;

now I am leaving the world and going back to the Father" (23-28).

Here Jesus is telling them that when He leaves them to go to the Father's house, they will not be able to bring their requests to Him, as they were accustomed to doing. Then they can ask the Father in His name and He will answer them. He will do anything we ask that is consistent with Jesus' name. To use His name means to pray in His authority. He has said many things to them using figures of speech, but after His resurrection and sending the Holy Spirit, this will not be necessary. They will be able to understand from experience about the Father.

Then they will ask the Father in Jesus' name. They will go to the Father as they had done with Jesus. For the Father loves them because they love Jesus and believed that He was the Savior who came from God and were united to Him. He came from the Father into the world on a mission. When His mission was accomplished, He would go back to the Father, and then the Holy Spirit would come and carry on His work through them.

Then Jesus' disciples said, "Now you are speaking clearly and without figures of speech. Now we can see that you know all things and that you do not even need to have anyone ask you questions. This makes us believe that you came from God."

"You believe at last," Jesus answered. "But a time is coming, and has already come, when you will be scattered, each of you to his own home. You will leave me alone. Yet I am not alone, for my Father is with me.

"I have told you these things, so that in me you may have peace. In this world, you will have trouble. But take heart! I have overcome the world" (29-33).

Now they grasped His words; His understanding of their very thoughts left no doubt that He knew all things even before they asked Him. Jesus said, *"You believe at last!"* Now they believed, but was the faith that they now had enough to carry them through what was coming? When they saw Him crucified? When they buried His dead body?

They must understand what they would be called upon to endure. The long-awaited hour, when He would be taken from them, was at hand. They would be scattered like sheep without a shepherd. Despite their assurances of faith, they would abandon Him. He had been warning them to prepare them for this hour. He wanted them to know that they could have peace in Him; that no matter what trials and tribulations they would find in the world, they were to maintain their faith and courage, because He had already overcome the world. *"I have overcome the world."* Here the "I" is emphatic. Only HE has won the complete victory, and they also will win through Him.

JOHN 17

After Jesus said this, he looked up toward heaven and prayed: "Father, the time has come. Glorify your Son, that your Son may glorify you. For you granted him authority over all people that he might give eternal life to all those you have given him. Now this is eternal life: that they may know you, the only true God, and Jesus Christ, whom you have sent. I have brought you glory on the earth by completing the work you gave me to do. And now, Father, glorify me in your presence with the glory I had with you before the world began" (1-5).

While the rest of the city slept, they stopped on the quiet road for the High Priest to pray before the sacrifice was made. Jesus was both the Sacrifice to be offered and the Priest who would offer it up, and the cross would be the altar. With infinite love the Son addresses the Father. The hour toward which Jesus, and indeed all history, had been moving had arrived. His one desire, as it had been throughout His life, was that, as He was lifted up in the agony of the cross, He would glorify the father.

He had known that the cross was His destiny from before the world was. In fact it was for the cross that the world was created. As the Last Adam, Jesus was given power over all flesh that He should give eternal life to all those who the Father gives Him. All those who would believe in Him, the Father gives to Him. They are removed from being "in Adam" and placed "in Christ." As we are told in 2 Corinthians 15:22: *For as in Adam all die, so in Christ all will be made alive.*

1 Corinthians 15:47-48 expands on this: *The first man was of the dust of the earth, the second man from heaven. As was the earthly man, so are those who are of the earth, and as is the man from heaven, so also are those who are of heaven.* The first man was Adam, the first representative of the human race. The Second Representative Head of the race is Christ.

Those who are still "in Adam," as we all are at one time, are of the earth, and those who have been placed "in Christ" are of heaven. According to verse 3, "Eternal Life" consists of knowing the Father and the Son in an intimate and personal way. Being "in Christ," believers possess eternal life and have a vital union with the Father and the Son. Jesus says He has finished His work on earth that was assigned to Him by the Father and He has glorified the Father on earth. Here He anticipates the cross, which was at hand. He had prepared the disciples to carry on His work and would soon be restored to the eternal glory with the Father, which He had laid aside at His incarnation.

"I have revealed you to those whom you gave me out of the world. They were yours; you gave them to me and they have obeyed your word. Now they know that everything you have given me comes from you, for I gave them the words that you gave me and they accepted them. They know with certainty that I came from you, and they believed that you sent me" (6-8).

All believers have been given to Jesus by the Father. Here He refers specifically to the eleven disciples, minus Judas, who was never really one of them. They were far from perfect but they held to the message of the Father in the midst of severe testing. Though they were flawed, they knew Jesus had come from God. Jesus is God's gift to the lost world (John 3:16). And those who believe in Christ are the Father's gift of love to His Son.

"I pray for them. I am not praying for the world, but for those you have given me, for they are yours. All I have is yours, and all you have is mine. And glory has come to me through them. I will remain in the world no longer, but they are still in the world. Holy Father, protect them by the power of your name – the name you gave me – so that they may be one as we are one. While I was with them, I protected them and kept them safe by that name you gave me. None have been lost except the one doomed to destruction so the Scripture would be fulfilled" (9-12).

Jesus has others, but now He prays for those who were to carry on His work after His departure. They belong to God and God has given them to Him. This reveals the oneness of the Father and the Son and the love they share. Despite the disciples' short comings, Jesus is glorified in them. As the Son brought glory to the Father through IIIS love and obedience, they would bring glory to the Son through THEIR love and obedience.

Jesus was about to leave the world and they would be left to carry on His work. In His prayer He anticipates the cross and speaks as though it had already happened and His resurrection has occurred. His concern for the disciples here is that they would be united in a relationship of intimacy like the Father and the Son: a family unity.

Until now, while He was with them, He protected them and kept them safe – all but one, who did not truly belong to Him, as the Scripture foretold. He was concerned for them in His absence when they would face the world's hostility as they carried on His work.

"I am coming to you now, but I say these things while I am still in the World, so that they may have the full measure of my joy within them. I have given them your word and the world has hated them, for they are not of the world, any more than I am of the world.

"My prayer is not that you take them out of the world but that you protect them from the evil one. They are not of the world, even as I am not of it. Sanctify them by the truth. Your word is truth. As you sent me into the world, I have sent them into the world. For them I sanctify myself, that they, too, may be sanctified" (13-19).

Jesus prays that as they carry on His work they will also share His joy in doing the Father's will. This would be fulfilled after the Holy Spirit takes up Jesus' work in them. The Holy Spirit would recall His word to equip them to overcome the world. The world would hate them as it hates Jesus, because, like Jesus, they do not belong to the world. Their identity with Jesus would mark them for hatred.

Jesus is sending them INTO the world, but they must not become LIKE the world; they must not adopt its standards or they will be of little use in the world. He prays that they will be kept from the evil one.

In John 8:23-24 speaking to those who did not believe in Him, Jesus said: *"You are from below; I am from above. You are of this world; I am not of this world."*

Believers are no longer "in Adam," which is synonymous with being "of the world." But are "in Christ," *Born from above* and *partakers of the Divine nature* (2 Pet 1:4). They share in everything with Him, including the hatred of the world.

They were to be sanctified by His word. The word "sanctify" means "to set apart for God," as does the word "holy." This is brought about by separation from worldly things that might dishonor God and living in communion with God, absorbing and reflecting His love and interests through His Word. Sanctification is progressive. It begins by being set apart by God for Heaven. This is what the Bible means by the word "saint," which describes a person "set apart for God." This is also what it means to be "in

Christ." The person "in Christ" is set apart or separated from the condemned world that is in Adam and is "set apart" for God's glory. There is a two-fold aspect to sanctification: (1)We are sanctified by God once and for all at conversion.

(2) We become God's possession when we are born again. We belong to him. This is referred to in Hebrews 10:10: *By God's will we have been made Holy through the sacrifice of the body of Christ once for all.* But on our side, it is progressive as we set ourselves apart from what displeases God, to learn and follow God's Word with the mind-set to love and please God. They were IN the world, while not being OF the world.

As the Father sent the Son, the Son sent His disciples and all believers. Jesus, who always set Himself apart to God's service, now set Himself apart to the specific service of the cross. The disciples were sanctified by God the moment they trusted in Christ. However, here Jesus prays for their sanctification to the work He would leave to them.

"My prayer is not for them alone. I pray also for those who will believe in me through their message, that all of them may be one, Father, just as you are in me and I am in you. May they also be in us so that the world may believe that you have sent me. I have given them the glory that you gave me, that they may be one as we are one. I in them and you in me. May they be brought to complete unity to let the world know that you sent me, and have loved them even as you have loved me.

"Father, I want those you have given me, to be with me where I am, and to see my glory, the glory you have given me because you loved me before the creation of the world. Righteous Father, though the world does not know you. I know you, and they know that you have sent me. I have made you known to them, and I will continue to make you known in order that the love you have for me may be in them, and that I myself may be in them" (20-26).

Jesus was praying for other sheep that were not yet in the flock, all those who would believe through the testimony of these disciples. All the other things that He prayed for also apply to these other sheep. He prays for a love and devotion to the Father and the Son.

He prays that despite their differences, there will be a unifying purpose for God that will manifest itself to the world so that others will believe. Believers are so united with Christ and one with Him that they are loved as Jesus is loved.

He prays that they will be with Him to see His glory. He was about to return to His Father and He longed for them to be there to see the glory and love that has existed for all eternity between the members of the Trinity. In verse 22 He refers to the glory that they will share with Him, glories which He won through the cross, as the Last Adam. This is the *"glory which you gave me,"* that Christ won in our behalf. In verse 24 He refers to His eternal glory before the world was created. This is the eternal, uncreated glory of the Triune God.

He prays that the love the Father has for Him will be in them, bringing great joy and glory through Him.

CHAPTER ELEVEN
Gethsemane – His Arrest and Trial

When he had finished praying, Jesus left with his disciples and crossed the Kidron Valley. On the other side there was an olive grove, and he and his disciples went into it (John 18:1).

Jesus, as the Last Adam, stepped forth on the road to the cross. As Priest He was to teach and pray, then offer the sacrifice. Having taught them and prayed, it was now time to offer the sacrifice. He would offer HIMSELF up for sin. He was both the Priest and the sacrifice. The Perfect High Priest who would offer up the Perfect Sacrifice. After preparing His disciples for this dreaded hour, He went to meet it.

He left the house with eleven disciples and they crossed the Brook Kidron that ran between Jerusalem and the Mount of Olives, where the Garden of Gethsemane was located. The Brook ran through a very narrow valley. It was a narrow stream about seven or eight feet across. It was dry now, as it always was, except in the rainy season.

The name "Gethsemane" means "oil press." It was a garden in the eastern sense – a small enclosed area with an olive press and many olive trees. Jesus would come here often for prayer, rest, and maybe to sleep. He said to His disciples, *"Sit here while I go over there and pray"* (Matt 26:36). *On reaching the place, He said to them, "Pray that you will not fall into temptation"* (Luke 22:40). They would come under great pressure to forsake Him.

Then leaving the eight disciples there, He took Peter, James, and John with Him. They had been with Him at His transfiguration and witnessed His coming glory and saw Moses and Elijah (Matt 17:1-2). He wanted their fellowship as He prayed to His Father. Having seen His future glory, they were best prepared to witness His agony.

As He went ahead, He *began to be deeply distressed and troubled* (Mark 14:33). He was literally filled with fearful astonishment at what lay ahead of Him. *Then he said to them, "My soul is extremely sorrowful, to the point of death; stay here and watch with me." Then going a little further, he fell on his face and prayed saying, "My Father, if it be possible, let this cup pass from me. Nevertheless, not my will but your will be done."* (Matt 26:42)

He had asked them to watch with Him. It was late and they were under great strain. It would be a great comfort to Him to know that those who were closest to Him were watching and praying with Him. This was the beginning of the fulfillment of Psalms 22:14, which referred to His sufferings, *I am poured out like water.*

His prayer shows the natural shrinking from the horror ahead of Him. The cup was associated with the wrath of God (Rev 16:19). The emphasis of His prayer was on the Father's will rather than on His being spared. This was indeed a bitter cup: Judgment for all the sin of the world. It contained all the abhorrence of God toward sin.

Jesus did not make any demands; He only asked that the cup pass from Him *"if it be possible"* to redeem mankind without His drinking it. But if not, He would drain the cup to its last horrible drop. This is what motivated His every move: the will of the Father.

Then He returned to His disciples and found them asleep. *"Could you men not keep watch with me for one hour?" He asked Peter. "Watch and pray so that you will not fall into temptation. The spirit is willing, but the body is weak"* (Matt 26:40-41).

Jesus came to them expecting encouragement and comfort. It was a great disappointment to find them asleep after He exhorted them to watch with Him. Peter awoke as He approached: *"Could you not even stay awake with me for one hour?"* This simply added to His sorrow. They, no doubt, thought Jesus would use His power to avoid harm. Jesus knew this and He also knew that He would not do that. He was concerned for their faith when they saw him taken by the Romans and crucified.

Then He left them again the second time, knowing that the cup could not be avoided, and prayed again, saying: *"My Father, if it is not possible for this cup to be taken away unless I drink it, may your will be done"* (Matt 26:42). *An angel from heaven appeared to Him and strengthened him* (Luke 22:43). He could have called many angels to deliver Him; instead, He allowed the angel to strengthen His resolve and determination. The angel reminded Him of His Father's will and the glory and the joy that was set before Him: all those who would believe in Him and would be given to Him so they could have eternal life.

And being in anguish, he prayed more earnestly, and his sweat was like Drops of blood falling to the ground (Luke 22:44). Being in agony, as He considered what lay ahead of Him, He grew more intense in His praying, and He broke out in a bloody sweat. In the Greek, Luke the physician uses the word "Clots." Great clots of blood oozed through His pores, staining His clothing. His soul was in great travail and agony.

When He rose from prayer and went back to his disciples, He found them asleep, exhausted from sorrow. "Why were you sleeping?" He asked them. "Get up and pray so that you will not fall into temptation" (Luke 22:45-46).

So he left them and went away once more and prayed the third time, saying the same thing. Then he returned to his disciples and said to them, "Are you still sleeping and resting? Look, the hour is near and the Son of Man is betrayed into the hands of sinners" (Matt 26:44-45).

When He prayed the third time He prayed the same words with greater intensity. He was saddened to find them sleeping again, but He had won the victory. He was prepared to face what was before Him. The time for watching was over. A long, trying night lay ahead of them.

"The hour is near, and the Son of Man is betrayed into the hands of sinners." The dreaded hour that had awaited Him His whole earthly life was here.

Then Jesus saw the light from the torches and heard the approaching crowd. He had known they were coming and said, *"Rise, let us go! Here comes my betrayer!"* He raised His voice to awaken them as He moved toward the gate at the entrance of the Garden (v. 46). Judas knew the place well, for Jesus often went there for prayer and rest. He planned to capture Jesus when He was alone at night during the feast (John 18:2).

Judas, having plotted with the chief priests, had left the upper room and gone to the Sanhedrin. The Romans allowed the Jews their own government within the province. The Temple police sent by the Sanhedrin would make the arrest. Roman soldiers were summoned from the Tower of Antonia near the Temple area in case there was a riot.

Judas returned from the upper room and saw that Jesus had left, so he led them to His usual place of prayer at Gethsemane, also called the Mount of Olives. He led a great multitude of Roman soldiers carrying swords. A detachment of peacekeepers of 300 to 600 soldiers were sent the arrest Him. Judas gave them a sign so they would not mistakenly think that one of the disciples was Jesus and arrest the wrong man. The sign was a kiss on the cheek. *"The one I kiss is the man; arrest him"* (Matt 26:48).

As he approached Jesus, Judas as usual, addressed Him as "Master," rather than "Lord," as the others did, and he kissed Him. Then Jesus said to Judas, *"Friend, why are you here?" Then looking Judas in the eye, He said, "Judas, do you betray the Son of Man with a kiss?"* (Matt 26:50; Luke 22:48). *Jesus therefore, knowing all things that would come upon Him, went out and said to the crowd, "Who is it you want?" "Jesus of Nazareth," they replied. "I am he," Jesus said (and Judas the traitor was standing there with them). When Jesus said, "I am he," they drew back and fell to the ground* (John 18:4-6). He was not taken by surprise. He was already surrendered to die.

When the soldiers came to arrest Jesus, He did not hide or run; He was volunteering to be arrested. He calmly told them, "I Am." The word "he" is not in the Greek. He was claiming the eternal self-existence that belongs only to God! They were stunned and fell backward to the ground. His exerted power thrust them back. This was to make it obvious to all that they could not have taken Him had He not gone willingly.

Again He asked them, "Who is it you seek?" Again they said, "Jesus of Nazareth" (John 18:7-8). They clearly know who He is, but they are still overwhelmed by Him. He offered Himself to them but asked that His disciples be allowed to go. *This happened so that the words He had spoken would be fulfilled: "I have not lost one of those you gave me"* (v. 9). *Then Simon Peter, who had a sword, drew it and struck the High Priest's servant, cutting off His right ear (The servant's name was Malchus)* (v. 10).

Peter was true to his word; he was willing to lay down His life for Jesus. Impulsively he grabbed his sword, ready to fight to the finish! *When Jesus' followers saw what was going to happen, they shouted, "Lord, should we strike with our swords?"* (Luke 22:49). Not waiting for an answer, Peter swung his sword at the high priest's servant's head, but the man ducked his head to the left and Peter missed and cut off his right ear!

Jesus cried out to Peter to put away his sword. Then He said pleadingly, *"Shall I not drink the cup the Father has given me?"* The bitter cup was given to Him from the hand of His Father. It was not what He suffered from man that made atonement for sin: the beatings, the mocking. These were merely the hatred of fallen and sinful humanity.

It is what He suffered from the Father's hand as He took upon Himself the penalty for our sins. Revelation 16:19 speaks of the cup filled with the wine of the fury of His wrath. He drinks it all so that those who trusted in Him would not have to drink any. But, rather, He would extend to them the cup of salvation. *I will lift up the cup of salvation and call upon the name of the Lord* (Psa 116:13)

> Death and the curse were in our cup;
> O Christ, 'twas full for thee
> But thou hast drained the last dark drop,
> 'Tis empty now for me:
> That bitter cup – love drank it up;
> Now blessing's draught for me!

But Jesus answered, "No more of this!" And he touched the man's ear and healed him (Luke 22:51).

"Do you think I cannot call on my Father, and He will at once put at my disposal more than twelve legions of angels? But how then should the Scriptures be fulfilled that say it must happen this way?" (Matt 26:53-54). A Roman legion consisted of 6,000 soldiers.

Twelve legions of angels is a total of 72 thousand angels who were waiting for His call, who could have crushed this planet like an eggshell!

Then Jesus said to the chief priests, the officers of the Temple guard, and the elders, who had come for him, "Am I leading a rebellion that you have come with swords and clubs? Every day I was with you in the Temple courts, and you did not lay a hand on me. But this is your hour – when darkness reigns" (Luke 22:52-53). The hour He had spoken of before had arrived.

"But this has all taken place that the writings of the prophets might be fulfilled." Then all the disciples deserted Him and fled (Matt 26:56). Zechariah 13:7 foretold that the Shepherd would be struck and the sheep would scatter. He was left alone.

Then the detachment of soldiers with its commander and the Jewish officials arrested Jesus. They bound Him, and brought Him first to Annas, who was the father-in-law of Caiaphas, the high priest that year (John 18:12-13). So they led Him away to Annas, a former high priest, who was succeeded by each of his five sons; then Caiaphas, his son-in-law was made high priest.

While no longer high priest, Annas still had great influence with the people and was trusted by the Romans. He still occupied quarters in the high priest's residence. A charge brought by Annas would have great influence with both Rome and the Jews. This would be done while the Sanhedrin was being assembled, since it was night and they were unprepared.

JESUS' TRIAL
ISRAEL'S LAWS AND THE SANHEDRIN

The five books of Moses are the source from which came all the Jewish customs. As the Jews multiplied in number and their government became more and more complex, the need arose to increase and clarify laws and customs. The legal system was based on Exodus 18:25-26 and Deuteronomy 16:18, where Moses instructed the people to choose judges and officers: *"Appoint judges and officials for each of your tribes in every town the Lord your God is giving you, and they shall judge the people fairly."*

The great Sanhedrin was based on Numbers 11:16-17, where Moses was told by God to choose seventy men to stand before the Tent of the Covenant with him, to help him with his burden of leading God's people. The Sanhedrin was made up of three groups of 23 members each: priests, Scribes, and elders. Requirements for all three groups were that each member be at least 40 years old and have memorized the Law of Moses and the Talmud, which contained all the Laws and traditions, and even the commentaries by the Rabbis. They also had to be married and have children.

The high priest was the 70th member and the head of the Sanhedrin. He was supposed to be elected by the people but, by the time of Jesus, the Roman Government sold the position to the highest bidder. The house of Annas was very influential and ruthless. Caiaphas was high priest and son-in-law to Annas, but Annas was the real power of the Sanhedrin and most of its members were his sons and other relatives. The Sanhedrin that sat at the trial of Jesus had plotted against Him. This was illegal. The leaders of the Jewish aristocracy were stirred up by the public and the "radical" teachings of Jesus, while the crowds listened to Him with delight (Mark 12:37).

When the Pharisees and Sadducees invited Jesus to dine with them, all their questions were directed to trying to catch him saying something that they might use to accuse Him of breaking the Laws of Moses (Luke 11:37-57). When He reminded them that God's house was a house of prayer for all people (Isa 56:7), but they have made it a den of robbers, *they sought how they might destroy Him* (Matt 21:12-16; Mark 11:15-18; 19:45-47).

They tried to trap Him on a political hook with the hope of being able to accuse Him of treason, but failed. *"Is it right to pay taxes to Caesar or not?" they asked.* His answer made them fail miserably. He asked them for a coin, a denarius. *He asked them: "Whose portrait is this? And whose inscription?" "Caesars," they* replied. Then He said to them, "Give to Caesar what is Caesar's, and to God what is God's." They made up their minds to get rid of Him under any circumstances, so long as they avoided showing their treacherous plotting and did not excite the multitudes who believed in Him and loved Him (Matt 26:3-5; John 11:47-54). Accordingly, they made an arrangement with Judas Iscariot, one of His disciples, who, like themselves, loved the wealth of this world more than the Lord.

So they bought the traitor for 30 pieces of silver, the price of a slave (Matt 27:3-9), as foretold by Jeremiah and Zechariah, to arrange for Jesus' arrest while Jerusalem slept. Caiaphas interrogated Jesus, who remained silent. This angered Caiaphas, who was disappointed in his ability to make Jesus incriminate Himself. As High Priest He was not to question witnesses or give his opinion about the accused, so as not to influence the verdict.

Caiaphas was the one who had advised the Jews that it would be good if one man died for the people (John 18:14). This refers back to John 11:49- 52. Verses 51-52 tell us: *Caiaphas did not say this on his own, but as a high priest that year he prophesied that Jesus would die for that nation and not only for that nation but also for the scattered children of God.* The Holy Spirit had moved him to say this as a prophecy of Jesus' sacrificial death. However, from Caiaphas' perspective he meant that Jesus must be given to the Romans lest there be a disturbance and the Romans, in retaliation, destroy the nation.

Annas then probed Jesus on what basis he made disciples and what was His teaching? Did He claim to be the Messiah? (John 18:19). The law said that a man could not incriminate himself. It took the testimony of two or three witnesses (Deut 17:6; 19:15; Num. 35:30). Jesus knew the law: *"I have spoken openly to the world,"* Jesus replied. *"I always taught in synagogues or at the temple, where all the Jews came together. I said nothing in secret."* Then He added: *"Why question me? Ask those who heard me. Surely they know what I said"* (John 18:20-21).

When Jesus said this, one of the officials nearby struck him in the face. *"Is this the way you answer the high priest?"* he demanded" (John 18:22). This fulfilled Micah 5:1b: *They will strike Israel's ruler on the cheek with a rod.*

"If I said something wrong," Jesus replied, *"testify as to what is wrong. But if I spoke the truth, why did you strike me?"*

This ended any pretense of a fair trial. Annas and Caiaphas lived in the same palace, with only a courtyard separating them

(Matt 26:57). It was now about midnight. The trial, legally, should have waited until morning. But they wanted to avoid a lengthy daytime trial that would have attracted Jesus' followers. By trials' end it was morning (Matt 27:1). *Those who had arrested Jesus took Him to Caiaphas, the high priest, where the teachers of the law and the elders had assembled* (Matt 26:57).

Simon Peter and John followed Jesus from the Garden of Gethsemane to the palace of the high priest. John, who was known by the high priest, went in with Jesus into the palace (John 18:15). John was recognized by the guard at the door and allowed in. Annas failed to bring any real charges against Jesus. The Sanhedrin sought to make up their own. They made a search for false witnesses to bring charges to put Him to death. The result they sought was predetermined. They only needed to manufacture the proper evidence (Matt 26:59). A witness had to be a person of good character. He was forbidden to take a bribe.

Though many false witnesses came forward, no evidence to put Jesus to death was found. Finally, two came forward and declared, "This fellow said, 'I am able to destroy this Temple of God and rebuild it in three days.'" This was said about three years earlier and was misquoted (John 2:19). What Jesus really said was, YOU *"destroy this temple, and in three days I will raise it up"* (John 2:21-22). Caiaphas probably made note of this statement by Jesus and may have coached these false witnesses with this false meaning or he may have actually misunderstood Jesus' words.

But even if this statement were true, it was not sufficient to bring the death sentence. Caiaphas, trying to push Jesus to incriminate himself, arose and said to Him: *"Are you not going to answer? What is this testimony that these men are bringing against you?"*

But Jesus remained silent (Matt 26:62-63). Legally, He did not need to answer since no evidence had been introduced, so Jesus remained silent. Out of desperation the high priest put Jesus under oath: *"I charge you under oath by the living God: tell us if you are the Christ, the Son of God"* (v. 63). By law Jesus could not be forced to incriminate Himself. The high priest was not to interrogate the witness or the accused.

"I am," said Jesus, "and you will see the Son of Man sitting at the right hand of the Mighty One and coming on the clouds of heaven" (Mark 14:62). Jesus makes His answer unmistakable by quoting two messianic passages. All of them would have

understood His meaning. Psalms 110:1 makes this clear: *The Lord says to my Lord: "Sit at my right hand, until I make your enemies a footstool for your feet."* The right hand of God was the place of power and authority.

Daniel 7:13 says of the Messiah: *In my vision by night I looked, and there before me was one like a Son of Man, coming with the clouds of heaven. He approached the ancient of days and was led into his presence. He was given authority, glory, and sovereign power; all peoples, nations and men of every language worshipped him. His dominion is an everlasting dominion that will not pass away, and his kingdom is one that will never be destroyed.*

They ridiculed him that one in such lowly circumstances could be the glorious Messiah. Jesus boldly told them that they would indeed see Him coming with power and glory.

The high priest was not to tear his clothes (Lev. 21:10) or give his opinion until AFTER all the others had given theirs, so as not to influence their vote. But now the high priest tore his clothes, saying, *"Why do we need any more witnesses? You have heard the blasphemy! What do you think?" "He is worthy of death,"* *they answered* (Matt 26:56-66). The voting of the Sanhedrin was supposed to begin with the youngest members, so that they would not be influenced by the older members, and was to end with the oldest member, and finally the high priest was to cast the final vote.

They had already passed the sentence of death in this mock trial. Then the Temple police who were holding Jesus abused Him. *Then they spit in his face and struck him with their fists. Others slapped him, and said, "Prophesy to us, Christ, who hit you?"* (Matt 26:67-68).

They blindfolded him and demanded, "Prophecy! Who hit you?" And they said many other insulting things to him (Luke 22:64-65).

Isaiah 50:6 prophesied, *I offered my back to those who beat me, my cheeks to those who pulled out my beard: I did not hide my face from the mocking and the spitting.* This was prophesied by Isaiah about 700 years before: Here we are told that they ripped Jesus' beard off His face. No wonder we are told: *Many were appalled at him – his appearance was so disfigured – beyond that of any man and his form marred beyond human likeness* (Isa 52:14).

Simon Peter and another disciple were following Jesus. Because this disciple was known to the high priest he went in with Jesus into the high priest's courtyard, but Peter had to wait outside at the door. The other disciple came back, spoke to the girl on duty there and brought Peter in. "Are you not one of his disciples?" the girl asked Peter. He replied, "I am not." It was cold and the servants and officials stood around a fire they had made to keep warm. Peter also was standing with them, warming himself (John 18:15-18).

Peter, trying to appear like he belonged, joined those around the fire. The palace where the Sanhedrin was holding their trial had several rooms that opened to the courtyard in the center. As Peter faced the fire, he was recognized and asked: *"You are not one of his disciples, are you?" Then, for the second time, Peter denied it, saying, "I am not."*

One of the high priest's servants, a relative of the man whose ear Peter had cut off, challenged him, *"Didn't I see you with him in the olive grove?"* (John 18:26).

He began to call down curses upon himself, and he swore to them, "I don't know this man you're talking about" (Mark 14:71). Then Peter, realizing that he had been seen in Gethsemane trying to kill the high priest's servant and afraid of being arrested, made his third denial while looking upon Jesus at His trial. At that moment a rooster began to crow. Then the Lord's attention was turned from His trial and He turned and looked straight at Peter. Then Peter remembered the word the Lord had spoken to him: *"Before the rooster crows today, you will disown me three times." And Peter went outside and wept bitterly* (Luke 22:61-62).

HIS TRIAL BEFORE PILATE

They led Jesus before Pilate, the Roman Governor, at the Hall of Judgment because Rome reserved the right to hand down the death penalty. The Judgment Hall was the Governor's place of residence, located in the Fortress of Antonia, the garrison of Roman soldiers, north of the temple area in the eastern part of Jerusalem. Pontius Pilate ruled Judea from 26 A.D. to 36 A.D. and was the fifth Roman Governor of Judea. He was not on good footing with the Jews.

His problem with them began soon after his appointment to Judea. He entered Jerusalem with troops bearing their banners with their images of Caesar. The Jews protested this as idolatry, and they sent a delegation to Caesarea, the Governor's residence in Judea. They made a loud protest of those banners.

Then Pilate placed Roman shields bearing the names of pagan deities on the walls of Herod's palace. Again the Jews protested and the shields were removed on orders of Emperor Tiberius. Pilate also used sacred money taken from the temple treasury to build an aqueduct. The Jews responded with a violent riot that resulted in many Jews being put to death, including Galileans who were worshipping in the temple, which resulted in their blood being mingled with that of the sacrifices, which was a very serious defilement of the temple and altar (Luke 13:1).

There was no love lost between Pilate and the Jews. They despised each other. Pilate lived in Caesarea and only went to Jerusalem when it was absolutely required. The Passover season was one such occasion, with Jewish passion at its height.

Jesus had been severely beaten and had been allowed no rest. He was brought to Pilate's Judgment Hall early in the morning. When they arrived with Jesus, their prisoner, they refused to enter the residence of a gentile because this would have made them unclean for a month and would have prevented them from eating the Passover Lamb that night.

Jesus would die while the Passover lambs were being killed. He was the True Lamb of God, of which all the others were but types and shadows. Jesus was not merely a lamb of God, but THE Lamb of God. Little did they realize that while they were concerned about eating the type, they were plotting the death of the True Lamb.

So Pilate came out to them and asked, "What charges are you bringing against this man?" "If he were not a criminal," they replied, "we would not have handed him over to you." Pilate said: "Take him yourselves and judge him by your own law." "But we have no right to execute anyone," the Jews objected. This happened so that the words Jesus had spoken indicating the kind of death he was going to die would be fulfilled (John 18:29-32).

Pilate met them outside in the courtyard on the palace steps. Pilate knew they must have a good reason to come to him since only he can give the death penalty.

When asked what charge they brought against him, they did not bring a charge against him but they clearly expect the death penalty. They answered that if he were not a criminal they would not have handed him over to him. These words "handed him over" meant they were bringing him for execution.

Pilate, assuming that it concerned one of their religious customs, told them to deal with it themselves. But they reminded him that it was not lawful for them to carry out the death penalty, which they were seeking. Rome's death penalty was by crucifixion. Jesus spoke of the need for him to be lifted up on the cross. *"As Moses lifted up the serpent in the wilderness, even so must the Son of Man be lifted up"* (John 3:14).

In John 12:32 He said: *"But I, when I am lifted up on the earth, will draw all men to myself."* And in John 8:28 we read: *So Jesus said, "When you have lifted up the Son of Man, then you will know that I am the one I claim to be, and that I do nothing on my own but speak just what the Father taught me; He has not left me alone, for I always do what pleases Him."*

And they began to accuse him, saying, "We have found this man subverting our nation. He opposes payment of taxes to Caesar and claims to be the Christ, a king" (Luke 32:2).

Pilate then went back inside the palace, summoned Jesus, and asked him, *"Are you the king of the Jews?" "Is that your own idea or did others talk to you about me?" Jesus asked. "Am I a Jew?" Pilate replied. "It is your own people and your chief priests who handed you over to me. What is it you have done"* (John 18:33-35).

Here Pilate, realizing that the charges against Jesus were more serious than he at first thought, went back inside and called for Jesus. He now knew that he would have to handle the case since Jesus was charged with being a king. Jesus asked if this question was part of the trial or if he just wanted to know for his own information. "Am I a Jew?" showed Pilate's disinterest and his confusion.

This should be of no interest to him, but rather it was religious bickering among the Jews, and should be settled by them not him. He was really saying: "Your own nation and your own chief priests delivered you over to me. I am simply trying to understand what crime you have done. Why are you here?"

Jesus answered, "My kingdom is not of this world; if it were, my servants would fight to prevent my arrest by the Jews. But now my kingdom is from another place" (John 18:36).

His kingdom is not of this world. It is a spiritual kingdom, not a political kingdom in competition with Rome. His followers were a small, scattered group, not an organized military force to fight Rome. *"You are a king, then!" said Pilate* (John 18:37).

Jesus did not speak openly of being the Messiah because the term had become greatly misunderstood and would be misinterpreted as a political leader, even among His disciples. Israel had lost its independence to Rome in 63 B.C., when the Roman general Pompey took Jerusalem. This caused the Jews to anticipate a military Messiah who would overthrow Rome and give Israel the military supremacy of the world. Here Jesus corrects this view. His coming had far greater significance.

Jesus answered, "You are right in saying I am a king. In fact, for this reason I was born, and for this reason I came into the world, to testify to the truth. Everyone on the side of truth listens to me" (John 18:37).

Jesus here does not refer to His second coming when He will rule all nations in a literal kingdom, But to His first coming when He would bear witness to Himself as the Way, the Truth, and the LIFE, and that no one could come to the Father but through Him. He came to die for the sins of mankind and establish His spiritual kingdom, as He said in Matthew 20:28: *"Just as the Son of Man did not come to be served, but to serve, and to give His life a ransom for many."*

Those who receive Him now become members of His spiritual kingdom and will enter His literal kingdom at His return.

Then Pilate said with a sneer, *"What is truth?"* With this he went out again to the Jews and said, *"I find no basis for a charge against him"* (John 18:38). At this point Pilate should have released him. *But they insisted, "He stirs up the people all over Judea by His teaching. He has started in Galilee and has come all the way here." On hearing this, Pilate asked if the man was a Galilean. When he learned that Jesus was under Herod's jurisdiction, he sent him to Herod, who was also in Jerusalem, at that time* (Luke 23:5-7).

Jesus had been charged with insurrection and Pilate would be held accountable if there was a riot. He wanted to pass the problem on to Herod. Herod Antipas was Tetrarch, or governor, of Galilee, and he was in Jerusalem at that time for the Feast of Passover. Galilee was his jurisdiction, so here was a legal loophole for Pilate to make amends with Herod.

They were on bad terms as a result of Pilate's disastrous massacre of the Galileans in the temple during sacrifice (Luke 13:1). Herod did understand Jewish religious law better than Pilate would have, so the decision seemed logical. By sending

Jesus to Herod, Pilate could get rid of the problem with Jesus and also show respect for Herod's jurisdiction.

JESUS BEFORE HEROD

When Herod saw Jesus he was greatly pleased, because for a long time he had wanted to see him. From what he had heard about him, he hoped to see Him perform a miracle. He plied him with many questions, but Jesus gave him no answer. The chief priests and the teachers of the law were standing there, vehemently accusing him. Then Herod and his soldiers ridiculed and mocked him. Dressing him in an elegant robe, they sent him back to Pilate. That day Herod and Pilate became friends – before this they had been enemies (Luke 23:8-11).

Herod was glad to see Jesus. He had heard of Jesus' ability to perform miracles and hoped to see one for himself, like a magic trick. He asked Jesus many questions but Jesus would not answer. The chief priests and scribes shouted many accusations. Then they mocked him and put a royal robe on him. Jesus still refused to speak, spoiling their fun, so they sent him back to Pilate still wearing the elegant robe. Herod Antipas was tetrarch, meaning "ruler of a quarter," which referred to Palestine. He was the son of Herod Archelaus, known as Herod the Great. Archelaus was king at the time of Jesus' birth and he was the builder of the temple. The Tetrarch's rule included Galilee and the lands to the east of the Dead Sea. Archelaus had once ruled Judea, but fell out of favor with Rome and was exiled in 6 A.D. Then a series of governors were appointed to govern Judea, the present one being Pilate.

Then Antipas and Pilate shared authority over Palestine. Antipas, being ambitious, sought to better Pilate in the eyes of Rome. He greatly embarrassed Pilate by sending to the emperor Tiberius a letter of protest against Pilate because his soldiers brought banners into Jerusalem that had the image of Caesar, which was considered idolatry to the Jews.

Rome allowed the Jews to make their own laws regarding their religious customs and when they demanded the removal of images of Caesar, Pilate had his soldiers surround them! When the Jews were threatened with death, according to the historian Josephus, they prostrated themselves, showing a readiness to die. Pilate had them physically removed. This resulted in Pilate being placed on probation by Rome.

Pilate, therefore, wanted to extend an olive branch by giving Jesus to Herod. This was more advantageous than revenge – for now. Herod was very pleased. For a long time he had wanted to meet Jesus. After he had John the Baptist killed, Herod heard of this miracle worker and even thought that Jesus might be John the Baptist risen from the dead (Matt 14:1-2).

Herod wanted Jesus to perform a miracle (Luke 23:8). But to Herod's dismay, Jesus did nothing and said nothing (Luke 23:9). Embarrassed and angry, Herod and his men mocked Him and put a robe on Him, as the Messiah might wear, and sent Him back to Pilate. The Jews probably expected more from Herod and felt betrayed. But Herod was still enduring the contempt of the people for his murder of John the Baptist. He did not want to risk killing another prophet who was even more popular than John.

Then Pilate called the chief priests and rulers of the people and said to them, "You brought this man to me as one who was inciting the people to rebellion. I have examined him in your presence and found no basis for your charges against him. Neither has Herod, for he sent him back to us; as you can see, he has done nothing to deserve death. Therefore I will punish him and then release him" (Luke 23:13-17).

It was necessary to release one prisoner at feast time. Even though Jesus was declared innocent, Pilate would have Him beaten severely to satisfy the mob in hopes that they would feel compassion after seeing Him punished and allow him to release Him. During this time Pilate had received a letter from his wife saying, *"Have nothing to do with that righteous man, for I have suffered much over him today in a dream"* (Matt 27:19). Dreams were taken very seriously by the Romans, and Pilate was acutely aware that he was on thin ice with Rome and the Jews, and he wanted to be rid of this responsibility.

With one voice they cried, "Away with this man! Release Barabbas to us!" (Barabbas had been thrown into prison for an insurrection in the city, and for murder). Wanting to release Jesus, Pilate appealed to them again. But they kept shouting, "Crucify him! Crucify him!" For the third time he spoke to them: "Why? What crime has this man committed? I have found in him no grounds for the death penalty. Therefore I will have him punished and then release him."

But with loud shouts they insistently demanded that he be crucified, and their shouts prevailed. So Pilate decided to grant their demand. He released the man who had been thrown into prison for insurrection and murder, the one they had asked for, and surrendered Jesus to their will (Luke 23:18-25).

Barabbas was in prison for rebellion and murder. Pilate was sure that the crowd would have chosen Jesus over Barabbas, which may be true, but we are told in Matthew 27:20: *But the chief priests and elders persuaded the crowd to ask for Barabbas and have Jesus executed.*

This crowd consisted of those who had come to Jerusalem for the feast of Passover (about two million people from many nations who hardly knew about Jesus).

Then Pilate took Jesus and had him flogged (John 19:1). Flogging was done with a whip with leather straps, whose ends had two lead balls attached. This was done while the victim was bound face down to a whipping post. The lead balls fastened to the straps would tear out chunks of flesh. Jesus' body was literally torn to pieces.

Jewish law allowed only forty lashes (Deut 25:2-3). But the Romans had no such law. They lashed legs and buttocks and arms as well as backs, until muscles and tendons were severed. Sometimes the victim would be disemboweled and die on the spot. But Jesus could only die according to Scripture.

Then the governor's soldiers took Jesus into the praetorian and gathered the whole company of soldiers around him. They stripped him and put a scarlet robe on him, and then twisted together a crown of thorns and set it on his head. Then they put a staff in his right hand and knelt in front of him and mocked him, "Hail, king of the Jews!" they said. They spit on him and took the staff and struck him over the head again and again. After they had mocked him, they took off the robe and put his own clothes on him. Then they led him away to crucify him (Matt 27:27-31).

Then the soldiers took Jesus to the common hall, probably an open court. In Rome the Praetorian Guard had its own special quarters. But in the provinces, it was in the palace of the governor. Here in Jerusalem Pilate ordered the cohort of soldiers to bring Jesus into the Common Hall in front of the Seat of Judgment. The soldiers would show their contempt for the prisoner. They stripped Him publicly and put a scarlet robe on Him. It was common for the soldiers to mock the condemned before the execution. Since Jesus claimed to be a king, this is how He was mocked.

A king must have a royal robe. They placed upon him a short military cloak or cape worn by magistrates, kings, and military officers, probably belonging to one of the soldiers. They platted a crown from very sharp thorns that grew on the palace grounds and pushed it down on His head. Then they pulled up a tall reed growing in the area and put it in His hand as a scepter.

"Hail, king of the Jews!" they said as they did obeisance to him as king. So they knelt, probably each soldier in turn, bowed, and mocked Him imitating the "Ave Caesar." When man sinned, the earth was cursed and brought forth thorns and thistles (Gen 3:18). As the Last Adam, Jesus would bear the thorns, as a sign of the curse, and remove it from mankind and all creation by bearing the curse in His own body on the cross.

Christ redeemed us from the curse of the law by becoming a curse for us, for it is written: 'Cursed is everyone who is hung on a tree' (Gal 3:13). For tribute they spit on Him and took the reed out of His hand and beat Him over His thorn-crowned head.

The prophet Isaiah, looking down through the centuries of time, cried out, *His appearance was so disfigured – beyond that of any man and His form marred beyond human likeness* (Isa 52:14). Jesus was not recognizable. *Once more Pilate came out and said to the Jews, "Look, I am bringing Him out to you to let you know that I find no basis for a charge against him." When Jesus came out wearing the crown of thorns and the purple robe, Pilate said to them, "Here is the man!" As soon as the chief priests and their officials saw him, they shouted, "Crucify! Crucify! But Pilate answered, "You take him and crucify him. As for me, I find no basis for a charge against him"* (John 19:4-6).

Pilate brought Jesus out to the people like this to show them by this mock coronation of a king how ridiculous the charges were that Jesus claimed to be a king. He was attempting by this sadistic mockery to win the sympathy of the people. Jesus wore the robe and crown of thorns, while covered in His own blood, battered and bruised and severely lacerated.

WHY ISRAEL REJECTED THE MESSIAH

Israel had the true religion given to them by God Himself, but they had developed a counterfeit religion. They were God's chosen nation as a depository of divine truth. The sacrificial system pointed to Christ and the whole ritual system spoke of Him. But it developed into a man-made system by which the nation was made blind to the Messiah when He appeared.

This was brought about by the development of a collection of Rabbinic opinions that were compiled and organized into what was called the "Mishnah" meaning "Repetition," which codified the Mosaic Law into 613 precepts consisting of 365 prohibitions and 248 commands, with hundreds of nuances. These were developed into a man-made system of salvation by keeping the law of Moses, which was never meant to bring salvation, as we are told in Galatians 3:21: *So the law was put in charge to lead us to Christ, that we might be justified by faith.*

The law was given to reveal our need for Christ: *Through Him everyone who believes is justified from everything you could not be justified from by the Law of Moses* (Acts 13:39).

And Romans 3:20: *Therefore no one will be declared righteous in His sight by observing the law; rather, through the law we become conscious of sin.*

Their great failing here is brought out in Romans 10:3: *Since they did not know the righteousness that comes from God and sought to establish their own, they did not submit to God's righteousness.*

Their collection of rituals is known as the Talmud, meaning "Learning," which included the "Mishna" (repetitions of the law), and the "Gemera" (Interpretation of the Rabbis). They were all rooted in the "Traditions of the Elders," which by the time of Jesus carried greater authority than the law itself, as Jesus said in Matthew 15:6: *"Thus you nullify the Word of God by your tradition."*

It was concerning these traditions that Jesus pronounced His severest condemnations, *"Woe to you, teachers of the law and Pharisees, you hypocrites. You shut up the kingdom of heaven in men's faces, nor will you let enter those who are trying to"* (Matt 23:13).

"You are of your father, the devil" (John 8:44).

"Isaiah was right when he prophesied about you hypocrites; as it is written: 'These people honor me with their lips, but their hearts are far from me. They worship me in vain; their teachings are but rules taught by men.' You have let go of the commands of God and are holding on to the traditions of men" (Mark 7:6-8).

Jesus deliberately challenged their fanaticism concerning the Sabbath and rejected their traditions, *and they determined to kill Him* (Mark 3:1-6). They despised His lowly upbringing in the town of Nazareth. His disciples were lowly fishermen and tax collectors and He gathered around Him outcasts like lepers, harlots, and beggars. It was this conflict that would result in the cross and the offer of eternal salvation to all people. Isaiah prophesied that though Israel was as the sands of the sea, only a remnant would be saved.

This is quoted by Paul in Romans 9:27-29. The reason for their being only a remnant is given in Romans 9:30-33. They sought salvation through the keeping of the law and not by faith in Christ, which became a stumbling stone to them.

CHAPTER TWELVE
Crucifixion

Crucifixion was invented by the Phoenicians and perfected by the Romans. It was a cruel, horrible form of execution. Square spikes were driven into the wrists and heel bones of the feet, through the median nerve, sending powerful, throbbing bursts of extreme pain. Then it became a sadistic game of survival. If the nails were only through the wrists (which to the Jews was considered part of the hand), the body would sag and prevent breathing and quickly cause death.

In order to prolong the agony, the feet were nailed through the second metatarsal, giving the victim a cruel "Support" for the body, enabling the victim to breath with great struggle, by pulling the body up by the nailed hands and pushing up by the nailed feet, thereby tearing the lacerated back against the rough wood of the cross. As the hours wore on under the hot sun, the body became dehydrated from perspiring and loss of blood; thirst became intense and fatigue would set in, and the pain and shock would be unbearable. Then, sometimes after days of struggling, pain, and terror, the victim would be unable to pull himself up to breath and would suffocate.

Breaking the legs just below the knees would make it impossible to push up with the feet. Because of the extreme beatings and lack of sleep leading up to His crucifixion, Jesus could not even carry His own cross. It had to be carried by another (Matt 27:32; Mark 15:21; Luke 23:26). Jesus had already been dead when they came to break His legs, so the soldier simply made doubly sure that He was dead, as usual, by thrusting a lance under the right side of the sternum into His heart. If it was discovered that the victim survived the death penalty, it could cost the soldiers their lives and Pilate his job.

Stoning was the Jewish means of the death penalty (Deut 21:20-21). In case of repulsive crimes, the dead body would be hung on a tree or impaled on a stake as a symbol of being accursed and as a warning to all (Deut 21:23). The cross was referred to as a "tree" (Acts 5:30; 10:39; 1 Pet 2:24). Galatians 3:13 gives the clear meaning: *Christ redeemed us from the curse of the law by becoming a curse for us, for it is written: Cursed is everyone who is hung on a tree.* It was only the most despised criminals who were crucified, as were those who were hung on a tree in the Old Testament. This is one reason the cross was a *stumbling block to the Jews and foolishness to the Greeks* (1 Cor 1:23; Gal 5:11). Yet *it is the power of God and the wisdom of God to save* (1 Cor 1:24).

The Jews insisted, *"We have a law and according to that law he must die, because he claimed to be the Son of God."* When Pilate heard this, he was even more afraid, and he went back inside the palace. *"Where do you come from?"* he asked Jesus, but Jesus gave him no answer. *"Do you refuse to speak to me?"* Pilate said. *"Don't you realize that I have power either to free you or to crucify you?"* Jesus answered, *"You would have no power over me if it were not given to you from above. Therefore the one who handed me over to you is guilty of a greater sin"* (John 19:7-11).

Now the Sanhedrin gave the real reason for their hatred and hostility toward Jesus and the charge on which they had voted to condemn Him (Matt 27:23-66). The real charge was blasphemy. Pilate already had a fear of this trial when *his wife sent him this message: "Don't have anything to do with that innocent man, for I have suffered a great deal in a dream because of him"* (Matt 27:19). Now his claim to be the Son of God made Pilate all the more afraid. He asked Jesus, *"Where do you come from?"*

He knew that Jesus was from Galilee, what he meant was, "Where do you REALLY come from?" Pilate is all the more fearful because of Jesus' silence and asks him if he realizes Pilate's authority over Him. Then Jesus let Pilate know who was really in control. Pilate's only authority over Him came from God. Earlier Jesus had said: *"The reason my Father loves me is that I lay down my life only to take it up again. This commandment I received from my Father"* (John 10:17-18).

Caiaphas bore the greater blame because he had manufactured charges and brought Pilate into it for his own corrupt use. *From then on, Pilate tried to set Jesus free, but the Jews kept shouting, "If you let this man go, you are no friend of Caesar. Anyone who claims to be a king opposes Caesar."* When Pilate heard this, he *brought Jesus out and sat down on the judge's seat at a place known as the stone pavement (which in Aramaic is "Gabbatha"). It was the day of preparation of Passover week, about the sixth hour. "Here is your king,"* Pilate said to the Jews. *But they shouted, "Take him away! Take him away! Crucify him!"* (John 19:12-15).

The mob in front of Pilate's tribunal, shouting for crucifixion, was mostly made up of the temple police controlled by the priests.

They numbered ten thousand while Jesus' followers were just getting the news.

"Shall I crucify your king?" Pilate asked. "We have no king but Caesar," the chief priests answered. Finally Pilate handed him over to be crucified (John 19:15-16).

This was a very serious accusation. Jesus had allowed Himself to be called the king of Israel when He rode into Jerusalem on a donkey at His triumphal entry (John chapters 12-13; Luke 19:38). Pilate feared Caesar would hear that he had released a claimant to the throne of Israel. Pilate was in enough trouble with Caesar over his rule of Judea. This could mean his removal or even execution.

The judgment seat was a raised platform for the judge to sit on outside the palace. Pilate was now ready to give the final judgment. The pavement was the platform holding the judgment seat. It was called "Gabbatha" in the Hebrew, meaning "elevation." Then the Jewish leaders shouted out, *"If you let this man go, you are not Caesar's friend: anyone who claims to be a king is against Caesar."*

"Friend of Caesar" was a term referring to a political ally of the Roman emperor who showed exceptional devotion to him. They were warning him that his career was in danger of ruin for not looking after the interests of Rome and the Emperor Tiberius Caesar.

It was about noon on the day of the preparation of the Passover. The Passover here refers to the whole Feast of Unleavened Bread, which was really a festival. The Passover meal was eaten the night of the festival. It was the day of preparation for the Sabbath Passover that would begin at sundown. Israel's true King was God. But now Israel's leaders were about to have their true King, the Messiah, crucified, while claiming Caesar as their king!

CHAPTER THIRTEEN
Jesus' Crucifixion

Then Pilate turned Jesus over to be crucified, and Jesus was led to the site of crucifixion outside the city. *As they led him away, they seized Simon from Cyrene, who was on his way in from the country, and put the cross on him and made him carry it behind Jesus. A large number of people followed him, including women who mourned and wailed for him. Jesus turned and said to them, "Daughters of Jerusalem do not weep for me, weep for yourselves and your children. For the time will come when you will say, 'Blessed are the barren women, the wombs that never bore and the breasts that never nursed!' Then they will say to the mountains, 'Fall on us!' And to the hills, 'Cover us!' For if men do these things when the tree is green, what will happen when it is dry?" Two other men, both criminals, were also led out with him to be executed* (Luke 23:26-32).

A centurion would have led the procession along the road called the "Sorrowful Road," with four soldiers who formed the execution detail. Pilate's cohort of 600 soldiers would have lined the roadsides to control the mobs. The victim was forced to carry the heavy horizontal cross beam weighing 110 pounds, while the vertical beam was kept at the crucifixion site.

Crucifixion was a public spectacle that took place near the main roadways to serve as a warning to all. Jesus would have been greatly weakened from what He had suffered the night before: the scourging and beatings and the tremendous loss of blood. Simon, going out of the country, was forced to carry His cross. With Jesus' back lacerated and very painful, carrying the crossbeam would have been unbearable.

A large number of people followed Him, including some devout women who were grief-stricken by what was happening to Jesus. Turning to them, He told them not to weep for Him. He was doing what He came to do, as He told His disciples: *"For the Son has come to seek and save that which was lost"* (Luke 19:10), and *"Just as the Son of Man did not come to be served, but to serve, and to give his life as a ransom for many"* (Matt 28:20).

They were to weep for themselves and their children. He warned them of Jerusalem's coming destruction that would come in 70 A.D. The "green tree" represented Him and the "dry" tree represented Israel. The historian Josephus tells us that during the siege and destruction of Jerusalem, over a million Jews were killed. All the trees in the surrounding area were cut down to make crosses for crucifixion and many were sold into slavery.

Normally for a woman to be childless was considered a great shame, but during that time they would be glad that they would not have to see their children face torture, rape, starvation, and being butchered. They would cry to the mountains and the hills to cover them and hide them from the horrible slaughter. Death would be preferable to extended suffering. This would take place 37 years later.

If the Romans did this to Christ, who was innocent (as Pilate knew), and during a time of peace, what would they do when Jerusalem was in rebellion and the land was a tinderbox?

They came to a place called Golgotha (which means the place of the skull). There they offered Jesus wine to drink, mixed with gall; but after tasting it, he refused to drink. When they had crucified him they divided up his clothes by casting lots. And sitting down they kept watch over him there. Above his head they placed the written charge against him: "This is Jesus, The King of the Jews" (Matt 27:34-37).

While the soldiers nailed the charges against Jesus to His cross, Colossians 2:14 tells us that God did something: *He took the laws that we have broken, the written code, with its regulation, that was against us and that stood opposed to us; he took it away: NAILING IT TO THE CROSS.*

God nailed our sins or crimes to Christ's cross. The Law of God requires obedience that we have failed to give. The Law of God was against us because we had a debt to the law that we could not pay, but God forgives us our debt by nailing the charges to Christ's cross and judging Him for our sins. Because Christ paid the penalty for our sins, all that is necessary for our salvation is faith in Christ.

Two robbers were crucified with him, one on his right and one on his left. Those who passed by hurled insults at him, shaking their heads and saying, "You who are going to destroy the temple and build it in three days, save yourself. Come down from the cross, if you are the Son of God." In the same way the chief priests, the teachers of the law, and the elders mocked him. "He saved others," they said, "but he can't save himself! He's the king of Israel. Let him come down now from the cross, and we will believe in him" (Matt 27:38-42).

Psalms 69:20 prophesies this from the victim's point of view: *Scorn has broken my heart and has left me helpless; I looked for sympathy, but there was none; for comforters, but I found none.* The truth is that if he saved Himself, He could not have saved others.

"*He trusts in God. Let him rescue him now if he wants him, for he said, 'I am the Son of God!'" In the same way the robbers who were crucified with him also heaped insults on him* (Matt 27:43-44).

It was customary before crucifixion to give the condemned wine mixed with gall, which was made with a narcotic made from the oil of Artemisia, mixed with myrrh to numb the pain. But Jesus refused to drink it. Then they crucified him (Matt 27:34-35). God is love and He is holy. His holiness demands judgment for our sins, while His love takes this judgment on Himself.

Though no one could see it, the greatest miracle of all occurred while they nailed Him to the cross. It was the miracle that nothing happened. No angel intervened to help Him as it did with Isaac.

The crossbeam would have been fastened to the main upright beam while Jesus was stripped naked. Then to prevent resistance, his arms would have been yanked out of joint; then, using large square spikes, His wrists were nailed to the crossbeam, then His feet. This nailing of the victim to the cross was only the beginning of the agonies of crucifixion.

When the cross was stood upright, the whole weight of the victim's body was held by the nails, and then the cross was dropped into the stone socket, jarring every nerve with excruciating pain. The slightest movement would have been unbearable. Then the entire trauma would bring on tremendous thirst.

The victim would eventually become so weakened that he could no longer pull up with his hands and push up with his feet to breath, and finally died from asphyxiation. It was a gruesome and horrible death.

The soldiers took His clothes and cast lots for them, fulfilling Psalms 22:18, *They divided my garments among them and cast lots for my clothing.* Then the soldiers who had crucified Him sat and watched Him. The two thieves (or better, revolutionaries) were crucified on either side of Him, fulfilling Isaiah 53:12, *He was numbered with the transgressors.* They were probably members of Barabbas' band, condemned with their leader, whom Jesus replaced.

Golgotha was by the road leading to Jerusalem, where there would be many travelers. They, along with the chief priests, mocked Him. They implied that if He were the Son of God, he did not have much time to prove it. He certainly did not look like the Son of God now!

The Messiah dying on a cross was a stumbling block for the Jews, as Paul said, *But we preach Christ crucified, a stumbling block for the Jews and foolishness to the gentiles* (1 Cor 1:23). This is because it was done in WEAKNESS, not befitting the popular notion of the Messiah: *For to be sure, He was crucified in weakness* (2 Cor 13:4).

One of the criminals who hung there hurled insults at him: "Aren't you the Christ? Save yourself and us!" But the other criminal rebuked him, "Don't you fear God?" he said, "since you are under the same sentence? We are punished justly, for we are getting what our deeds deserve. But this man has done nothing wrong." Then he said, "Jesus, remember me when you come into your kingdom." Jesus answered him, "I tell you the truth, today you will be with me in paradise" (Luke 23:39-43).

Here one of the criminals asked Jesus to remember him when He comes into His kingdom. He had probably heard bits and pieces of Jesus' preaching and heard Him speak of His kingdom. Jesus assures him that however incomplete his understanding of His kingdom, that very day he would be with Him in Heaven.

Before that day ended, by simple faith in Christ, he would enter into glory through the merits of Christ. Here we see a demonstration of Romans 10:13: *Everyone who calls upon the name of the Lord will be saved.* He had no good works to offer God: *For it is by grace you have been saved, through faith – and this is not from yourselves, it is the gift of God – not by works, so that no one can boast* (Eph 2:8-9).

This man was saved without baptism or confession to a priest. He simply trusted Jesus and that moment, that very moment, he passed from death into eternal life. He was born again and entered into eternal life, directly from the cross he was hanging on.

Near the cross of Jesus stood his mother, his mother's sister, Mary the wife of Clopas and Mary Magdalene. When Jesus saw his mother there, and the disciple he loved standing nearby, he said to his mother, "Dear woman, here is your son," and to the disciple, "Here is your mother." From that time on, this disciple took her into his home (John 19:25-27).

Mary's children did not believe in Jesus at that time, so Jesus entrusted her to John, who loved both Jesus and Mary, and they both loved John. Jesus made it clear that He loved His mother dearly, but now His relation to her was as her Lord and Savior. From then on John took Mary as his mother.

From the sixth hour until the ninth hour darkness came over all the land. About the ninth hour Jesus cried out in a loud voice, "Eloi, Eloi, Lama Sabachthani?" – which means, "My God, my God, why have you forsaken me?" (Matt 27:45-46).

Jesus now senses a dreadful loneliness. He has experienced many disappointments. Many had forsaken Him, including His own disciples; Peter denied that he even knew Him. The horror of this cry is in the word "You," "Why have YOU, My precious Father, forsaken me – the one who always did what pleased You – The one You delighted in – WHY?"

This was so we would never be forsaken and He could say to us, *Never will I leave you; never will I forsake you* (Heb 13:5). David had prophesied this cry from the cross a thousand years before in Psalms 22:1.

From noon until 3 p.m., the land was covered in darkness, representing judgment from God, as Jesus experienced the wrath of God for the sins of humanity. He was drinking the cup of the wrath of God.

It was prophesied that Jesus would be put to death for our sins: *This man was handed over to you by God's set purpose and foreknowledge* (Acts 2:23). *By oppression and judgment he was taken away. And who can speak of his descendants. For he was cut off from the land of the living; for the transgressions of my people he was stricken* (Isa 53:8).

He was made an offering for sin: *The Lord makes his life a guilt offering* (Isa 53:10). The exact mode of His death was prophesied in Psalm 22. His crucifixion was foretold centuries before Rome came to power: *They have pierced my hands and feet* (v. 16).

He was condemned as a criminal: *He was numbered with the transgressors* (Isa 53:12).

The exact words describing His anguish were prophesied a thousand years before He cried them out: *My God, my God, why have you forsaken me* (Psa 22:1).

Many other details of the crucifixion were given in vivid detail, as through the prophetic writers had already watched Him die at Calvary! Earlier Jesus had said: *"Now is the time for judgment on* the world; now the prince of this world will be driven out. But I, when I am lifted up from the earth, will draw all men to myself" (John 12:31-32).

The judgment of the world fell on Christ and He would break Satan's power.

Satan's power was the law that condemned us. Christ would break Satan's power. The law demanded death for sin, and this was carried out on Christ to satisfy the demands of the law on our behalf. The preaching of the cross would be the means of drawing all people to trust in Him. God was in complete control.

Jesus was not only crucified on the day the Passover lambs died, but He died at the ninth hour (3 p.m.) when the Passover Lamb was killed. He died on the right day, at the right hour, for the Scripture to say: *Christ, our Passover Lamb, has been sacrificed* (1 Cor 5:7).

When the pioneers were settling this country, fires would flare up suddenly on the prairies, and the wind would cause it to travel very quickly through the dry grass that grew very high. Anyone within a certain distance was trapped. No horse could outrun it. The only thing they could do was to turn their backs to the wind and set fire to the grass in front of them.

They would then be standing between two raging infernos; the one behind them moving toward them, and one in front of them moving away from them.

When enough grass in front of them, moving away from them, was burned, they would simply step onto the ground where the fire had already been and they were safe. The fire of God's wrath had fallen on Christ on the cross, and those in Christ are safe because they are standing where the fire had already fallen.

Later, knowing that all was now completed, and so the Scripture would be fulfilled, Jesus said, "I am thirsty." A jar of wine vinegar was there, so they soaked a sponge in it, put the sponge on a stalk of the hyssop plant, and lifted it to Jesus lips. When he had received the drink, Jesus said, "It is finished." With that, He bowed His head and gave up his spirit (John 19:28-30).

He who stood in the temple during the Feast of Tabernacles and cried out, *"If any man thirst let him come to me and drink. Whoever believes in me, as the Scripture has said, 'Streams of living water will flow from within him'"* (John 7:37-38), now thirsted. Thirst was one of the agonies of the cross. His thirst was prophesied in Psalms 22:15: *My strength is dried up like a potsherd, and my tongue sticks to the roof of my mouth; you lay me in the dust of death.*

His mouth was dry. His tongue stuck to the roof of his mouth and made it difficult to speak. Before being crucified He had refused to drink the drugged wine to numb the pain (Matt 27:34). But now He needed to speak and would need to wet His mouth. Near the cross was a vessel full of vinegar or sour wine. Jesus knew that He would be given this to burn His cracked and dry lips and mouth as an added mockery of His sufferings, but it would serve His purpose.

Now before death He asks for a drink. Psalms 69:21 refers to this: *They gave me vinegar for my thirst.* A soldier filled a sponge with this drink that was connected to a reed of the hyssop plant about four feet long, and Jesus would have sucked on the sour, but drug-free wine. Thirst was part of the curse and because He thirsted, those who believe in Him would drink the "Water of Life": *"Whoever drinks the water I give him will never thirst. Indeed the water I give them will become to them a spring of water welling up to eternal life"* (John. 4:14).

After receiving the wine, Jesus cried out, *"It is finished."* In the Greek it is one word "Tetelestia." It was used in connection with a debt being paid and means that a debt is "finished" or "paid in full." It is the perfect tense of "Teleo," which is the tense of fullness. The debt is "ended" or "completed," "fulfilled" or "finished." And it is done so "forever" or "once for all."

Before the creation God knew that man would sin, and would take on a debt that he could not pay. Jesus gave a promissory note to pay the debt.

The animal sacrifices did not pay for sin but pointed to the True Lamb of God who would ultimately pay for our sins. By offering these sacrifices, the offerer was pointing to the One who would pay the debt in full. The Old Testament had the shadow of good things to come. That is, in types and symbols it foreshadowed the good things to come. But in the New Testament Jesus Christ was the substance or "reality" of what was foreshadowed in the Old Testament.

We are told in Hebrews 10:1-4: *For the law is only a shadow of the good things that are coming – not the realities themselves. For this reason it can never, by the same sacrifices repeated endlessly year after year, make perfect those who draw near to worship. If it could, would they not have stopped being offered? For the worshippers would have been cleansed once for all, and would no longer have felt guilty for their sins, because it is impossible for the blood of bulls and goats to take away sins.*

Those sacrifices could not take away sin, but rather in those sacrifices there is a reminder of our need of a Savior. Those sacrifices and offerings were required by the law to point the sinner to the True Lamb of God. Jesus' perfect sacrifice, offered in complete submission, superseded and therefore fulfilled all previous sacrifices.

Jesus called out with a loud voice, "Father, into your hands I commit my spirit." When he had said this, he breathed his last.

After the darkness ended and the penalty for sin was paid – the cup of judgment drunk, the Father's presence returned. Jesus was now out of the hands of sinful men and into the hands of his Father. From now on God would allow only loving hands to handle His Son.

His followers took Him down from the cross and placed Him in the tomb, and only they touched Him after His resurrection.

The Old Testament sacrifices did not take away sin but foreshadowed the one who would. Hebrews 10:5-12 makes this clear. *Therefore when Christ came into the world, He said: "Sacrifice and offering you did not desire, but a body you prepared for me; with burnt offering and sin offering you were not pleased, Then I said, Here I am – It is written about me in the scroll – I have come to do your will, O God."*

First he said, "Sacrifices and offerings, burnt offerings and sin offerings you did not desire." Then He said, "Here I am, I have come to do your will." He set aside the first to establish the second. And by that will, we have been made holy through the sacrifice of the body of Jesus Christ once for all. Day by day every priest stands and performs his religious duties; Again and again he offers the same sacrifices, which can never take away sins. But when this priest had offered for one time one sacrifice for sins, he sat down at the right hand of God.

On the cross Jesus paid the sin debt in full. "Paid in full" or "Finished" was written in his blood. The ceremonial laws were finished and His sufferings were finished. The cross was first in the heart of God and later on the hill of Calvary – The Lamb slain *from the foundation of the world* is holy love and holy justice in perfect union.

The very justice that demands judgment on us endures the judgment for us. The very unyielding holiness that condemns us suffers to restore us. The God who condemns us agonizes to save us. God's holiness and love are both perfect and meet perfectly in Christ on Calvary's cross – resulting in grace.

God was upholding His own holiness by suffering our penalty and calling us back to Himself. The Blood Atonement that changes his throne of judgment to a throne of mercy is His own. In Acts 20:28 Paul exhorts the elders of the church at Ephesus to *be shepherds of the church of God which He bought with His own blood.* Man's sin was met by a display of Divine holiness and love, the one demanding satisfaction and the other providing it. Redemption was provided by God and reveals the kind of God He is. in Christ, He gave Himself FOR and TO us.

The unity of the trinity is such that it is not possible for one to suffer without the others being involved. When Abraham and Isaac went up Mount Moriah, who suffered? The Son who must take the knife or the Father who must plunge the knife into His Son? Once we truly see Calvary, we can never get away from it and we can never be the same again. Even God cannot outdo Calvary! It is as big as the heart of God. Once you see that Calvary was for you, it is like being shot with the barbed arrow of God's love; you can never pull it out.

Through the incarnation Christ becomes our representative and bears the full penalty of the law on our behalf.

Now it was the day of preparation, the next day was to be a special Sabbath. Because the Jews did not want the bodies left on the crosses during the Sabbath, they asked Pilate to have the legs broken to make for a quick death, and the bodies taken down. The soldiers therefore came and broke the legs of the first man who had been crucified with Jesus and then those of the other. But when they came to Jesus and found that He was already dead, they did not break His legs.

Instead, one of the soldiers pierced His side with a spear, bringing a sudden flow of blood and water. The man who saw it has given testimony and his testimony is true. He knows that he tells the truth, and he testifies so that you also may believe. These things happened so that the Scriptures would be fulfilled: "Not one of His bones would be broken," and, as another scripture says, "They will look on the one they have pierced" (John 19:31-37). The importance of the fact that they did not break His legs (Psa 34:20) and the piercing of His side (Zech 12:10) was in the fulfillment of Scripture. It was the day of preparation, the day before the Sabbath. This Sabbath was a special Sabbath because it came during the Passover week and was one of the days of

Unleavened Bread. Every Sabbath was a holy day, but this was a special Sabbath. So the Jewish authorities, concerned about the Sabbath, asked Pilate to break the legs of the men on the cross to get the execution over with. The soldiers would break their legs just below the knees with a mallet.

Crucifixion brought about death by asphyxiation. The soldiers broke the legs of the other two. But when they came to Jesus, they found He was already dead and did not break His legs. Psalms 34:20 prophesied concerning Him: *He protects all His bones, not one of them will be broken.* And regarding the Passover Lamb, we read: *Do not break any of his bones* (Exod 12:46).

THE CURTAIN OF THE TEMPLE

At that moment the curtain of the temple was torn in two from top to bottom. The earth shook and the rocks split (Matt 27:51). It is emphasized that the curtain was torn from top to bottom, rather than from the bottom up, showing that it was not torn by the earthquake, but by the hand of God. This curtain separated the holy of holies through which the high priest would enter once a year with blood on the Day of Atonement.

The holy of holies was where God's symbolic presence, the Shekinah Glory, dwelt. Going about their duties, the priests were forbidden to enter here on pain of death. Moses' brother Aaron, the high priest, could only enter on the Day of Atonement. It was covered by a curtain sixty feet high, thirty feet wide, and four inches thick! This curtain separated the holy of holies from the people, and to look behind it meant death: *The Lord said to Moses: "Tell your brother Aaron not to come whenever he chooses into the most holy place behind the curtain in front of the atonement cover on the Ark, or else he will die, because I appear in the cloud over the atonement cover"* (Lev 16:2).

It was a monumental task to tear the veil. According to Matthew 27:45-51, Jesus died about the ninth hour, which would have been 3 p.m. by Jewish time. It was Passover and it was the time of the evening sacrifice, when the lamb was killed. The temple would have been full of priests performing their duties.

This opening to the holy of holies at the death of Christ indicated that from now on, it was through Christ that man has access to God. This is explained in Hebrews 10:11-12: *Day after day every priest stands and performs his religious duties; again and again he offers the same sacrifices, which can never take away sins. But when this priest had offered for all time one sacrifice for sin, he sat down at the right hand of God.*

Here we see that the Old Testament priests stood daily offering sacrifices over and over, that could not take away sin. There was no place for the priest to sit because he was constantly offering sacrifices that could never take away sin, but only typified and pointed to the One who would (v. 11). But this man, Jesus Christ, offered one sacrifice for sin (Only one perfect sacrifice that fulfilled all the Old Testament sacrifices – the sacrifice of Himself) and sat down at the right hand of God.

After only one Sacrifice, this Priest "sat down," because, as He had said from the cross, *"It is finished"* or "paid in full" Hebrews 10:14 adds: *Because by one sacrifice he has made perfect forever those who are being made holy.*

Hebrews 10:19 says: *Therefore, brothers, since we have confidence to enter the most holy place by the blood of Jesus, by a new and living way opened for us through the curtain, that is, his body.* This torn curtain represents entering the very presence of God. The believer is to have confidence entering God's presence through Jesus' blood.

Jesus has opened a new and living way into the very presence of God, through the curtain, that is to say his body. Here His flesh is likened to the curtain that was torn, opening the way to God. Jesus' torn body has given us perfect acceptance with God. It also revealed that God was finished with temple worship, and would show this by the destruction of the temple in 70 A.D. Israel had rejected their Messiah and God had rejected their worship.

This is what Jesus meant when He said, *"Destroy this temple, and in three days I will raise it up"* (John 2:19). *But the temple he had spoken of was his body* (John 2:21). Jesus was comparing Himself to the earthly temple. In Matthew 12:6 Jesus said: *"I tell you one greater than the Temple is here."* The Temple showed Him and His work in types and symbols. He was the SUBSTANCE, or the REALITY, to which it pointed. Earlier He had said: *"How dare you turn MY FATHER'S HOUSE into a market"* (John 2:16). Then when He was about to go to the cross and it was clear that they were going to reject Him, He told them: *"Behold YOUR HOUSE is left to you desolate"* (Matt 23:38). He no longer referred to it as "My Father's house," but as YOUR house. Here he referred to the Temple that would be destroyed in 70 A.D.

HIS BURIAL AND RESURRECTION

It was Preparation Day (that is, the day before the Sabbath). So as evening approached, Joseph of Arimathea, a prominent member of the council, who was waiting for the kingdom of God, went boldly to Pilate to ask for Jesus' body. Pilate was surprised to hear that he was already dead. Summoning the Centurion, he asked him if Jesus had already died. When He learned from the centurion that it was so, he gave his body to Joseph (Mark 15:42-45).

Joseph of Arimathea was a member of the council, that is, a member of the Sanhedrin, who had not consented to Jesus' death (Luke 23:51). He went boldly to Pilate and asked for Jesus' body. He took a risk making it known that he was a friend of Jesus. He was concerned about the body of Jesus, because had no one claimed it. It would have been thrown into the Vale of Hinnom (Later known as "Gehenna" in the Greek), the garbage dump of Jerusalem.

Before he gave consent, Pilate checked with the Centurion in charge. Pilate was very surprised to learn that he was already dead. Then Pilate allowed Joseph to have the body.

Joseph was accompanied by Nicodemus, the man who had earlier visited Jesus at night (John 3:1-21). Nicodemus brought a mixture of myrrh and aloes, weighing about seventy-five pounds.

Taking the body, the two of them wrapped it with the spices, in strips of linen. This was in accordance with Jewish burial customs. At the place where Jesus was crucified there was a garden, and in the garden a new tomb, in which no one had ever been laid. Because it was the Jewish day of preparation and since the tomb was nearby, they laid Jesus there (John 19:39-42).

Taking Jesus' body, Joseph and Nicodemus wrapped it with spices. Because it was preparation day, they worked quickly because no work could be done after sunset. They wrapped it with clean linen cloth soaked with a mixture of myrrh and aloes like a mummy. This was to prevent the smell of decay.

Near the place of crucifixion there was a garden in which was a new tomb, Joseph's tomb that had been hewn out of rock. They did this hurriedly before the special Sabbath and the eating of the Passover lamb at sundown. The women would return after the Sabbath to finish the burial properly.

The women who had come with Jesus from Galilee followed Joseph and saw the tomb and how the body was laid in it. Then they went home and prepared spices and perfumes. But they rested on the Sabbath in obedience to the commandment (Luke 23:55-56). The women wanted to see where the body of Jesus was laid, so they followed Nicodemus and Joseph of Arimathea. Then they went home where they would complete the Sabbath preparations and return after the Sabbath to complete the burial.

Now the next day, the day after preparation day, the chief priests and the Pharisees went to Pilate. "Sir," they said, "we remember that while he was still alive that deceiver said, 'After 3 days I will rise again.' So give the order to make the tomb secure until the third day, otherwise his disciples may come to steal the body and tell the people that he had been raised from the dead. This last deception will be worse than the first."

"Take a guard," Pilate answered. "Go and make the tomb as secure as you know how." So they went and made the tomb secure by putting a seal on the stone and posting a guard (Matt 27:63-66).

The next day that followed the day of preparation was the Sabbath. The chief priests and Pharisee came to Pilate requesting that Pilate secure the tomb to prevent the disciples coming at night and stealing the body of Jesus. They remembered His claim that after three days He would rise from the dead, while the disciples had forgotten this because they thought He was speaking in parables. It was completely contrary to their Messianic beliefs that the Messiah would die.

The third day was nearing, so the Jewish religious leaders were anxious for Pilate to guard the tomb. They believed that Jesus and His followers had perpetrated that Jesus was the Messiah, which error they believed they corrected by putting Him to death. But now they feared that if they allowed His followers to take his body and claim that Jesus rose from the dead, it would be worse for the religious leaders than what they claimed to be the first so-called error, that Jesus was the Messiah.

Pilate told them that they could have a "watch" or "guard," referring to the permanent guard of Roman soldiers stationed at the tower of Antonia. The Jewish leaders had been given the authority to use as many soldiers as needed as well as their own Temple police. They had the tomb sealed and set a watch.

This was no ordinary group of men, but well trained and well-armed Roman soldiers. To protect this seal was the soldiers' only concern, as servants of the empire to which they had sworn allegiance on pain of death.

They would have sealed the stone by placing a rope or cord across the stone and securing both ends with sealing clay and imprinting the clay with a signet of Roman authority. Breaking the seal would mean suffering a terrible death. Roman soldiers who did the sealing were then left to protect the seal of Roman power and authority. A Roman watch consisted of 16 soldiers, with four alternative watches every six hours.

There was a violent earthquake, for an angel of the Lord came down from heaven and, going to the tomb, rolled back the stone and sat on it. His appearance was like lightning, and his clothes were white as snow. The guards were so afraid of him that they shook and became like dead men (Matt 28:2-3).

Matthew 28:2 should be read with the meaning, "there HAD BEEN a violet earthquake earlier." The resurrection and the earthquake had taken place sometime before the women came to the tomb. The angel had already rolled back the stone: *They found the stone rolled away from the tomb* (Luke 24:2).

Early on the first day of the week, while it was still dark, Mary Magdalene went to the tomb and saw that the stone had been removed from the entrance (John 20:1). Earlier when the guards were there, the earthquake had occurred when an angel came and rolled the stone away from the tomb and sat on it. The stone was rolled away, not to let Jesus out, but to let the women in.

When the Sabbath was over, Mary Magdalene, Mary the mother of James, and Salome brought spices so that they might go to anoint Jesus (Mark 16:1). We can almost see a play-on-words here. "When the Sabbath was over" refers to Sunday. But it could also point out that the last Sabbath of the dispensation of the law had come to an end. A new era, ushered in by the resurrection of Jesus Christ, represented by a new day, had begun. These women had come to finish what they had hurriedly began, Jesus' burial. The Sabbath was not changed, but was fulfilled and done away with.

And they asked each other, 'Who will roll the stone away from the entrance of the tomb?" But when they looked up, they saw that the stone, which was very large, had been rolled away (Mark 16:3-4). It was a large disk-like stone fitted into limestone groves that weighed up to two tons. It had been rolled downhill to cover the opening of the tomb. Removing it by rolling it uphill would be much more difficult.

They were surprised to see the stone rolled away. They naturally would have thought that someone had moved the body. Luke 24:3 says: *But when they entered they did not find the body of the Lord Jesus.* At this point Mary Magdalene thought of Peter and John, who were probably staying together. They would know what to do.

In the meantime, other women arrived at the tomb and found it empty. *While they were wondering about this, two men in clothes that gleamed like lightning stood beside them. In their fright the women bowed down with their faces to the ground, but the men said to them, "Why do you look for the living among the dead. He is not here. He is risen! Remember how he told you, while he was still with you in Galilee:*

'The Son of Man must be delivered into the hands of sinful men, be crucified and on the third day be raised again.' Then they remembered his words.

As they stood there wondering over the empty tomb, two angels dressed in shining robes appeared suddenly before them. The women were terrified and bowed their faces to the ground. Then the Angels' words would have revived them with tremendous joy: *"Why are you looking for the living among the dead?"* Then the Angel reminded them that Jesus had told them in Galilee that He would be betrayed and be crucified and rise again on the third day. Then they remembered Him saying these words.

Meanwhile, Mary Magdalene had run to tell Peter and John about Jesus' body being gone. *So she came running to Simon Peter and the other disciple, the one Jesus loved, and said, "They have taken the Lord out of the tomb, and we don't know where they have put Him!" So Peter and the other disciple started for the tomb. Both were running, but the other outran Peter and reached the tomb first.*

He bent over and looked at the strips of linen lying there but did not go in. Simon Peter, who was behind him, arrived and went into the tomb. He saw the strips of linen lying there, as well as the burial cloth that had been around Jesus' head. The cloth was folded up by itself separate from the linen. Finally the other disciple, who had reached the tomb first, also went inside. He saw and believed (John 20:1-9).

When John and Peter heard from Mary Magdalene that Jesus' body was gone they both ran to the tomb. John, being much younger than Peter, arrived at the tomb first. He bent down and looked at the strips of linen lying there. First century sepulchers had round stone doors with openings about waist high, and people had to stoop down to look in. He did not go in at first but stood there contemplating what he saw. The grave clothes remained where the body had lain, without being unwound. The strips of linen wrapped around the body with the sticky glue-like spices remained intact with the body missing, like an empty mummy's shell. The body had passed through the linen wrappings without disturbing them.

The burial cloth that covered the face by tucking it under the chin and tied on the top of the head was not with the body wrapping but remained where the head had been, neatly wrapped up. All remained untouched. When Peter arrived he saw these things but did not understand. Then John entered and did comprehend and believed.

They did not yet understand from the Scriptures that He must rise from the dead, though Jesus had repeatedly told them that this would happen. Then they went to their homes.

But Mary stood outside the tomb crying. As she wept, she bent over to look into the tomb and saw two angels in white, seated where Jesus' body had been, one at the head and the other at the foot. They asked her, "Woman, why are you crying?" "They have taken my Lord away," she said, "and I don't know where they have put him." At this she turned around and saw Jesus standing there, but she did not realize that it was Jesus.

"Woman," he said, "why are you crying? Who are you looking for?" Thinking He was the gardener, and that Joseph perhaps may have changed his mind and may have had the body moved, she said, "Sir, if you have carried him away, tell me where you have put him, and I will get him." Jesus said to her, "Mary." She turned toward him and cried out in Aramaic, "Rabboni!" (which means Teacher). Jesus said, "Do not hold on to me, for I have not yet returned to my Father. Go to my brothers and tell them, 'I am returning to my Father and to your Father, to my God and your God'" (John 20:11-17).

Meanwhile, Mary Magdalene returned to the tomb. Peter and John had run ahead of her to the tomb and had already left, and she was alone. She stood outside the door weeping. She stooped down and through tear-filled eyes she saw two angels in white, one sitting at the head and one at the foot where Jesus body had been. The position of the intact body wrappings and the two angels sitting at the head and at the foot emphasized the missing body, and was reminiscent of the Cherubim at both ends of the mercy-seat.

Mary thought they were two men. They asked her why she was weeping: *"Because they have taken away my Lord and I don't know where they have laid him," she answered.* As she spoke, she sensed another presence behind her. Turning, she saw Jesus standing there, but not recognizing Him, she thought He was the gardener since the tomb was located in a garden.

He said to her, *"Woman, why are you weeping; who are you looking for?"* He repeats the angel's question. Then remembering the two inside, she said, *"Sir if you have moved Him, tell me where you have laid him, and I will get him."*

Jesus said to her "Mary." The way He said her name brought back many familiar memories and, turning to Him, she cried, *"Rabboni,"* meaning "Master" or "Teacher." Mary Magdalene was looking for His dead body, but she met her risen Lord! She was the first person to see the resurrected Lord! Jesus said, *"Do not cling to me, for I have not yet returned to my Father. Go instead to my brothers and tell them, 'I am returning to my Father and your Father, to my God and your God'"* (John 20:17). Mary seemed to think that Jesus was back to stay!

He had told them all earlier that it was expedient that He go to the Father and send the Holy Spirit. He wanted to show Himself to his followers after his resurrection and give them their final instructions and exhortations before going back to the Father, which He was in the process of doing. She was to go back and tell His disciples that He was about to ascend to His Father and their Father, to His God and their God. There was a difference in their relationship. His relationship to the Father was an eternal Oneness. Their relationship to the Father was because of the relationship with Jesus. Theirs came from being "in Christ," the eternal Son. And in His role as the Last Adam, sharing our humanity, the Father was His God and our God.

Mary Magdalene went to His disciples with the news: "I have seen the Lord!" And she told them that He had said these things to her (John 20:18).

When they heard that Jesus was alive and that she had seen him, they did not believe it (Mark 16:11).

It was fitting that Jesus first appeared to the women, to share in the joy of His resurrection, because of their great love and devotion to Him. *As the women were going to tell His disciples suddenly Jesus appeared to them. "Greetings," He said. They* came to Him, clasped His feet and worshipped Him. Then Jesus said to them, "Do not be afraid, go and tell my brothers to go to Galilee: there they will see me" (Matt 28:9-10).

The word for "greetings" could be translated "O Joy." It was the triumphant joy of victory over sin, death, and Hell. A new era had begun! The suffering and sorrow were over and joy lay ahead. Jesus told the Jews the one sign He would give them was the sign of Jonah: *"For as Jonah was three days and three nights in the belly of a great fish, so the Son of Man will be three days and three nights in the heart of the earth"* (Matt 12:40-41).

In John 8:28 Jesus said: *"When you have lifted up the Son of Man, then you will know that I am the one I claim to be."* We read in Romans 1:4: *Who through the Spirit of holiness Jesus was declared with power to be the Son of God by the resurrection from the dead.* Jesus did not become the Son of God by His resurrection, but the resurrection proved "with power" that Jesus WAS (eternally) the Son of God.

Now that same day two of them were going to a village called Emmaus, about seven miles from Jerusalem. They were talking with each other about everything that had happened. As they talked and discussed these things with each other, Jesus himself came up and walked along with them; but they were kept from recognizing Him.

He asked them, "What are you discussing together as you walk along? They stood still, their faces downcast. One of them, named Cleopas, asked him, "Are you only a visitor to Jerusalem and do not know the things that have happened there in these days?"

"What things?" he asked. "About Jesus of Nazareth," they replied. "He was a prophet, powerful in word and deed before God and all the people. The chief priests and other rulers handed him over to be sentenced to death, and they crucified him; but we had hoped that he was the one who was going to redeem Israel. And what is more, it is the third day since all this took place. In addition, some of our women amazed us. They went to the tomb early this morning but did not find his body. They came and told us that they had seen a vision of angels, who said he was alive. Then some of our companions went to the tomb and found it just as the women had said, but him they did not see."

Then He said to them, "How foolish you are, and how slow of heart to believe all that the prophets have spoken. Did not the Christ have to suffer these things and then enter his glory?" And beginning with Moses and all the prophets, he explained to them what was said in all the Scriptures concerning himself.

As they approached the village to which they were going, Jesus acted as if he were going further. But they urged him strongly, "Stay with us, for it is nearly evening; the day is almost over." So he went in to stay with them.

When he was at the table with them, he took bread, gave thanks, broke it and began to give it to them. Then their eyes were opened and they recognized him, and he disappeared from their sight. They asked each other, "Did not our hearts burn within us while he talked with us on the road and opened the scriptures to us?" (Luke 24:13-32).

Jesus had other disciples besides the twelve. Two of them were walking down the road to Emmaus about seven miles from Jerusalem, from which they were coming after observing the Passover. They were discussing the things that had recently happened to Jesus when Jesus Himself caught up with them. They were prevented from recognizing him. He began walking with them and asked them what they were discussing so seriously.

One of them named Cleopas was amazed that he could have been in Jerusalem and not be aware of the very public crucifixion of Jesus. They thought that perhaps he was a visitor to Jerusalem for the Passover and had not heard about the recent events. Jesus asked them what things they were referring to. They answered the things concerning Jesus of Nazareth who was a mighty prophet and how he was condemned and crucified. They had hoped he was the one to redeem Israel from Roman bondage, and to make things worse, now three days later, women, who also believed in him, went to the tomb early and found that the body was gone. They went to the disciples and said that an angel told them that he was alive.

Certain ones who were with them, Peter and John, went to the tomb and found it empty; this was before Mary Magdalene returned and saw Jesus. Then Jesus said, *"You foolish people who find it so hard to believe what the prophets have spoken in the Scriptures. Was it not predicted that Messiah would suffer these very things and enter into his glory?"*

The very things that were causing them to doubt were the very things that should have convinced them that he was the Messiah. Then He led them through the Old Testament explaining how it applied to Him. But now as they were coming near Emmaus where they were going. He acted as though He would continue on.

But they urged Him to stay the night as it was getting late. He went home with them, and as they sat down to eat, He took the bread and blessed it. Then He broke it and gave it to them when suddenly they recognized Him and He disappeared before them. Then they told each other how their hearts burned within them as He explained the Scriptures to them. We can only marvel at the privilege of hearing Jesus opening these Scriptures and applying them to Himself! He prevented them from recognizing Him because He first wanted them to see Him clearly in the Scriptures.

Then they hurried back to Jerusalem to the disciples. But before they could say anything to them, they were told that the Lord Had appeared to Peter. They had not accepted the testimony of the women, but they did Simon Peter. Then they told the disciples their story, how he appeared to them on the road and went home with them and was recognized by them as He broke bread.

On the evening of the first day of the week, when the disciples were together, with the doors locked for fear of the Jews, Jesus came and stood among them and said, "Peace be with you!" After he had said this, he showed them his hands and side. The disciples were overjoyed when they saw the Lord.

Again Jesus said, "Peace be with you! As the Father has sent me, I am sending you." And with that he breathed on them and said, "Receive the Holy Spirit. If you forgive anyone his sins, they are forgiven; if you do not forgive them, they are not forgiven." Now Thomas (called Didymus), one of the twelve, was not with the disciples when Jesus came. So the other disciples told him, "We have seen the Lord." But he said to them, "Unless I see the nail marks in his hands and put my fingers where the nails were, and put my hands into his side, I will not believe it" (John 20:19-25).

On the same day as the resurrection, the disciples were gathered in the upper room of the last supper, with the doors closed and locked for fear of arrest by the Jews for being Jesus' disciples. Jesus suddenly appeared in their midst and said to them, *"Peace be with you."* He showed them His hands and side. Luke 24:40 specifies that He also showed His scarred feet, as well as His hands and spear-torn side. These scars will be shown to the Jews when He returns, as we are told in Zechariah 12:10: *They will look upon the one they have pierced and mourn for him as one mourns for their only child.*

Now after His resurrection, He was sending them to spread the gospel and bring people into the kingdom that will be set up when He returns. In His high priestly prayer, He had stated this earlier: *"As you sent me into the world; I have sent them into the world"* (John 17:18). To enable them to do this, *He breathed on them and said, "Receive the Holy Spirit"* (John 20:22).

This is what He promised in John 7:37-39, *On the last day of the feast, Jesus stood and said in a loud voice, "If anyone is thirsty, let Him come to me and drink. Whoever believes in me, as the Scripture has said, 'Streams of living water will flow from within him.'" By this He meant the Spirit, whom those who were to believe in him were later to receive. Up to that time the Spirit had not been given, since Jesus had not yet been glorified.*

The Holy Spirit would be given after Jesus was glorified: after He was raised from the dead. From then on, the Holy Spirit immediately indwells the body of the believer upon faith in Christ. *And if anyone does not have the Spirit of Christ, he does not belong to Christ* (Rom 8:9). Later, at Pentecost, the Holy Spirit came to supply us with power to carry on Christ's work.

Only God can forgive sin. Jesus demonstrated His authority to do this, and here Jesus commits the responsibility and privilege, not of actually forgiving sin, but of proclaiming the conditions of forgiveness.

"I give you the keys of the kingdom; whatever you bind on earth will be bound in heaven, and whatever you loose on earth will be loosed in heaven" (Matt 16:19). Binding and loosing are associated with being freed by Jesus: *"If the Son sets you free, you will be free indeed"* (John 8:36). Greek Scholar A.T. Robertson says that "binding and loosing" are rabbinical metaphors for proclaiming and teaching.

The "keys to the kingdom" refers to proclaiming the gospel and opening the door to the kingdom by declaring the terms for entering the kingdom. The door or gate to the kingdom is Christ Himself: *"I am the gate for the sheep"* (John 10:7). The keys are given to all believers to give the terms of salvation to others, and opening the door for those who want to enter in. If they trust in Christ, their sins are forgiven, if they do not, their sins are not forgiven.

Thomas called Didymus (meaning Twin) was not there when Jesus came. He said he would not believe until he had seen and touched the wounds from the crucifixion. The other disciples did not believe the testimony of the women, until they saw Jesus for themselves. Thomas only wanted the same evidence that the others had. A week later the disciples were in the house again and this time Thomas was with them.

Though the doors were locked, Jesus came among them and said, *"Peace be with you!" Then He said to Thomas, "Put your finger here; see my hands and side, stop doubting and believe." Thomas said to Him, "My Lord and my God!" Then Jesus told him, "Because you have seen me you have believed, blessed are those who have not seen and yet have believed"* (John 20:26-29).

Now eight days later, probably in the same room, the doors shut and locked, once again, Jesus suddenly appeared in their midst and greeted them with *"Peace be with you."* Then He turned directly to Thomas and told him to touch His wounds and to put his hand in His side and stop doubting.

Thomas does not take Jesus up on His offer. He didn't need to, Thomas immediately gasps out, *"My Lord, and my God."* This was not merely an exclamation of surprise, but a heartfelt worship. Jesus did not protest Thomas' words but commended them.

Afterward Jesus appeared again to his disciples by the Sea of Tiberius. It happened this way: Simon Peter, Thomas (called Didymus), Nathanael from Cana in Galilee, the sons of Zebedee, and two other disciples were together. "I'm going out to fish," Simon Peter told them. And they said, "We'll go with you." So they went out and got into the boat, but that night they caught nothing.

Early in the morning Jesus stood on the shore, but the disciples did not realize that it was Jesus. He called out to them, "Friends haven't you any fish?" "No," they answered. He said, "Throw your net on the right side of the boat and you will find some." When they did, they were unable to haul the net in because of the large number of fish. Then the disciple whom Jesus loved said to Peter, "It is the Lord!"

As soon as Simon Peter heard him say, "It is the Lord," He wrapped his outer garment around him (for he had taken it off) and jumped in the water. The other disciples followed in the boat, towing the net, full of fish, for they were not far from shore, about a hundred yards. When they landed, they saw a fire of burning coals there with fish on it, and some bread.

Jesus said to them, "Bring some of the fish you have caught." Simon Peter climbed aboard and dragged the net ashore. It was full of large fish, 153, but even with so many the net was not torn. Jesus said to them, "Come and have breakfast." None of the disciples dared ask him, "Who are you?" They knew it was the Lord. Jesus came, took the bread and gave it to them, and did the same with the fish.

Now this was the third time Jesus appeared to his disciples after he was raised from the dead. When they had finished eating, Jesus said to Simon Peter, "Simon son of Jonas, do you truly love me more than these?" "Yes, Lord," he said, "you know that I love you." Jesus said, "Feed my lambs." And Jesus said again, "Simon son of Jonas, do you truly love me?" He answered, "Yes lord, you know that I love you." Jesus said, "Take care of my sheep." The third time he said to him, "Simon, son of Jonas, do you love me?"

Peter was hurt because Jesus asked him the third time, "Do you love me?" He said, "Lord you know all things; you know that I love you." Jesus said, "Feed my sheep" (John 21:1-17).

Tiberius was the Greek name for the Sea of Galilee. Jesus appeared again to His disciples. Among them were Peter, Thomas who was also called (or nicknamed) the twin, Nathanael, and the sons of Zebedee: John and James. Peter said he was going fishing, and the others came too. After fishing all night they caught nothing. About dawn Jesus stood on the shore, but because of the distance and the morning fog, the disciples could make out a figure, but could not recognize who it was.

He called out to them, *"Friends, did you catch any fish yet?" "No," they called back. "Throw your nets on the right side of the boat and you will find some."* These experienced fishermen knew that His advice was a waste of time. But they did as He said and they immediately had a tremendous catch. John knew who it was and cried out to Peter, *"It is the Lord!"*

Peter, who had stripped down to his waistcloth, which was common while fishing, quickly put on his tunic and swam to meet the Lord, not waiting for the slow-moving boat that would draw the fish. The other disciples came in the "little ship" of verse 8, which was attached to the large fishing boat. This little boat rowed to shore dragging the net filled with fish, a distance of about a hundred yards. This was about as close to shore as it could come.

When they arrived they found that the resurrected Lord had prepared a standard Galilean breakfast of fish and bread on a charcoal fire for these tired and hungry men. The aroma of the charcoal would have made Peter uncomfortable, remembering how he had denied Jesus while he sat with soldiers by a charcoal fire (John 18:18). Jesus said to bring some of the fish they had caught and Peter came dragging the net to shore. Jesus, in His resurrected body, looked as though it could not have possibly been the same that had so recently been crucified. They knew it was Jesus but were amazed at His appearance.

This was the third time that Jesus had appeared to the disciples as a group. They sat down to eat with Him. When they finished eating, Jesus abruptly asked Peter a question: *"Simon, son of Jonas, do you love me more than these?"* Jesus will ask him three questions to renew his devotion to everything he had denied earlier. Peter had boasted that he would be faithful, even if the others abandoned Him. Jesus causes Peter to do some heart searching to prepare him for service.

Peter answered, *"Yes, Lord, you know I love you."* He brushes aside the words "more than these." He does not use the same word for "love" that Jesus uses, "Agapao," the Greek word for the highest devotion, but uses the word "Phileo" for fondness of a friend. Jesus understood that Peter truly did love Him, as Peter's bitter tears had showed, and He knew that Peter's failure had wrought a greater commitment to Him, so He tells Peter to shepherd his precious sheep.

Jesus asks the same question again, to which Peter repeats his answer. Again Jesus charges him to care for His sheep. Again, the third time He asks the same question. Peter got the meaning of why Jesus asked him for the third time, corresponding to Peter's three denials. However, this third time, Jesus uses Peter's word for "love." The first two times Jesus asked Peter if he loved Him, Jesus used the highest word for love, and both times Peter answered using a lower word for love. The third time that Jesus asked Peter if he loved Him, he used the word for the lower kind of love that Peter had used. This stung Peter's heart. He had been humbled for service. Peter answers that Jesus knew all things and he was confident that Jesus knew that he truly loved Him. And Jesus confirmed His command to feed His sheep.

"I tell you the truth, when you were younger you dressed yourself and went where you wanted (Peter was in control of where he went)*; but when you are old you will stretch out your hands, and someone else will dress you and lead you where you do not want to go"* (someone else would bind him and be in charge of where he went). *Jesus said this to indicate the kind of death by which Peter would glorify God. Then he said to him, "Follow me"* (John 21:18-19).

Peter would die a martyr's death. Peter, who had denied Jesus three times, would in the end, be faithful to the Lord he truly loved, and die a martyr's death. Peter had many weaknesses as we all do but loving Jesus was not one of them.

Peter turned and saw that the disciple whom Jesus loved was following them (This was the one who had leaned back against Jesus at the supper and had said, "Lord, who is going to betray you?"). When Peter saw him, he asked, "Lord what about him?" Jesus answered, "If I want him to remain alive until I return, what is that to you? You must follow me" (John 21:20-22).

When Peter asked how it would be with John, Jesus answered him abruptly; He was not to be troubled about John but about himself. Then Jesus summed it all up for Peter, *"Follow me."*

Then the eleven disciples went to Galilee, to the mountain that Jesus had told them to go. When they saw him they worshipped him but some doubted (Matt 28:16-17). A short time before, as they went toward Jerusalem, Jesus warned His disciples of His approaching death and resurrection: *Then Jesus told them, "This very night you will all fall away on account of me, for it is written: 'I will strike the shepherd, and the sheep of the flock will be scattered.' But after I have risen, I will go ahead of you into Galilee"* (Matt 26:31-32).

Here on a mountain, they met with Jesus and worshipped Him. But others, who were there besides the eleven, doubted. These doubts would be overcome. But the resurrected body was so different from the torn and battered body that had so recently been crucified.

He said to them, *"This is what I told you while I was still with you: Everything must be fulfilled that is written about me in the Law of Moses, the prophets and the psalms. Then He opened their minds so they could understand the Scriptures. He told them, "This is what is written: 'The Christ will suffer and rise from the dead on the third day, and repentance and forgiveness of sins will be preached in his name to all nations, beginning at Jerusalem.' You are witnesses of these things. I am going to send you what my Father has promised; but stay in the city until you have been clothed with power from on high"* (Luke 24:44-49).

The things that had happened to Him, His death and resurrection, were the fulfillment of the things He said before, that were written in the law and prophets and the psalms. This refers to the three divisions of the Old Testament. The whole Old Testament points to salvation through Christ. Now He showed them how these things, now in light of their fulfillment, were according to Scripture, proving that He was the Messiah.

The Old Testament also foretold that the gospel would be proclaimed to all the nations: Jesus is the promised *Light for the Gentiles* (Isa 42:6; 49:6); *I will pour out My Spirit on all people* (Joel 2:28).

They were witnesses to the very things that the Messiah would fulfill, and they would be the ones to bring the gospel to the whole world.

Jesus was about to send the Holy Spirit in fulfillment of the Old Testament Scriptures (Joel 2:28-32 with Acts 2:17-21; 13:47; 15:16-18; See also Isa 32:15, Jer. 31; 33): *I will give you a new heart and put a new Spirit in you; I will remove your heart of stone and give you a heart of flesh. And I will put My Spirit in you and move you to follow my decrees and be careful to keep my law* (Ezek 36:26-27).

They were to remain in Jerusalem until "you cause yourselves to be covered with power from on high" (Literally, in the middle voice, meaning something they were doing for themselves). God would send the Holy Spirit, but His empowerment was not automatic; they must seek the power for witnessing for Christ and be submissive to Him. The Spirit's indwelling is automatic the moment we believe in Christ, but the filling is for service, and is not automatic.

Then Jesus came to them and said, "All authority in heaven and on earth has been given to me. Therefore go and make disciples of all nations, baptizing them in the name of the Father and of the Son and of the Holy Spirit, and teaching them to obey everything I have commanded you. And surely I am with you always to the very end of the age" (Matt 28:18-20).

Jesus, as the eternal Son of God, always had all power and authority. The point here is that, as the Son of Man, the Last Adam, He has been given all authority. He who went down as low as He could go, to lift humanity to heaven, has been exalted to the preeminence of all things. As we are told in Philippians 2:5-11 concerning Christ:

Who, being in very nature God, did not consider equality with God something to be grasped, but made himself nothing, taking the very nature of a servant, being made in human likeness.

And being found in appearance as a man, humbled himself and became obedient to death, even death on a cross!

Therefore God exalted him to the highest place and gave him the name that is above every name, that at the name of Jesus every knee should bow, in heaven and on earth, and every tongue confess that Jesus Christ is Lord, to the glory of God the Father.

Here we are told that Jesus has always been God by nature but He did not hold onto His inherent right of equality with God. Christ could not set aside His divine nature, but He could and did set aside His glory or outward manifestation of His deity. He did not MANIFEST His divine nature. While retaining all His divine attributes He divested Himself of all OUTWARD appearance of glory.

The human race was dragged down by the first Adam yielding to the temptation to be as God: *"For God knows when you eat of it your eyes will be opened, and you will be like God, knowing good and evil"* (Gen 3:5). The Last Adam, Christ, lifted the race by not clinging to what was His by right: equality with God. He denied Himself His essential rights and privileges of deity. He did not cease being deity, but only set aside its outward display.

As He existed in the nature of God, sharing His nature and attributes, now He took upon Himself the nature and attributes of a human servant. While not giving up His deity, He took upon Himself another form or appearance, that of Adam, but apart from sin. He did give up His divine manifestation, veiling it in the manifestation of a human servant.

The words *being made in human likeness* (v. 7) is used not because He was not truly Man, but because He was also Deity. He was "like us" but not identical to us. He was a genuine human being, but without a sin nature, and He was also Deity. As the Last Adam, He represented the human race. As we are told in 1 Corinthians 15:22: *For as in Adam all die, so in Christ all will be made alive.*

He looked like a normal man and did have a human nature. This is how He was regarded by the people; this was His outward appearance, but He was much more. His humanity was manifested or showed forth while His deity was veiled or hidden.

He humbled Himself by taking on humanity, but He humbled Himself even further by taking on the form of a servant. He passed from the appearance of equality with God – from absolute sovereignty to the appearance of absolute humiliation of a lowly servant. His essential nature as God did not change, but only the method of His manifestation.

But we see Jesus, who was made a little lower than the angels, now crowned with glory and honor because he suffered death, so that by the grace of God he might taste death for everyone. In bringing many sons to glory, it was fitting that God, for whom and through whom everything exists, should make the author of salvation perfect through suffering (Heb 2:9-10).

Since the children have flesh and blood, he too shared in their humanity so that by his death he might destroy him who holds the power of death – that is the devil – and freed those who all their lives were held in slavery by their fear of death. For surely it was not angels he helps, but Abraham's descendants. For this reason he had to be made like his brothers in every way, in order that he might become a merciful and faithful high priest in service to God, and that he might make atonement for the sins of the people (Heb 2:14-17).

Jesus humbled Himself still further by being obedient even to the point of dying.

All others die because they have no choice, but Christ's death was a choice, an act of obedience to the Father. This was in contrast to the first Adam who disobeyed a simple command in the Garden of Eden: not to eat from one of many trees.

But Jesus humbled Himself even further, to the farthest extreme of death on a cross, the humiliating death of a criminal. Rome reserved crucifixion for slaves and the lowest criminals. Cicero said, "No adequate word can be found to describe so execrable an enormity. And far be the very name of the cross, not only from the body, but even from the thought, the eyes, and the ears of Roman citizens."

To the Jew His death was even more humiliating. Hanging on a cross was considered being accursed by God. According to Deuteronomy 21:22-23, certain criminals were so vile that they were cut off from God's covenant: *For he that is hanged is accursed of God.* Paul refers to this as the stumbling block of the cross to the Jew. They could not accept a Messiah who died the accursed death of a blasphemer and to the Gentile, a Messiah executed as a criminal was foolishness.

But Christ was accursed for OUR sakes. HE bore the curse WE deserved. This is the heart of the message of the cross and reconciliation to God: *But we preach Christ and him crucified: a stumbling block to the Jews and foolishness to the Gentiles, but to those whom God has called, both Jews and Greeks (Gentiles), Christ is the power of God and the wisdom of God.*

For the foolishness of God is wiser than man's wisdom, and the weakness of God is stronger than man's strength (1 Cor 1:23-25).

But God chose the foolish things of the world to sham the wise; God chose the weak things of the world to shame the strong. He chose the lowly things of this world and the despised things – and the things that are not – to nullify the things that are, so that no one may boast before him. It is because of him that you are in Christ Jesus, who has become for us the wisdom of God – that is our righteousness, holiness, and redemption. Therefore, as it is written: "Let him who boasts boast in the Lord" (1 Cor 1:27-31).

Christ redeemed us from the curse of the law by becoming a curse for us, for it is written: "Cursed is everyone who is hung on a tree" (Gal 3:13).

The "curse of the law," that is, the curse that comes from breaking the law. This is what is meant in Colossians 2:14-15: *God forgave us all our sins, having cancelled the written code, with its regulations, that was against us and that stood opposed to us; he took it away, nailing it to the cross. And having disarmed the powers and authorities, he made a public spectacle of them, triumphing over them by the cross.*

The written codes and regulations that were against us refer to the laws that were broken by all humanity. When Christ was crucified, Rome nailed the charges against Him to the cross. While God took all the broken laws and ordinances committed by the human race and nailed them to Christ's cross and judged Him for those offences. Christ suspended His rights as Creator to stoop to the dredges of the degradation of the cross. *And being found in appearance as a man, He humbled himself and became obedient to death – even death on a cross* (Phil 2:8).

The Angels' greatest joy was to serve Jesus' every desire. But now He humbled Himself to be born in a stable, to labor in Joseph's carpenter shop, and to do what no one could have imagined, wash the feet of those who would run away and abandon Him. He removed His robe of glory and put on the rags of a beggar. He *"did not come to be served, but to serve, and give His life a ransom for many"* (Matt 20:28).

When He returned to heaven in triumph, He not only resumed the eternal glory He had before His incarnation, but also the added glory of redemption over sin and death, the glorious victory of fulfilling the Father's will as the Last Adam. He now stood as the Head of the new creation as the God-man: *Every knee will bow and every tongue confess that Jesus is Lord* (Phil 2:9-11).

CHAPTER FOURTEEN
The Great Commission

"Therefore go and make disciples of all nations baptizing them in the name of the Father and of the Son and of the Holy Spirit, and teaching them to obey everything I have commanded you. And surely I am with you always, to the very end of the age" (Matt 28:19-20).

The Church's main duty and the job of every believer is to make disciples – this is called the Great Commission. There are three parts to the Great Commission. The first part is we must first give them the gospel and lead them to trust in Christ for salvation. We are told in Mark 16:15: *"Go into all the world and preach the good news to all creation."* The primary commission is to preach the gospel and instruct them in the way of life.

Second, we are to baptize them. Those who believe are then to be baptized as an outward expression of their faith in Christ, thus joining the outward fellowship of believers. Baptism does not save. The Bible is clear that only by faith in Christ alone is a person saved. The thief on the cross next to Jesus was not baptized and that very day he was in heaven with Jesus.

Many times in the Scriptures people were saved without being baptized. A few of them are Mark 2:5; Luke 7:37-50; and Luke 18:9-14. We show, by going under the water, that we have trusted in Christ and share in His death; the old sinful life is gone. Then, we share in His resurrection and newness of life. We illustrate this fact by coming up out of the water.

Going under the water does not wash away sin – only the blood of Jesus can do that, and coming out of the water does not raise us to new life – only faith in Christ can do that. Going under the water illustrates that we died with Christ. Our position in the old Adam is dead and buried. Coming up out of the water pictures our new life in Christ, the New Adam. We share in His new resurrection life as Jesus tells us in John 14:19: *"Because I live, you also will live."* And they are to be baptized in the singular name of "The Father, Son, and Holy Spirit," the source of salvation.

The third part of the commission is *"teaching them to obey everything I have commanded you."* We are to make disciples, not just winning them to Christ but teaching them to witness. We are to make disciples who will make disciples. We are to teach them to obey everything Jesus commanded in the Great Commission. In John 17:18 Jesus prays to the Father referring to His disciples: *"As you sent me into the world, I have sent them into the world."* Then in John 17:20 Jesus says: *"My prayer is not for them alone, I pray also for those who will believe in me through their message."*

So not only is Jesus sending His disciples to proclaim His message but also those who are won through the disciples. So from that day until today everyone who is won to Christ is given the same commission as His disciples. The Great Commission covers total evangelism: We are to WIN them, TEACH them, and send them out as evangelists. This is discipleship.

Jesus promises to enable all believers everywhere to carry out the Great Commission. He promises to be with them always. The One who has all power is with us. He is with all believers in the Person of the Holy Spirit. Here, He promises to be, in a special way, with those who carry out His work of bringing the gospel to the lost. This is a hostile world toward Christ and His gospel, and His presence with us is necessary.

He promises to be with His people until the "end of the Age." This refers to the end of this present age of proclaiming the gospel after which Jesus will set up His kingdom.

After his suffering he showed himself to these men and gave many convincing proofs that he was alive. He appeared to them over a period of forty days and spoke about the kingdom of God. On one occasion while he was eating with them, He gave this command, "Do not leave Jerusalem, but wait for the gift my Father promised, which you have heard me speak about. For John baptized with water, but in a few days you will be baptized with the Holy Spirit."

So when they met together, they asked him, "Lord, are you at this time going to restore the kingdom to Israel?" He said to them, "It is not for you to know, the times or dates the Father has set by his own authority. But you will receive power when the Holy Spirit comes on you; and you will be my witnesses in Jerusalem, and in all Judea and Samaria, and to the ends of the earth."

After he had said this, he was taken up before their very eyes, and a cloud hid him from their sight. They were looking intently up into the sky as he was going, when suddenly two men dressed in white stood by them. "Men of Galilee," they said, "why do you stand here looking into the sky. This same Jesus who has been taken from you into heaven, will come back in the same way you have seen him go into heaven (Acts 1:3-11).

Jesus showed himself after his resurrection for a period of forty days. "Convincing proofs" consisted of face-to-face conversations. He spent forty days with them to confirm their faith and instruct them in carrying on His work. He walked and talked with them. They touched His wounds.

The promise of the Father refers to the promises of the Old Testament of the outpouring of the Holy Spirit, like Joel 2:28, *And afterward, I will pour out my Spirit on all people.* John the Baptist said that Jesus *"shall baptize you with the Holy Spirit and with fire"* (Matt 3:11).

When they asked Him if he would now restore the kingdom to Israel, He answered that it was not for them to know the times or the seasons, which was in the Father's hand. He would not bring in the literal kingdom at this time. But would bring in His spiritual kingdom with the coming of the Holy Spirit. The concern now was to spread the gospel. They would receive power after the Holy Spirit came upon them. After receiving this anointing, they would be His witnesses, beginning at Jerusalem, Judea, Samaria, and to the ends of the earth.

This is how the gospel was spread out to the Gentiles. It began in Jerusalem, then moved to Judea among the Jews, and then to the Samaritans who were of a mixed blood of Jews and Gentiles and were looked down upon by the Jews as being unclean, and the Jews would not associate with them (John 4:9). This would prepare them to go to the full Gentiles and to the ends of the earth.

We see this movement in the Book of Acts: The gospel is spread to Jerusalem in Chapters 1-7; to Judea and Samaria in chapters 8-12; and to the uttermost parts of the earth in chapters 13-28. This can be broken down in the lives of believers today for evangelization: Your "Jerusalem" would be where you are: your immediate family; "Judea" would be relatives and friends; "Samaria" would be neighbors; then to the ends of the earth.

The Great Commission is for every believer in Christ. Every person is the center of an ever-widening circle. Its program is to begin at home and spread out. Its power is the Holy Spirit. The Holy Spirit baptizes or buries the believer into the body of Christ. *For by one Spirit we are all baptized into one body* (1 Cor 12:13). This unites us to Christ. He places the believer "in Christ." The

Spirit is the agent and Christ is the element. There, the believer is baptized by the Holy Spirit into Christ.

But here, we have the believer baptized by Christ with the Holy Spirit.

HIS ASCENSION

After He said this, he was taken up before their very eyes, and a cloud hid Him from their sight. They were looking intently up into the sky as He was going, when suddenly two men dressed in white stood beside them. "Men of Galilee," they said, "why do you stand here looking into the sky? This same Jesus who has been taken from you into heaven, will come back in the same way you have seen him go into heaven" (Acts 1:10-11).

As the Last Adam, the glorified Son of Man, eternally incarnated, Jesus ascended to heaven and today sits at the right hand of the Father *with great power and glory* (Matt 24:30), and is given *everlasting dominion* (Dan 7:14). His death and resurrection is the basis for the renewal of all things. *For God was pleased to have all His fullness dwell in Him, and through Him to reconcile to himself all things, whether things on earth or things in heaven, by making peace through his blood, shed on the cross* (Col 1:19-20).

Here the scope of reconciliation is "all things," things on Earth and things in heaven. Satan and all his fallen angels, all unsaved humanity will be forever banished, ending all possibility of broken harmony in the future. *The reason the Son of God appeared was to destroy the devil's work* (1 John 3:8). The destruction of the devil's works will be total. Humanity will be glorified.

The resurrection of believers is based on the resurrection of Christ as the Last Adam. *"Because I live, you also will live"* (John 14:19). The earth will become the kingdom of God and the universe will be renewed. *Behold, I create new heavens and a new earth. The former things will not be remembered* (Isa 65:17). *But in keeping with his promise we are looking forward to a new heaven and a new earth the home of righteousness* (2 Pet 3:13).

When Jesus returned to His throne with the Father, His glorified human body still carried the scars from the cross. Now in Heaven, as the Last Adam, He represents His people. We are told in Hebrews 10:19-21: *Therefore, brothers, since we have confidence to enter the most holy place by the blood of Jesus, by a new and living way opened for us through the curtain, that is, His body, since we have a great priest over the house of God . . .*

Here we are told that His body that was torn at His crucifixion is likened to the curtain that was torn covering the holy of holies. As the torn curtain opened the way into the Holy Place, the torn body of Jesus opened a new and living way into the presence of God. We have a sure approach to God. Our High Priest has opened the way by removing every barrier. He is both the sacrifice and the High Priest Who offered the sacrifice, and the cross was the altar on which He was sacrificed: *He sacrificed for their sins once and for all when He offered Himself* (Heb 7:27).

We are assured that we rose with Him and have already entered into Heaven through Him, our Representative and High Priest: *Since then, you have been raised WITH Christ, set your hearts on things above, where Christ is seated at the right hand of God. Set your minds on things above, not on earthly things. For you died and your life is now hidden with Christ in God. When Christ, who is your life, appears, then you also will appear with Him in glory.*

But you have come to Mount Zion, to the heavenly Jerusalem, the city of the living God. You have come to thousands upon thousands of angels in joyful assembly, to the church of the firstborn, whose names are written in heaven.

You have come to God, the judge of all men, to the spirits of righteous men made perfect, to Jesus the Mediator of a new covenant, and to the sprinkled blood that speaks a better word than the blood of Abel (Heb 12:22-24).

This is the City that Abraham looked for whose Architect and Builder is God (Heb 11:10). Where believers have an inheritance (1 Pet 1:4).

The thought here is not that we shall come in the future, but that we are come because our great High Priest is there as our Representative.

APPENDIX I
The Kingdom of Heaven

In my vision at night I looked, and there before me was one like a son of man, coming with the clouds of heaven. He approached the ancient of days and was led into his presence. He was given authority, glory and sovereign power; all peoples, nations, and men of every language worshipped him. His dominion is an everlasting dominion that will not pass away, and his kingdom is one that will never be destroyed (Dan 7:13-14).

Here we see the Messianic kingdom referred to as the kingdom of the "Son of Man."

"At that time the sign of the coming of the Son of Man will appear in the sky and all the nations will mourn. They will see the Son of Man coming on the clouds of the sky with power and great glory" (Matt 24:30).

"In the future you will see the Son of Man sitting at the right hand of the mighty One, and coming on the clouds of heaven" (Matt 26:64).

King David referred to the son of man being made ruler over God's works: *You made him ruler over the works of your hands; you put everything under his feet* (Psa 8:6). However, mankind lost his dominion by the fall. Jesus, as the "Last Adam" was appointed to restore the fallen creation.

The writer to the Hebrews refers to this in Hebrews 2:6-8: *But there is a place where someone has testified: "What is man that you are mindful of him, the son of man that you care for him? You made him a little lower than the angels; you crowned him with glory and honor and put everything under his feet." In putting everything under him, God left nothing that is not subject to him. Yet at present we do not see everything subject to him.*

But we see Jesus, who was made a little lower than the angels, now crowned with glory and honor because he suffered death, so that by the grace of God he might taste death for everyone.

Jesus, as Head of the restored dominion over the earth, took upon Himself humanity and became, in His humanity, a little lower than the angels. Now, as man, He is crowned with honor and glory at God's right hand, because by his death on the cross,

He has redeemed mankind and will bring about the ultimate fulfillment of Psalm 8, through the establishment of His kingdom.

"The Son on Man is going to come in his Father's glory . . ." (Matt 16:27).

"I tell you the truth, at the renewal of all things, when the Son of Man sits on his glorious throne . . ." (Matt 19:28).

As Prophet, Jesus proclaimed the kingdom (Matt 4:17; Luke 24:19).

As Priest, He has provided the basis for the kingdom (Heb 9:14; Rev 5:10).

As King, He will establish and rule the kingdom at His second coming (Matt 16:27; 19:28). It will be perfect and eternal.

But until then it is the rule of God in the hearts of men and women on this earth upon which Christ suffered and died to provide redemption. Those who believe the gospel become members. The Church is the kingdom in its "mystery" or "Secret" form. As Jesus told His disciples: *"The knowledge of the secrets of the kingdom of heaven have been given to you, but not to them"* (Matt 13:11).

For he has rescued us from the dominion of darkness and brought us into the kingdom of the Son he loves, in whom we have redemption, the forgiveness of sins (Col 1:13).

Jesus' miracles were done to confirm the coming of the kingdom: *"But if I drive out demons by the Spirit of God, then the kingdom of God has come upon you"* (Matt 12:28).

"Do not be afraid, little flock, for your Father has been pleased to give you the kingdom" (Luke 12:32).

It is a very unique kingdom where the King of Glory was crowned with thorns, where the king suffers and dies for his subjects. Whose subjects were once slaves who have become aristocrats, who were once enemies, and now they reign with Him.

For if, when we were God's enemies, we were reconciled to him through the death of his Son, how much more, having been reconciled, shall we be saved through his life (Rom 5:10).

To him who loved us and has freed us from our sins by his blood, and has made us to be a kingdom and priests to serve his God and Father to him be glory and power forever and ever! Amen (Rev 1:6).

The church is the kingdom in this present age, the kingdom in mystery form. *Consequently, you are no longer foreigners and aliens, but fellow citizens with God's people and members of God's household* (Eph 2:19). The purpose of the church in the present age is to be the instrument of God *to take out of the nations a people for His name* (Acts 15:14). *And you also are among those who are called to belong to Jesus Christ* (Rom 1:6).

Jews and Gentiles have become citizens of heaven. *But our citizenship is in heaven. And we eagerly await a Savior from there, the Lord Jesus Christ* (Phil 3:20).

They will become future administrators of the future kingdom. *Do you not know that the saints will judge the world? Do you not know that we will judge angels?* (1 Cor 6 :2-3). Here the word "judge" has the meaning of "rule."

In the Old Testament, Israel was called an "ecclesia" as the people of God. By the time of Jesus, there was only a remnant of the faithful. Paul tells us that New Testament believers were the true Israel after the Spirit. *Peace and mercy to all who follow this rule, even to the Israel of God* (Gal 6:16).

Now we, like Isaac, are children of promise (Gal 4:28). *There is neither Jew nor Greek, slave or free, male nor female, for you are all one in Christ Jesus. If you belong to Christ, then you are Abraham's seed, and heirs according to promise* (Gal 3:28-29).

Abraham believed the Lord and He credited to him as righteousness (Gal 3:6).

So those who have faith are blessed along with Abraham, the man of faith (Gal 3:9).

He redeemed us in order that the blessing given to Abraham might come to the Gentiles through Jesus Christ (Gal 3:14).

The creation of the New Heaven and New Earth is the renewal of the old heaven and earth where Christ suffered and died, much like the believer in Christ becomes a new creation and yet is the same person. Christ will remain the God-Man; this earth the dwelling place of mankind will become the home of the Triune God and the capital of the universe, with God's throne on earth. For the heavenly Jerusalem descends to the earth.

And he carried me away in the Spirit to a great and high mountain and showed me the great city, the holy Jerusalem, descending out of heaven from God (Rev 21:10). The scene of Christ's redemption will be the site of God's kingdom. No longer will there be any curse. *The throne of God and of the Lamb will be in the city, and His name will be on their foreheads* (Rev 22:3).

The earth will become heaven and we will dwell with God. *But you have come to mount Zion, to the heavenly Jerusalem, the city of the living God. You have come to thousands upon thousands of angels in joyful assembly, to the church of the Firstborn, whose names are written in heaven. You have come to God, the judge of all people, and the spirits of righteous men made perfect, to Jesus the mediator of a new covenant, and to the sprinkled blood of Abel* (Heb 12:22-24).

An untold number of angels are there and all the saints throughout history. It is the city Abraham looked for, *whose Architect and builder is God* (Heb 11:10), and for which God's people are *strangers and pilgrims on the present earth* (Heb 11:13). It is the longed-for inheritance of all the redeemed.

All honor to the God and Father of our Lord Jesus Christ! For it is by His boundless mercy that God has given the privilege of being born again. Now we live with a wonderful expectation because Jesus Christ rose from the dead. But God has reserved for us a priceless inheritance for His children. It is reserved in heaven for you, pure and undefiled, beyond the reach of change and decay (1 Pet 1:3-4).

We will share in His glory: *When Christ, who is your life, appears, then you also will appear with him in glory* (Col 3:4).

You are a chosen people; you are a kingdom of priests, God's holy nation, His very own possession. This is so you can show others the goodness of God, for he called you out of darkness into his wonderful light (1 Pet 2:9).

The believer's relationship to the kingdom is clear. They are citizens and ambassadors (2 Cor 5:20).

We are given this authority by the King himself with the promised certainty of His Presence, while in the meantime we await His return to establish His glorious kingdom.

The message of the gospel is at the same time the proclamation of the kingdom. As we see from Paul's words: *But my life is worth nothing unless I use it for doing the work assigned me by the Lord Jesus – the work of telling others the good news about God's wonderful kindness and love. And now I know that none of you to whom I have preached the kingdom will ever see me again* (Acts 20:24-25). So the *preachers of the gospel* are at the same time *fellow workers for the kingdom of God* (Col 4:11).

Like the Old Testament saints, we are strangers here *looking forward to the city with foundations, the Architect and Builder of which is God* (Heb 11:9-10). Here below we are strangers, while above in the heavenly city we are citizens. *But our citizenship is in heaven. And we eagerly await a Savior from there, the Lord Jesus Christ* (Phil 3:20).

Today there is being fought on this planet a great battle for the souls of men, between God and Satan. God has appeared on earth and made covenants with its inhabitants. The Son of God became the Son of Man to die for their sins and make them the sons of God. He rose from the dead and ascended back into heaven from which He will return to this planet. All history is moving toward this goal.

Believers will be glorified with Christ and will enter their eternal inheritance, and will forever be inseparable from Him, and will make up His ruling administration. Today when believers die, they go to heaven, the Father's house. They are at home with the Lord. Jesus said He was going there to prepare a place for New Testament believers. The Father's house is also called a city. Hebrews 11:16 tells us that God has prepared a city for Old Testament saints. This is where Jesus went to prepare dwelling places for New Testament believers.

The believer goes to be with the Lord, as 2 Corinthians 5:8 tells us: *We are confident, I say, and would prefer to be away from the body and at home with the Lord.* The life of the body is the Spirit. When the Spirit leaves the body, it is immediately present with the Lord. The body becomes lifeless and awaits the resurrection, when the spirit enters back into its glorified body.

This is what is taught in the Old Testament as well: *The dust returns to the ground it came from, and the spirit returns to God who gave it* (Eccl 12:7).

Jesus said to the thief on the cross: *"I tell you the truth, today you will be with me in paradise"* (Luke 23:43). His spirit would go to paradise with the Lord while his lifeless body would be buried. In 1 Thessalonians. 4:13 the body of the believer whose spirit had gone to be with the Lord is said to have fallen asleep because it is waiting to be awakened at the resurrection.

And in Acts 7:55 we read: *But Stephen, full of the Holy Spirit, looked up into heaven and saw the glory of God, and Jesus standing at the right hand of God.* Then in verse 59 we read that he prayed while being stoned to death: *"Lord Jesus, receive my Spirit,"* while his body fell asleep.

The present heaven is where the redeemed spirits of believers dwell until the return of the Lord when their bodies will be resurrected.

Ultimately, the New Jerusalem will come out of heaven to the new earth: *I saw the holy city, New Jerusalem. Coming down out of heaven from God, prepared as a bride beautifully dressed for* her husband. *And I heard a loud voice from the throne saying, Now the dwelling place of God is with men, and he will live with them. They will be his people and God himself will be with them and will be their God. He will wipe away every tear from their eyes. There will be no more death or mourning or crying or pain, for the old order of things has passed away. He who was seated on the throne said, "I am making everything new"* (Rev 21:2-5).

God's dwelling place in heaven will be moved to the new earth. It has always been God's will to dwell with His people. It began with the incarnation and will culminate in the New Jerusalem on the new earth.

This is the city that Abraham longed for, *whose Architect and Builder is God.* This is the place that Jesus told the thief on the cross they would go that very day: *"Today you shall be with me in paradise"* (Luke 23:43). And the place where Paul was *caught up to paradise* (2 Cor 12:4). And ultimately it is the city that all God's people are looking for.

We are told in Hebrews 13:14: *For here we do not have an enduring city, but we are looking for the city that is to come.* This world is not our home but we are looking for our city in heaven, which is yet to come.

Jesus said: *"Heaven and earth will pass away, but my words will never pass away"* (Matt 24:35).

But the day of the Lord will come like a thief. The heavens will disappear with a roar; the elements will be destroyed by fire, and the earth and everything in it will be laid bare. Since everything will be destroyed in this way, what kind of people ought you to be? You ought to live Holy and godly lives as you look forward to the day of God and speed its coming. That day will bring about the destruction of the heavens by fire, and the elements will melt in the heat. But in keeping with His promise we are looking forward to a new heaven and a new earth, the home of righteousness (2 Pet 3:10-13).

The thought here is not that the earth will pass away in the sense of passing out of existence, but that its present character will pass away and be changed. Just as believer's old bodies will not be discarded or cease to be, but rather the old will be changed. It is the same identity but in a changed or renewed character.

So too the New Creation will be the continuation of the old creation, but purged of all its imperfections and transformed and made a fitting place for God and His people. God will merge His dwelling place with the renewed creation to form a perfect and glorious domain of love and beauty. God's purpose in creation was to have an intimate relationship with mankind who was to rule the creation for God's glory. But mankind rebelled and brought the whole creation to sin and ruin.

God knew this before creation and appointed Christ, the Son of His infinite love, as redeemer, to buy back His fallen creation and restore it to God's original purpose. This is why the great words of redemption refer to a return to what was lost through sin.

God's plan was *to bring all things in heaven and on earth together under one head, even Christ* (Eph 1:10). History is moving toward this goal. Hebrews 1:3 tells us that Jesus is *sustaining all things* – In the Greek, it means not only preserving creation, but moving it toward a goal. The world as it is now is not our home. We are waiting for a restored earth, no longer under the curse, without sin and suffering and death.

Christ died to reclaim creation for God's glory and our good. His miracles were a demonstration of this. His blood on Calvary flowed down to the earth and claimed its redemption. There will be the satisfying exercise of all the faculties of all God's people and the gratifying of all holy desires in ruling for God's glory in the designated authority given to them by the Head of the creation, the Son of Man, Jesus Christ. He will retain His humanity forever and His people will have resurrected and glorious bodies like His.

Jesus resurrection was physical and required an empty tomb. When He appeared to His disciples, they handled His body and He ate food to show them that He was not a spirit. As the two who had met Jesus on the road to Emmaus were telling the other disciples about how they recognized Jesus as He broke the bread, He was suddenly standing there among them and said, *"Peace be with you."*

But they were frightened thinking they were seeing a ghost, but He said to them: *"Look at my hands and my feet. It is I Myself! Touch Me and see; a ghost does not have flesh and bones as you see I have"* (Luke 24:37-38). *Then they gave him a piece of fish and he ate it* (42-43). The believer's resurrected body will be like Jesus' resurrected body: *But our citizenship is in heaven. And we eagerly await a savior from there, the Lord Jesus Christ, who, by the power that enables him to bring everything under his control, will transform our lowly bodies so that they will be like his glorious body* (Phil 3:20-21).

Dear friends now are we the children of God, and what we shall be has not yet been made known. But we know that when he appears, we shall be like him, for we shall see him as he is (1 John 3:2).

Now we know that if the earthly tent we live in is destroyed we have a building from God, an eternal house in heaven, not built by human hands. Meanwhile we groan, longing to be clothed with our heavenly dwelling (2 Cor 5:1-2). Here our earthly bodies are compared to tents that are our temporary homes while our new bodies are likened to a permanent building made by God. These bodies that we have now serve their purpose for the time being; like tents on a camping trip, they serve a temporary purpose.

For God was pleased to have his fullness dwell in Him, and through him to reconcile to himself all things, whether things on earth or things in heaven, by making peace through his blood, shed on the cross (Col.1:19-20).

Here we see that the *reconciling to himself all things* goes as far as the fall and curse. It covers mankind, nature, and the earth. All will be restored to God's original "very good" before sin entered in. For all creation longs for and anticipates the resurrection of God's children as we are told in Romans 8:19-23: *The creation waits in eager expectations, for the sons of God to be revealed. For the creation was subjected to frustration, not by its own choice, but by the will of the one who subjected it, in hope that the creation itself will be liberated from its bondage to decay, and brought into the glorious freedom of the children of God. We know that the whole creation has been groaning in the pains of childbirth right up to the present time. Not only so, but we ourselves, who have the first fruits of the Spirit, groan inwardly as we wait eagerly for our adoption as sons, the redemption of our bodies.*

The believer's resurrection depends on Christ's resurrection. *"Because I live, you also will live"* (John 14:19). We see in Romans 8:19-21 that the rest of creation depends on the resurrection of mankind: *The creation waits in eager expectation for the sons of God to be revealed. For the creation was subjected to frustration, not by its own choice, but by the will of the one who subjected it, in hope that the creation itself will be liberated from its bondage to decay and brought into the glorious freedom of the children of God.*

Here we see that the redemption of believers' bodies will not only bring deliverance to them, but also to the rest of creation, over which mankind is the head. The earth will be renewed as our eternal home.

These have been groaning in suffering though having committed no sin. These will join God's children in deliverance from the bondage of death and decay. God cares for His animals and expects His people to care for them as well. Proverbs 12:10 says: *A righteous man cares for the needs of his animal.* Examples of God's care for animals are found in Exodus 20:9-10 in the giving of the Ten Commandments, where the whole household is commanded to rest on the Sabbath, including their animals.

When God sent Jonah to warn Nineveh and Nineveh repented, Jonah was angry and God said to him: *"But Nineveh has more than a hundred and twenty thousand people who cannot tell their right hand from their left and many cattle as well. Should I not be concerned about that great city?"* (Jonah 4:11).

Animals, who had never sinned, fell when man sinned and were used to picture Christ's sacrifice on the cross and the horror of sin. When Nathan came to David with the story of the rich man who took a poor man's only lamb who was his pet and killed it to serve to his guests, David said the rich man should die (2 Sam. 12:1-5). The pet lamb *"shared his food, drank from his cup and even slept in his arms. It was like a daughter to him"* (v. 3). There is no suggestion that the affectionate attachment was wrong. All creation will share in the restoration of "all things."

Man's original position in paradise was to *"rule over the fish of the sea and the birds of the air and over every living creature that moves on the ground"* (Gen 1:28). *You made him ruler over the works of your hands; you put everything under his feet: all flocks and herds, and the beast of the field, the birds of the air, and the fish of the sea, all that swim in the paths of the seas* (Psa 8:6-8).

God delights in the animals: *For every animal of the forest is mine, and the cattle on a thousand hills. I know every bird in the mountains, and the creatures of the field are mine* (Psa 50:10-11). God will restore all that He had said was "very good."

Adam was told to name the animals in Gen 2:19-20. He also named Eve, his wife (Gen 3:20), implying a relationship of headship over them.

When Noah left the ark to rule the new earth, God filled it again with animals. When Jesus, the Last Adam, came into the world, He was laid in a manger, a feeding trough for animals in a stable surrounded by animals. And they would have brought the infant many smiles and giggles. And when God brings in a new earth, He will fill it with animals.

We have no idea how animals were before the fall. They were given to us to love and to love us back. And we do not need to feel ashamed to love them. Christ's resurrection was the guarantee that God's people and all creation will be resurrected.

The present sufferings of creation are likened not to death, but to the temporary pains of childbirth, anticipating the bursting forth of life into a new and glorious creation. The old creation is dying, but its death will give birth to the new creation. What was created and lost in Genesis 1 and 2 are at last recreated and restored in Revelation 21 and 22. The whole creation waits in expectation. Something is coming, causing the creation eager anticipation. It was subjected *in hope that the creation itself will be liberated from its bondage to decay and brought into the glorious freedom of the children of God.* The curse is only temporary; it was done "in hope." God intends to remove it. The new creation will be brought forth FROM the old creation, not in place of it. It is not the earth itself but its *subjection to frustration* that will cease to be, as a result of its purifying fire of judgment. In Matthew 19:28 Jesus calls this the *"renewal of all things."* And Acts 3:21 refers to it as the time *for God to restore everything, as he promised long ago through the holy prophets,* referring to passages such as Isaiah 11:6-9: *The wolf will live with the lamb, the leopard will lie down with the goat, the calf and the lion and the yearling together; and a little child will lead them. The cow will feed with the bear, their young will lie down together, and the lion will eat straw like the ox. The infant will play near the hole of the cobra, and the young child put his hand in the viper's nest. They will neither harm nor destroy on all my holy mountain, for the earth will be full of the knowledge of the Lord as the waters cover the seas.*

And Isaiah 65:25: *The wolf and the lamb will feed together, and the lion will eat straw like the ox, and dust will be the serpent's food. They will neither harm nor destroy on all my holy mountain,"* says the Lord.

Mankind is by nature both spiritual, connecting us to God, and physical, connecting us to the animals and the earth. Mankind was created from the earth and for the earth and in the image of God to rule the glorified earth for God's glory. Acting as God's representative, Adam ruled over God's creation with loving care for God's glory.

It is God's pleasure and our eternal destiny to rule forever as His children and heirs. *The Spirit Himself testifies with our spirit that we are God's children. Now if we are God's children, then we are heirs – heirs of God and co-heirs with Christ, if indeed we share in his sufferings in order that we may also share in his glory* (Rom 8:16-17).

When Jesus said, *"My kingdom is not of this world"* (John 18:36), He meant that it did not originate from this Fallen, cursed, and sinful world. But His kingdom will be on this planet that has been redeemed, when sin and the curse have been removed.

Revelation 5:1-10 is a scene in heaven where God the Father is seated on the throne of the universe. *Then I saw in the right hand of Him who sat on the throne a scroll with writing on both sides and sealed with seven seals. And I saw a mighty angel proclaiming in a loud voice, who is worthy to break the seals and open the scroll? But no one in heaven or on the earth or under the earth could open the scroll or look inside.*

In verse 1 this scroll contains God's will for the management of His creation. A scroll is written on one side, but here it is written on both sides to indicate how full and complete God's plan for His beloved creation is. Usually one seal is used to seal a scroll to keep it rolled up and closed. Here this scroll has seven seals to keep its purposes secure until the rightful heir opens it. God's plan will be carried out only when each seal is broken.

God's purpose was that mankind would rule the earth as God's representative. All Heaven waited for the one who was worthy to receive the scroll and break the seals. But no one was found worthy to rule as God's representative, even though a mighty angel called out in a loud voice for the rightful heir to come forward and John, the human writer of the Book of Revelation, wept when no one came forward. All of Adam's descendants had sinned and failed and forfeited all rights (2-4).

Then one of the elders said to me, "Do not weep! See, the lion of the tribe of Judah, the root of David, has triumphed. He is able to open the scroll and its seven seals." Then I saw a Lamb, looking as if it had been slain, standing in the center of the throne, encircled by four living creatures and the elders. He had seven horns and seven eyes, which are the seven spirits of God sent out into all the earth. He came and took the scroll from the right hand of him who sat upon the throne. And when he had taken it, the four living creatures and twenty-four elders fell down before the Lamb. Each one had a harp and they were holding golden bowls full of incense which are the prayers of the saints. And they sang a new song: "You are worthy to take the scroll and to open its seals, because you were slain, and with your blood you purchased men for God from every tribe and language and people and nation. You have made them to be a kingdom and priests to serve our God, and they will reign on the earth" (Rev 5:5-10).

"The Lion of the tribe of Judah" and the "Root of David" were Messianic terms for the heir of David's throne. One of the elders said to John that the Messiah, Jesus Christ has triumphed to open the scroll and to break the seven seals (v. 5).

John looks around to see the Lion of Judah in the midst of the throne but instead he sees a lamb, as Israel had expected the Messiah to come as a lion, but instead He came as a Lamb. The Lamb John saw had been slain for sacrifice, but he was standing as resurrected. Horns were symbolic of power and seven horns would symbolize perfect or absolute power. Eyes were symbols of knowledge and seven eyes represent perfect or absolute knowledge. The *seven spirits of God* refer to the seven-fold Holy Spirit. Perfect power and wisdom are characteristics of the fullness of the Holy Spirit (v. 6).

John watches as the Lamb stepped forth and took the scroll from the right hand of the Father (v. 7).

When he had taken the scroll the four beasts fell down and worshiped before the Lamb and each had a bowl full of incense, which are the prayers of the saints for the establishment of Christ's kingdom, as Jesus taught us to pray: *Your kingdom come, your will be done on earth as it is in heaven* (Matt 6:8).

They sang a new song of praise to the worthiness of the Lamb to take the scroll and open the seals and bring about the fulfillment of God's purpose because He died to redeem mankind for God and made them kings and priests or a *Kingdom of priests* (9-10). Thus the fulfillment of God's purpose for mankind will be fulfilled through the Last Adam the new Head of redeemed humanity, Jesus Christ.

As Head of redeemed humanity, God the Father has delegated to Him sovereignty over His redeemed creation. Christ, in turn, shares His rule with His redeemed brethren as co-heirs of His Father's kingdom. Today they share in His sufferings and fight to advance His rule by spreading His gospel to bring redemption to those who are now His enemies. God's does not want us to destroy His enemies but to bring them into His kingdom.

Now we must share in His sufferings because this earth, the scene of His coming kingdom, is at war. It is being claimed by a false king, Satan, and his fallen angels, who are the real rulers behind those human rebels, and with whom the followers of the true king engage in spiritual warfare for the souls of mankind: *For our struggle is not against flesh and blood, but against the rulers, against the authorities, against the powers of this dark world and against the spiritual forces of evil in the heavenly realms* (Eph 6:12).

Jesus said: "Fear not, little flock for it is your Father's good pleasure to give you the kingdom" (Luke 12:32).

"Then will the King say to those on His right, 'Come, you who are blessed by my father, inherit the kingdom prepared for you from the foundation of the world'" (Matt 25:34).

All believers will have their works judged at the Judgment Seat of Christ. Referring to believers Paul wrote: *For we must all appear before the Judgment Seat of Christ, that each one may receive what is due him for the things done in the body, whether good or bad* (2 Cor 5:10).

This is the judgment of believers' works after being saved. It is for rewards not salvation, which is by faith alone. Rewards are based on our faithfulness in serving Christ. *Now it is required that those who have been given a trust must prove faithful* (1 Cor 4:2).

The believers' judgment will spotlight their personal stewardship of their abilities and opportunities. *"Behold, I am coming soon! My reward is with me, and I will give to everyone according to what he has done"* (Rev 22:12).

Our service now will determine how we will serve in the kingdom. Some misunderstand when the Bible refers to "resting" from our labors in heaven and they think there will be no work in heaven.

Actually, work is part of our reward. Believers will rest from their present labors, but in the kingdom we will have new assignments and new bodies that will never tire. We will enjoy serving God. There will be no suffering or labor (in the sense of hardship) in our new, glorified, eternal bodies.

What awaits us is incomprehensible. We have never experienced how God intended things to be. How men and women created in the image of God were meant to be. We have never seen animals before the fall, or the earth and universe as they were originally created. We only see the feeble remains of what they once were.

The greatest joy of Heaven will be to be with God Himself. He Himself is our greatest gift. Because of our union with Christ, we will have such closeness and intimacy with God that we will see His face. *And they shall see His face, and His name will be written on their foreheads* (Rev 22:4). His name upon us will mark us as His possession. We were created for Him.

Even now we have spiritual access into His presence: *Therefore, brothers since we have confidence to enter the most holy place by the blood of Jesus* (Heb 10:19). As His blood-bought children, we will spend eternity knowing Him, worshipping Him, and serving Him. We will always be in His immediate presence. Revelation 21:22 tells of the New Jerusalem: *I did not see a temple in the city, because the Lord God Almighty and the Lamb is its temple.* There will be no temple because we will have direct access to God's presence. God the Father and God the Son are seen as seated together on a single throne.

Concerning the Holy Spirit, we are told in John 14:16: *"And I will ask the Father, and he will give you another Counselor to be with you forever."* Forever means forever, so the Holy Spirit will continue to indwell believers to empower us to serve in the kingdom. Those in heaven will be supremely and eternally filled with joy because they will participate in the very life of the Triune God.

Colossians 3:1-4 tells us: *Since then you have been raised with Christ set your hearts on things above, where Christ is seated at the right hand of God. Set your mind on things above, not on earthly things. For you died and your life is now hidden with Christ in God. When Christ, who is your life, appears, then you also will appear with Him in glory.*

The Greek has the thought of "fervently and continuously seeking those things that are above." Physically we dwell on this earth but spiritually we are in Christ. We died with Him and our lives are forever identified with the risen Christ who is seated at the right hand of God.

And God raised us up with Christ and seated us with him in the heavenly realms in Christ Jesus. In order that in the coming ages he might show the incomparable riches of his grace, expressed in his kindness to us in Christ Jesus (Eph 1:6-7).

Our identity is in Christ and our hearts and lives are centered in Him at the right hand of God and not on things on the earth. He is our life and we are to seek to please Him, and when he returns to set up His glorious kingdom, then we will share in His glory. While here on earth, we draw our strength and resources from Him. Positionally, we are already with Him in Heaven. Our vital union with Him makes us inseparable from Him even now.

When we see God as He really is and we realize His love for us, we will overflow with praises and worship. It will burst forth as a river of joy to Him who is more than we could ever hope – or dream. Our awe and amazement will never end. To honor and please Him will motivate everything we do. Our unending joy will be to know that we are His and He is ours forever.

In 1 Corinthians 15:22-26 the triumphant Son of God, the Last Adam, returns the redeemed, restored kingdom back to His Father. Here we have the climax of history. *For as in Adam all die, so in Christ all will be made alive. But each in his own turn: Christ the first fruits; then, when he comes, those who belong to him. Then the end will come when He hands over the kingdom to God the Father after he has destroyed all dominion, authority and power, for he must reign until he has put all his enemies under his feet. The last enemy to be destroyed is death.*

Here the mission that was foretold in the Garden of Eden in Genesis 3:15 of the *Seed of the woman,* the Last Adam, taking upon Himself the responsibility for our sin, has been accomplished in a demonstration of love for His fallen and rebellious creation to whom He gave everything. After man's sin no one could have imagined the blood and tears it would cost the Son of God. He will return the redeemed and restored kingdom to the Father. Mission accomplished.

Those in the kingdom will never doubt His love as our first parents did, for in His glorified body He will still carry the scars of their redemption forever. What is God's goal for His people in eternity? This is revealed in Ephesians 2:7: *In order that in the coming ages He might show the incomparable riches of his grace, expressed in his kindness to us in Christ Jesus.*

The Resurrection of Jesus Christ

The Resurrection of Jesus Christ from the dead is referred to directly more than a hundred times in the New Testament. Paul refers to it in 1 Corinthians 15:1-4 as one of the essential and foundation truths of the gospel. *Now, brothers, I want to remind you of the gospel I preached to you, which you received and on which you have taken your stand. By this gospel you are saved if you hold firmly to the word I preached to you. Otherwise you have believed in vain. For what I received I passed on to you as of first importance. That Christ died for our sins according to the Scriptures, that he was buried, that he was raised on the third day according to the Scriptures.*

When the apostles chose a replacement for Judas, his replacement had to be *"a witness with us of His resurrection"* (Acts 1:21-22).

The accounts of the resurrection of Jesus Christ show clear evidence for eyewitness accounts. Apparent contradictions give convincing evidence that these accounts could not have been agreed-upon fabrications.

I say "apparent" contradictions because upon closer investigation, these "contradictions" vanish.

In a court of law, the strongest evidences come from witnesses who agree on the main points while having apparent contradictions that upon further probing disappear. The writers would have been aware of these apparent discrepancies and did not change them.

The first point of the gospel message is that Christ died for our sins. One thing we know for certain is that the Roman military knew how to kill. If there was any doubt about crucifixion doing its job of bringing about the death sentence, a lance was thrust under the ribs into the victim's heart. If they were in a hurry to bring about death, they would break the legs of the victim and suffocation would soon take place.

Either way, the executioner had to certify the death of the victim. If he got it wrong, he could lose his life. But they did not get it wrong. The victim was dead before he was taken down from the cross. The fact of his death would have been obvious; the victim simply was not pulling himself up to breathe! There was no reviving in the tomb. The fact that the tomb was empty that first Easter morning is indisputable.

That left only two options: The tomb was empty because the body was stolen or that Jesus rose from the dead. Who would have removed it? There were only two options: either His enemies or His friends. His enemies? Why? They had nothing to gain, whether as a prank or some other perverse reason. If it was his enemies, then they would have been in the enviable position to refute the claim that He rose from the dead and make a laughingstock out of His disciples. Why didn't they? Because they couldn't: It's that simple.

But what about His friends? For one thing there was a Roman guard posted outside the tomb (Matt 27:65). The Roman guard consisted of four well-armed and well-trained soldiers who would be relieved every six hours.

Imagine stepping over these guards and rolling away the huge stone without alerting them, even if they WERE sleeping, which held the death penalty. The watch was for too short a time to worry about them falling asleep. Especially ALL of them!

Rome was an occupying army and they ruled the Mediterranean with an iron fist. The disciples did not want to be anywhere near a Roman Soldier. They were not interested in taking Jesus' body; they were interested in their own safety. If Rome had executed their leader, how far away would their arrests be?

If the disciples had stolen His body, would they have gone around preaching His resurrection, facing torture and death? Would they have been willing to die for what they knew was a lie? People might die for what they THINK is true, but not for what they know is a lie.

The disciples were totally transformed from being fearful and hiding behind closed doors, to fearlessly facing death by boldly declaring that Jesus had risen from the dead. Only one reason is possible: They had seen their risen Lord.

If the disciples were fabricating Jesus' resurrection, why would they have had the women be the first to see him? Women were looked down upon in this oriental culture; their testimonies were not even accepted in court.

Shortly after Jesus had been executed as a criminal, His disciples were on the run, and His movement all but dead; something happened that changed the Christian movement from one facing extinction to a movement exploding like wildfire. It has spread to every country on earth and has changed the world with the message of God's love and Christ's power to save. What happened? They had seen the risen Lord!

Consider that from Israel's beginning, the Jews had kept the Sabbath to honor the work of God as Creator, thereby honoring the completion of creation. There was no work on the Sabbath as a memorial day set by God when He ceased creating. It was God's day and was set aside as a day of rest and worship.

Those first Christians were devout Jews. But they were so convinced of the resurrection of Jesus that they made the first day of the week the day of honoring God's work of redemption. They simply could not ignore it. They called it the "Lord's day." This is very powerful evidence for Jesus' resurrection.

Then there is Christian baptism that took on the meaning of Jesus death and resurrection. The rite symbolized that the believer had entered into Christ's death by going under the water, and His resurrection by rising up out of the water.

Other theories have been advanced to explain the empty tomb. One theory that liberal scholars came up with is "the wrong tomb theory." So saying that because of the chaos caused by Jesus' hurried burial at the dawning of the Sabbath, and the fact that the women came back very early Sunday, in the dim morning light they became confused where Joseph of Arimathea's tomb was located. As such they entered the wrong tomb and found it empty, whereupon hearing the grave-keeper, whom they mistook for an angel, say: "He *is not here.*" They became hysterical and ran away announcing an empty tomb and the rest is history! Or is it?

Surely it would not have taken long, once their story got out, for people to see their error, or for Joseph to point out his tomb to them. Certainly the Roman guard would have been happy to tell them their mistake. Even the Sanhedrin would have been happy to straighten them out. And most certainly Peter and John would not have run to the wrong tomb!

Another theory advanced is what is called the "Swoon theory." According to this theory, Jesus never really died. Somebody slipped Him a very powerful drug, putting him into a coma-like state, giving the appearance of death. Then after His burial He revived in the cool, damp tomb, changed into grave clothes left there by the gardener, and removed the large stone that was shaped like a wheel and weighed as much as two tons.

Then He crawled out of the tomb and happened to run into Mary Magdalene, who ran and told His disciples, who nursed Him back to health as best they could and then they declared Him the risen Lord, but forty days later he succumbed to his wounds. Before he died he called his disciples to meet him on a mountain and there disappeared into a cloud which they believed was his ascension into heaven!

The soldiers had seen hundreds of men killed by crucifixion. It was routine for them to know when a man was dead. He simply was not rising up and down to breathe!

But let's suppose Jesus had survived a Roman crucifixion? Would this crawling near-corpse have convinced his disciples that he was the Lord of Life, the great conqueror of death? And let us not forget the spear thrust under his ribcage and into his heart. Roman soldiers were very efficient in their jobs. Victims of a Roman crucifixion were not allowed to escape with their lives.

Then there is the psychological theory, which says that the disciples missed Jesus so much that they subconsciously invented His resurrection in order to feel his presence psychologically. Then they began to imagine seeing him, including more than five hundred at one time.

Some believe that the disciples were merely referring to a spiritual resurrection. But this was unknown to Jews and Christians. Resurrection can only apply to the body because only the body dies. Only in second century gnostic texts do historians find the concept of spiritual resurrection.

Those who claim a spiritual resurrection base it on a misunderstanding of Scripture. I Corinthians 15:44, referring to the resurrection body says: *It is sown (buried) a natural body, it is raised a spiritual body.* But the contrast here is not between a physical or material and a spiritual or immaterial body, but between a carnal or sinful body subject to death and a body that is sinless and not subject to death – one that is immortal. The same contrast is found in Romans 7:14, *We know that the law is spiritual; but I am unspiritual, sold as a slave to sin.* Only the body dies, so only the body can be resurrected. Jesus told the believing thief on the cross next to Him that on that very day they would both meet in paradise. *"I tell you the truth, today you will be with me in paradise"* (Luke 23:43). So that very day their dead bodies were placed in tombs, while their spirits, which do not die, went to paradise until Jesus' human spirit entered back into His body, giving it life. When the Bible speaks of spiritual death, it refers to the spirit being separated from God.

Then there is the twin brother theory with the predictable outcome. Jesus' twin pops up after His death and claims to be the risen Lord. Or his twin is crucified, thinking it was Jesus, and then the real Jesus appears! The remaining theories are just as flimsy as this and not worthy of consideration. The resurrection of Jesus is the only explanation for the empty tomb on that first Easter morning.

Many today assume that the ancients were quick to believe what we now know to be unscientific claims of people rising from the dead, but this is not true, especially with the Jews. They did believe in resurrection but this was a general resurrection at the end of history, as Martha said to Jesus after He told her that her brother, Lazarus, would rise again: *Martha answered, "I know he will rise again in the resurrection on the last day"* (John 11:24).

There were others in the first century who claimed to be the Messiah and were also executed. But with none of them was a resurrection mentioned. They knew better. It was not even considered. Nor was it with Jesus own followers – at first, until they saw Him in His resurrected body. There never could have been a belief in His resurrection among Jews without His appearing to them.

They walked and talked with Him and saw His wounds. The Christian movement sprang up immediately after His death. How could it rise so soon and so powerfully? Just when it should have died, it exploded into life. How could devout Jews worship a man who they also believed was God? These Jews faced persecution and horrible deaths defending their faith in Jesus resurrection from the dead. All the apostles and many early Christians were tortured and /or killed.

Jesus had predicted His death and resurrection many times. In fact He never predicted His death without adding that He would rise again.

From that time on Jesus began to explain to his disciples that he must go to Jerusalem and suffer many things at the hands of the elders, chief priests and teachers of the law, and that he must be killed and on the third day be raised to life (Matt 16:21).

When they came together in Galilee, he said to them, "The Son of Man is going to be betrayed into the hands of men. They will kill him, and on the third day he will be raised to life" (Matt 17:22-23). Also in Matthew 12:38-40; 17:9; 26:32; 27:63; Mark 8:31-9:1; 9:10; 9:31; 14:28, 58; 10; 32-34; Luke 9:22-27; and John 2:19-22; 12:34.

Paul, in Romans 1:4 tells us: *Who through the Spirit of holiness was declared with power to be the Son of God by his resurrection from the dead.*

Here the word "declared" has the meaning "shown" or "demonstrated." Jesus did not become the Son of God by His resurrection, but rather Jesus, Who always was the Son of God, humbled Himself and in lowliness died in "weakness," and was the demonstrated to be the Son of God with "power" by His resurrection from the dead.

A very significant change came about in Israel's social institutions for those first Jewish Christians. They rightly believed that these institutions were given to them by God. The Sacrificial systems, the Sabbath, and Circumcision, were all abandoned. A mere five weeks after His crucifixion, more than ten thousand Jews were following Him as the Son of God.

These were not minor adjustments but monumental changes in social structures of thousands of years. The Apostle Paul tells us that everything in the Christian faith depends on the resurrection of Christ: *If Christ has not been raised, your faith is futile; you are still in your sins* (1 Cor 15:17).

If you confess with your mouth, "Jesus is Lord" and believe in your heart that God raised Him from the dead, you will be saved (Rom 10:9).

Peter writes: *Praise be to the God and Father of our Lord Jesus Christ! In his great mercy he has given us new birth into a living hope through the resurrection of Jesus Christ from the dead* (1 Pet 1:3).

CONVERSION OF SKEPTICS:
JESUS' BROTHER – JAMES

1 Corinthians 15:7: *Then Jesus appeared to James.* We are told in the Gospels that Jesus brothers did not believe in Him: *"When the Jewish feast of Tabernacles was near, Jesus' brothers said to Him, "You ought to leave here and go to Judea, so that your disciples may see the miracles that you do. No one who wants to be a public figure acts in secret. Since you are doing these things, show yourself to the world." For even his own brothers did not believe in him* (John 7:2-5).

Jesus' brothers, half-brothers really, are named in Matthew 13:55 and Mark 6:3: James, Joseph, Judas, and Simon. The Feast of Tabernacles was one of the annual feasts that all Jewish males were required to attend. His brothers were mocking Him. They were saying: "Don't stay here where no one can see you; if you can do such great works, go to the feast and impress not only your disciples, but the whole world."

This was prophesied of Him in Psalms 69:8: *I am a stranger to my brothers, an alien to my own mother's sons.* This is why at his crucifixion Jesus left His mother in the care of His disciple John.

But after His resurrection, His brothers became believers. They were among those gathered in the upper room in Acts 1:13-14: *When they arrived they went upstairs to the room where they were staying. Those present were Peter, John, James and Andrew; Philip and Thomas, Bartholomew and Matthew; James son of Alphaeus and Simon the Zealot, and Judas son of James. They all joined together constantly in prayer, along with the women and Mary the mother of Jesus, and with his BROTHERS.*

This was done in obedience to Jesus' command just before His ascension: *"I am going to send you what my Father has promised; but stay in the city until you have been clothed with power from on high"* (Luke 24:49). They were associated with the other disciples and played an important role among them, including the writing of the epistles James and Jude.

James became the leader of the Jerusalem church (Gal 1:19). Josephus, the Jewish historian, informs us that James, the brother of Jesus, was the leader of the church of Jerusalem, and he was stoned to death because of his faith in Jesus.

CONVERSION OF SAUL/ PAUL

Paul describes his past in Philippians 3:4-6: *If anyone thinks he has reason to put confidence in the flesh, I have more: Circumcised on the eighth day, of the people of Israel, of the tribe of Benjamin, a Hebrew of Hebrews; in regard to the law, a Pharisee; as for zeal, persecuting the church; as for legalistic righteousness, faultless.*

He was the son of a Pharisee, a model Pharisee himself. He rigorously followed and defended the law. He learned the law under Gamaliel, one of Israel's most famous Rabbis. His zeal for the law drove him to persecute the church. After he encouraged the murder of Stephen, he began a career to exterminate Christianity.

In his own words: *For you have heard of my previous way of life in Judaism, how intensely I persecuted the church of God and tried to destroy it* (Gal 1:13). *But Saul began to destroy the* church. *Going from house to house, he dragged off men and women and put them in prison* (Acts 8:3).

Saul was still breathing out murderous threats against the Lord's disciples (Acts 9:1). Believers were scattered to other cities and Paul pursued them. He had the authority of the Sanhedrin behind him and he was able to travel to the synagogues in the farthest reaches of the Roman Empire. He carried credentials giving him full power to pursue Christians and bring them back in shackles to Jerusalem.

He went to the high priest and asked him for letters to the synagogues of Damascus, so that if he found any there who belonged to the Way (A name for Christianity) *whether men or women, he might take them back to Jerusalem* (Acts 1:2).

As he neared Damascus on his journey, suddenly a light from heaven flashed around him. He fell to the ground and heard a voice say to him, "Saul, Saul, why do you persecute me?"

"Who are you, Lord?" Saul asked.

"I am Jesus, whom you are persecuting," he replied. "Now get up and go into the city, and you will be told what you must do." The men travelling with Saul stood there speechless; they heard the sound but did not see anyone. Saul got up from the ground, but when he opened his eyes he could see *nothing, so they led him by the hand into Damascus. For three days he was blind, and did not eat or drink anything* (Acts 9:3-9).

Saul later recounted as he neared Damascus about noon, he saw a *light from heaven, brighter than the sun, blazing around me and my companions* (Acts 26:13). It was a display of the glory of the One who appeared to him. Saul was blinded, and he heard the voice of the holy One of Israel.

We all fell to the ground, and I heard a voice saying to me in Aramaic, "Saul, Saul, why do you persecute me. It is hard for you to kick against the goads." (Acts 26:14).

Saul knew what those goads were. It was the prayer of Stephen in Acts 7:59-60: *While they were stoning him, Stephen prayed, "Lord Jesus, receive my spirit." Then he fell on his knees and cried out, "Lord, do not hold this sin against them." When he had said this, he fell asleep.*

It was the sight of those humble believers who would rather die than deny the One whom Paul was now facing. He remembered Stephen's dying words: *"Look," he said, "I see heaven open and the Son of Man standing at the right hand of God!"* (Acts 7:56).

Now the one who had kept watch over the coats of those who were stoning Stephen, Saul, the persecutor, was lying on the ground before the risen Christ.

Overwhelmed, Paul gasps out *"Who are you Lord?* Then stripped of all his pride, Saul felt a terrible dread when he heard, "I *am Jesus whom you are persecuting."* But there was no anger in His voice, only sadness. Saul's fear turned to shame.

Now everything that Paul once held dear had suddenly lost its charm. While blinded and stripped of everything, Paul had found what he had sought for his whole Life. He would later write: *For God, who said, "Let light shine out of darkness" made his light to shine in our hearts to give us the light of the knowledge of the glory of God in the face of Jesus Christ* (1 Cor 5:6).

He also later wrote in his letter to the Philippians: *But whatever was to my profit I now consider loss for the sake of Christ. What is more, I consider everything loss compared to the surpassing greatness of knowing Christ Jesus my Lord, for whose sake I have lost all things. I consider them rubbish, that I may gain Christ and be found in Him, not having a righteousness of my own that comes from the law, but that which is through faith in Christ – the righteousness that comes from God and is by faith.*

Paul was brought to Damascus. God gave a disciple named Ananias a vision in which he was told to go to Saul and restore his sight and welcome him as a new believer! Ananias was afraid of Saul because of his reputation as a persecutor of Christianity, but he obeyed and laid his hands on Saul, who was filled with the Holy Spirit and could see again. Then Ananias baptized Saul. Jesus had told Ananias that Saul was His "chosen instrument" to bring His name to the Gentiles and their kings and before the people of Israel. *I will show him how much he must suffer for my name* (Acts 9:8-16).

Paul explained that he received his gospel directly from God by revelation from the risen Christ: *I want you to know brethren that the gospel I preached is not something that man has made up. I did not receive it from any man, nor was I taught it; rather, I received it by revelation from Jesus Christ* (Gal 1:11-12). After Paul's conversion he spent time in the desert of Arabia near Damascus and received his gospel from Jesus Christ.

But when God, who set me apart from birth and called me by His grace, was pleased to reveal His son in me so that I might preach Him among the Gentiles, I did not consult any man, nor did I go up to Jerusalem to see those who were apostles before I was, but I went immediately into Arabia and later returned to Damascus (Gal 1:15-17). Paul did not receive his gospel from the twelve apostles but directly from the risen Jesus while in the Arabian Desert. After three years Paul would meet with Peter to show him the gospel that he had received from Jesus so they could see that it was the same gospel that they preached.

From the very beginning, the resurrection of Jesus was vital to the apostolic teaching. It was the motivating force of Paul's life and ministry. After meeting the resurrected Christ, he was forever changed. Christ was now the center of his life and the driving force of his ministry. After recounting the facts of the gospel and Christ's resurrection appearances, Paul says concerning himself and the other apostles: *Whether, then, it was I or they, this is what we preach, and this is what you believed* (1 Cor 15:11).

Paul suffered innumerable dangers and hardships, and severe persecution. *I have worked much harder, been in prison more frequently, been flogged more severely, and been exposed to death again and again. Five times I received from the Jews the forty-nine lashes minus one. Three times I was beaten with rods, once I was stoned, three times I was shipwrecked, I spent a night and a day in the open sea, and I have been constantly on the move.*

I have been in danger from rivers, in danger from bandits, in danger from my own countrymen, in danger from Gentiles; in danger in the city, in danger in the country and in danger at sea; and in dangers from false brothers.

I have labored and toiled and have often gone without sleep; I have known hunger and thirst and have often gone without food; I have been cold and naked besides everything else, I face daily the pressure of my concern for all the churches (2 Cor 11:23-28).

Paul labored under these conditions for 25 years, until he was tortured and beheaded in Rome by order of Emperor Nero in 67 A.D.

Jesus was the Messiah, the Last Adam, the promised one who fulfilled the types and shadows of the Old Covenant and brought in the New Covenant in His blood.

In 1 Corinthians 1:23-24 we read; *We preach Christ crucified: a stumbling block to Jews and foolishness to Gentiles, but to those whom God has called, Jews and Greeks (Gentiles), Christ is the power of God and the wisdom of God.*

The great offence to Paul's Jewish hearers which had also become a stumbling block to himself, was the fact that a suffering Messiah went against all the preconceived ideas of the Jews. The Messiah suffering and dying was to them a contradiction in terms. It was sheer madness. It was a sign of a divine curse to be crucified as Jesus was. For it is clearly written in Scripture: *Anyone who is hung on a tree is under God's curse* (Deut 21:23).

To claim that the long-awaited Messiah would die such a shameful death would have been considered blasphemy. Paul did not try to avoid this paradox. Rather, it was the heart of his message. The curse Jesus bore was not His own, but ours, in accordance with prophetic Scriptures, such as Isaiah 53.

However, this was not the end, for He rose from the dead, also according to Scripture: *Because you will not abandon me to the grave, nor will you let your Holy One see decay* (Psa 16:10). Then Paul lists the eyewitnesses to whom He appeared, many of which would have still been alive.

Paul first came upon the scene as a persecutor who is suddenly converted by the resurrected savior. He then disappears to Arabia to prepare for his ministry, where he is taught by the risen Lord Himself. Then Paul reappears to proclaim the message of a risen Savior with the same intensity that he once fought against it.

His conversion was not only the turning point in his own life, but also in the history of the church and, thus, the history of mankind. Alongside the achievements of this former persecutor of Christians, blasphemer and murderer, all the achievements of those whom the world holds to be great fade into insignificance. The only explanation for the life of this man is that he met the risen Savior and was forever changed

Writing from prison at the end of his life, Paul wrote: *So do not be ashamed to testify about the Lord, or ashamed of me His prisoner. But join with me in suffering for the gospel, by the power of God, who has saved us and called us to a holy life– not because of anything we have done but because of his own purpose and grace. This grace was given to us in Christ Jesus before the beginning of time, but it has now been revealed through the appearing of our Savior, Jesus Christ, who has destroyed death and has brought life and immortality to light through the gospel. And of this gospel I was appointed a herald and an apostle and a teacher of Gentiles. That is why I am suffering as I am. Yet I am not ashamed, because I know whom I have believed, and am convinced that He is able to guard what I have entrusted to Him for that day* (2 Tim 1:8-12).

Paul had met the resurrected savior and served Him for about 25 years and wrote a third of the New Testament. This is irrefutable evidence for the resurrection of Jesus Christ from the dead! And so is the fact that the apostles who were commissioned by the resurrected Christ to preach the gospel faced severe persecution and torture until they were silenced, by sealing their testimonies with their blood.

APPENDIX 3
Did the Story of Jesus Evolve over Time?

The unique and essential truth of Christianity centers around the stupendous teaching of the incarnation: that Jesus Christ was God who took upon Himself humanity and gave His life for the sins of the world and rose from the dead.

Christianity reversed the initiative of redemption of paganism, from man who works his way to God – to God who comes to us in our helplessness and unworthiness and, in an unparalleled demonstration of love, took upon Himself the judgment of our sins.

The implication of this is staggering and grips the heart like nothing else can. That the Lord of glory could reach so low to redeem us who were so vile and unworthy; it will take eternity to tell that story, and it will be told by the redeemed who will never tire of telling it or of hearing it.

Myths take time to evolve – at least a generation – and for all the eyewitnesses to die off. The Jesus seminar and other liberal scholars tell us that the "Jesus of history" was merely a charismatic teacher of wisdom. Then a generation later, the tradition of the wisdom teacher was radically transformed and overlaid with apocalyptic traditions, miracles, and claims of being the Messiah until the "Jesus of history" is now unrecognizable as the "Jesus of faith," resembling a pagan myth.

But the greatest myth of all is that there is a difference between the Jesus of history and the Jesus of faith. These so-called "scholars," removed from the accounts of eyewitnesses by two thousand years, write endless books about stripping away the layers of myth from the Jesus of faith in order to "liberate" the Jesus of history – the real Jesus; and this is where the real myth is created.

The truth is that there is virtually no time between the crucifixion of Jesus and the fully developed Christology of the budding Christian church. Jesus was executed as a criminal on a cursed cross (Deut 21:23). This was totally unacceptable to the Jewish concept of the Messiah, even among His own disciples. When He told them that He would be killed, He was rebuked by Peter and the others were shocked (Mark 8:31-33).

They expected the Messiah to crush their enemies. Crucify the Messiah? Preposterous! Then Jesus was dead and His disciples were afraid and on the run. His movement, humanly speaking, was dead. But suddenly it exploded. Within months, thousands of Jews formed the church. Israel's social institutions – sacrifices, Sabbaths, ceremonial laws, etc. – in place for centuries – were changed by these first century Jewish Christians.

This sudden change came about because of the sincere belief of thousands of Jews that Jesus arose from the dead – not just from hearsay, but many who had seen Him. But even more, as Jesus would later explain, this was based on the Old Testament prophecies concerning Him. He was worshipped, not a generation later, but by the infant church made up mostly of Jews.

The power of this movement came not from some memories of a once great leader but from a risen Christ who has accomplished eternal salvation by His suffering and death on the cross, and has risen to carry out those benefits. He has sent forth the Holy Spirit to care for His people and empower them for service to proclaim His gospel.

The earliest records of Christianity are the epistles of Paul. They were written within twenty years of the death and resurrection of Jesus. What these letters reveal is the fact that the fully developed Christology that Paul was writing about was already believed by the church. These letters are not evangelistic in nature, but rather exhort and encourage Christians in their faith.

When Paul presented his Christology (his teaching about Christ) to these infant churches, it was a fully developed body of teaching. He fully expected them to understand his teaching. From these letters we know what the early church believed. They were written to those who were already Christians and under the supervision of elders, in churches already formed.

Jesus was already worshipped and called Lord (Yahweh). So within the time Paul wrote these letters, these believers had already been evangelized and instructed in these doctrines of the church. We must also remember that Paul, sometime before this, had to be converted and instructed by Jesus Himself in Arabia (Gal 1:11-12).

This means that there was no time gap for the development of myths, especially within the Jewish context of the early church. There was literally only time for Jesus to rise from the dead and make His appearances. There is no other explanation other than the one given by the apostles and other eyewitnesses, many of who died for their testimony.

There was no gap between the church and its Christology. In fact, without the church's Christology there could not have been a church or Christianity. The church's Christology was not simply a set of beliefs, but a Person; The risen Savior who had left His glory with the Father to go on a mission of suffering and death to redeem a lost and rebellious world.

Though we had forfeited and were unworthy of His love, yet He loved us and gave us His all – by entering into our darkness and sorrow and taking upon Himself the full force of the curse and exhausting the wrath we all deserve. It is the fact that He loved us so much that gives us our worth. This has always been the secret of the church. Behind this ordinary and flawed group of people stands the unchanging love of God.

It is from Paul that we learn that the Christians worship of Jesus did not develop over time but was there from the beginning. At the time of Jesus, devout Jews considered God's name too holy to speak. His name consisted of four Hebrew letters (YHWH) (pronounced "Yahweh"), known as the Hebrew Tetragrammaton. So in order not to speak the name out loud, they replaced Yahweh with the Hebrew word "Adonai," while the Greek speaking Jews used the Greek word Kyrios for the Tetragrammaton, Yahweh, when spoken.

For the first century Jews, including Paul, the title "Kyrios" was the equivalent of Yahweh, when used in the religious context where Paul refers to Jesus as "Lord" in Phil 2:9-11: *Therefore God exalted Him to the highest place and gave Him a name that is above every name, that at the name of Jesus every knee should bow, in heaven and on earth and under the earth and every tongue confess that Jesus Christ is Lord* (Kyrios) *to the Glory of God the Father.*

The apostles' teaching was that Jesus was Lord: *Therefore let all Israel be assured of this: God has made this Jesus, whom you crucified, both Lord* (Kyrios) *and Christ* (Messiah) (Acts 2:36).

With great power the apostles continued to testify to the resurrection of the Lord (Kyrios) *Jesus* (Acts 4:33).

There are passages in the Old Testament that apply to Yahweh that are applied to Jesus (Kyrios) in the New Testament, such as:

Joel 2:34: *And everyone who calls on the name of the Lord (Yahweh) will be saved.*

Romans 10:9: *That if you confess with your mouth Jesus is Lord* (Kyrios), *and believe in your heart that God has raised Him from the dead, you will be saved.*

Romans 10:13: *For everyone who calls on the name of the Lord* (Kyrios) *will be saved.*

To confess that Jesus is Lord or Kyrios means to confess Him as God.

Amos 5:18: *Woe to you who long for the day of the Lord* (Yahweh)*! Why do you long for the day of the Lord* (Yahweh)*? That day will be darkness, not light.*

2 Thessalonians. 2:2-3: *Concerning the coming of the Lord* (Kyrios) *Jesus Christ and our being gathered to Him; we ask you, brothers, not to become easily unsettled or alarmed by some prophecy, report or letter supposed to have come from us, saying that the day of the Lord* (Kyrios) *has already come.*

Stephen prays to Jesus while dying: *While they were stoning him, Stephen prayed, "Lord Jesus receive my spirit." Then he fell on his knees and cried out, "Lord, do not hold this sin against them." When he had said this, he fell asleep* (Acts 7:59-60).

Jesus was called God: *While we wait for the blessed hope – the glorious appearing of our great God and Savior, Jesus Christ* (Titus 2:13).

Theirs are the patriarchs (referring to the Jews) *and from them is traced the human ancestry of Christ, who is God over all, forever praised! Amen* (Rom 9:5).

They also believed that Jesus was crucified for our sins and resurrected from the dead. Paul says in 1 Corinthians 15:3-4: *For what I received I passed on to you as of first importance that Christ died for our sins according to the Scriptures, that he was buried, and that he was raised on the third day according to the Scriptures.*

These were clearly not new or controversial doctrines that Paul was teaching. They were firmly established and needed no explanation or to be defended. There was no window of time for the historical Jesus to evolve into the Jesus of faith. Too many eyewitnesses made it impossible to distort the facts amide the Jewish social and educational structures. It was simply the wrong historical setting for a pagan myth to take root and develop.

The theology of the Christian church was fully developed by the time Paul wrote in 60 A.D.

The church did not create its doctrine. In a literal sense, its doctrine is what formed the church.

There are many historical references to Jesus from pagan and Jewish sources outside of the Bible. One such source is the great historian Tacitus, who wrote about events in Rome in 64 A.D., when Rome burned and the emperor Nero blamed the Christians. Tacitus agreed with the popular belief that Nero was the cause of the fire because he wanted to rebuild a large area in the middle of the city for his palace.

He wrote: "To dispel the rumor, Nero substituted culprits and treated them with the most extreme punishments – those people popularly known as Christians, whose disgraceful activities were notorious. The originator of the name Christus had been executed when Tiberius was emperor by order of the procurator Pontius Pilitus. But the deadly cult, though checked for a time, was spreading out again, not only in Judea, the birthplace of this evil, but even throughout Rome where all nasty and disgusting ideas from all over the world pour in and find a ready following" (Annals 15:44). He goes on to tell how these Christians were killed by being covered with animal skins and torn apart by wild beasts, by crucifixion, and by being burned alive.

From this we learn some important facts about Christ and His followers who lived in Rome about thirty years after Jesus' crucifixion.

1. The followers of Christ were called Christians after their leader "Christus" (from the Latin for Christ).
2. Jesus was executed by Rome (crucified) under the Roman Procurator Pontius Pilitus (from the Latin for Pilate).
3. This occurred during the reign of the Emperor Tiberius.
4. His death ended the movement for a short time.
5. It broke out again (doubtless referring to after His resurrection).
6. It was especially strong in Judea where the movement began.
7. His followers carried His message to Rome.
8. A fire, probably caused by Nero, destroyed a large part of the city and he blamed the Christians.
9. Christians were hated for their disgraceful activities (refusing to offer worship to the emperor or the gods of Rome and celebrating communion, which was understood as cannibalism, partaking of Christ's body and blood).

10. They were arrested and tortured and killed by wild beasts, crucified, and burned alive.

Tacitus refers to them again his book, *Histories*, which was lost, but an excerpt was copied and preserved by another writer, in which he says that Christianity sprang from Judaism and that the Roman general Titus tried to put an end to both Christianity and Judaism by destroying Jerusalem in 70 A.D.

Pliny the younger, governor of Bithynia, a Roman province in Turkey, during the reign of Trajan, wrote the emperor requesting instruction on how to interrogate Christians. In letter 10:96 he writes that the Christians would not worship Emperor Trajan or the gods and even under torture would not curse Christ. He gives us important information on the worship service.

He writes that the Christians were "in the habit of meeting on a certain fixed day (Sunday) before light and would sing a hymn to Christ as God and bound themselves by a solemn oath not to do any evil; no fraud, theft, adultery, not to falsify their word or deny the truth when called upon."

He described how many were tortured and killed. He said that they did nothing to be punished for – their only guilt was their refusal to worship the Emperor's image or images of the gods.

Christianity was spreading rapidly in his province and it was becoming a social and economic problem because the temples to the gods were closing down for lack of worshipers, as were their festivals. The lack of demand for sacrificial animals had almost stopped those businesses.

Pliny had many of them executed. This was bothering him so he wrote to the emperor for instructions on how to proceed. He added that at their common meal they ate food of an "ordinary and innocent kind." Here he was referring to communion, a memorial symbolic of partaking the Lord's body and blood that was rumored to be cannibalism. He was obviously saying that the rumors were false and he also referred to their calling Christ "Lord" and said that they refused to call others by that title.

A second century satirist name Lucian spoke with disdain about Jesus and Christianity. He wrote: "The Christians to this day worship a man who introduced their rites and was crucified because of that . . .You see, these misguided creatures start with the general conviction that they are immortal for all time, which explains their contempt for death and their own self devotion. Taught by their original lawgiver that they were all brothers, from the moment that they are converted and deny the gods of Greece and worship the crucified sage and live after His laws."

Here again we learn some important things about Jesus and the early Christians from a secular source.

1. Jesus was worshiped by Christians.
2. Jesus' teachings were new.
3. Jesus was crucified because of His teachings.
4. Jesus taught that all believers are brothers upon conversion and they demonstrated this by denying the false gods and worshiping Jesus and living according to His teachings.
5. They believed themselves to be immortal, and this is the reason for their willingness to die.
6. They had contempt for self-devotion.

The Roman philosopher Celsus was a monotheist who wrote a treatise around 170 A.D. "Now if the Christians worshiped only one God, they might have reason on their side. But as a matter of fact they worship a man who appeared only recently. They do not consider that they are doing a breach to monotheism; rather, they think it perfectly consistent to worship the great God and to worship His servant as God. Their worship of Jesus is the more outrageous because they refuse to listen to any talk about God, the Father at all, unless it includes some reference to Jesus; tell them that Jesus, the author of the Christian insurrection, was not His Son and they will not listen to you. When they call Him Son of God, they are not really paying homage to God; rather they are attempting to exalt Jesus to the heights."

Celsus was a monotheist and could not understand how Christians could worship Jesus as God without going into Polytheism.

ORAL TRADITION

Tradition is simply a body of teaching handed down. It may be good or bad, depending on the teaching. The traditions of the Scribes and Pharisees conflicted with God's commandments: *And Jesus said to them: "You have a fine way of setting aside the commands of God in order to observe your own traditions"* (Mark 7:9). The traditions of the Scribes and Pharisees were teachings that conflicted with the revelation of God given in the Scriptures. Apostolic traditions were the life and teachings of Jesus handed down by those commissioned by Christ.

We live in a culture of the written or printed word. Instead of memory we rely on the writing of even small and simple things like telephone numbers and lists for everything from shopping, household chores, and appointments.

Memorization is depended on less and less in our educational system due to the easy availability of the printed text in books and on the computer. Birger Gerhardsson notes: "In the tradition of western culture, it is only in our own day that the memory has been effectively unloaded into books. Not until our own day have we learned to accept a form of education which to a great extent consists of being able to find the material which is required in the right books without needing to carry it all in the memory. Not until our day has the pedagogical revolution taken place that has been called the "dethronement of memory" (Memory and manuscript, pg. 123).

James D. G. Dunn writes: "Guttenberg and Caxton had instituted a revolution in human perspectives in sixteenth century Europe . . . consequently, we in the West simply take it for granted that the basis of a sound education is the ability to read and write . . . in a word, we are all children of Guttenberg" (A new perspective on Jesus: what the quest for the historical Jesus missed).

The world of Jesus was defined by the spoken word. Written records were of secondary importance to spoken narratives. The modern mind finds it difficult to understand, but the tendency to prefer oral teaching over the written was partly because many could not read or write and the written form was relatively new in the first century A.D.

When Jesus was born, reading and writing was taught for the Jews at the local synagogue school and at home with repetition and memorization. It was taught amazingly well. Studies in middle east villages where repetition and memorization are still used, as in first century Palestine, confirms that the oral tradition maintains faithful adherence to the vitally important details of a saying or of an event.

For the early followers of Jesus, this emphasis would have been demonstrated by accurately maintaining the meaning and significance of Jesus' teaching and deeds in their writings. While oral tradition was important to every society, it was especially important to Jewish society. Repetition and memorization was the norm and was very effective.

Jews memorized the law and large portions of the Old Testament and the teachings of the Rabbis. They practiced very effective memory development techniques to study the teachings of the True God. Jesus was educated in the synagogue learning system.

Using the example of passing on a story from person to person or the "telephone game" is a far cry from the teaching tradition established in the first century synagogues.

For the Jewish community, reading and writing were crucial for the teaching and learning of the Scriptures and maintaining their culture. As a result, the method of teaching in the synagogues was unsurpassed in the ancient world. Thus, the Jewish world was uniquely prepared to learn and pass on the incomparable teachings of Jesus Christ. The early Christians, who were mostly Jews, were the inheritors of the synagogue method of learning and teaching.

The ability of the Jews to read and write in the first century was not as rare as we might think. We know that it was the Jewish custom in the synagogues to allow those present to give the Scripture reading and to comment on it. This is how Jesus began His ministry.

He went to Nazareth, where he had been brought up, and on the Sabbath day he went into the synagogue, as was his custom. He stood up to read. The Scroll of the prophet Isaiah was handed to him (Luke 4:16-17).

And we know that when Paul went to a new area of the Roman Empire to proclaim the gospel, he began at the local synagogue. This is what is meant when the Scripture says: *But when the time had fully come, God sent His Son* . . . (Gal 4:4). The stage was set for maximum effect for the appearing of the "Coming One," the central Figure around whom all God's plans for time and eternity revolved.

Jesus clearly was not illiterate, and there is every reason to believe that the disciples could read and write. Papias, an early second century church father, who had close contact with the Apostle John, tells us that Matthew, who was a tax collector, was chosen among the disciple to take notes. There is no reason to suppose that, while Jesus' words and deeds would primarily have been passed on orally, they would not have been written down as well.

His disciples would have been memorizing His words during His ministry. Their purpose was to carry on the tradition of their Teacher. They knew that theirs was no ordinary Rabbi, but the Messiah, the coming king and the very Son of God. And they may have been taking notes as well.

A "disciple" was a "learner." They were to be trained until they "graduated" and were qualified to teach as "apostles," which means "sent ones." As disciples, they were being trained. We know that during His ministry in Galilee, Jesus sent them out to teach and preach (Luke 10:1-16). We can assume, because of the importance of their mission, that this was typical of many areas besides Galilee.

But even after all their training, after His resurrection they were strictly told not to begin their ministries until they had waited in Jerusalem and were filled with the Holy Spirit: *"I am going to send you what my Father has promised; but stay in the city until you have been clothed with power from on high"* (Luke 24:49).

Only then were they ready to represent Him as His apostles or "sent ones." *"But you will receive power when the Holy Spirit comes upon you; and you will be my witnesses in Jerusalem and in Judea and Samaria, and to the ends of the earth"* (Acts 1:8). To do God's work, they needed God's power.

Even in modern times, oral narratives lasting many days have been documented.

Lauri Honko documents an oral narrative lasting seven days (Lauri Honko, *Textualizing the Siri Epic*, Helsinki, Finland, 1998).

One characteristic of oral tradition is flexibility on how the material is presented, with strict restraints on altering the core content. The particular order it is presented in and what minor details are added or omitted are left up to the deliverer of the oral message.

The community, or those associated with this particular tradition, would interrupt and correct any errors to assure its truthfulness. We find the same freedom and restraint when we compare the four Gospels. The essential content is totally consistent, but there is a freedom with how it is presented in its incidental details.

Also Jesus used rhythm, word play, and poetry that greatly enabled His hearers to remember His teachings. These are much easier to see in the Aramaic language of Jesus. Joachim Jeremias says that when Jesus' sayings are translated back into the Aramaic language, it further increases the ability to remember His sayings. The artistic styles of the sayings were a remarkably memorable method of communicating and transmitting His sayings. The poetic form He used was much easier for His hearers to memorize and pass on to others.

And Birger Gerhardsson notes: "It is obvious that we are dealing with carefully thought out and deliberately formulated statements." Jesus' sayings were often short and had rhythm, with words that rhymed in Aramaic

The presence of so many eyewitnesses would serve to keep the tradition accurate. It was a collective witness based on written sources and memories of eyewitnesses. The earliest written documents were hymns, devotional creeds, and confessions. These preceded the written sources and were incorporated into them. This means that Jesus was worshipped as a Divine Being Who died for our sins and rose from the dead from a time almost contemporaneous with the events they describe.

These documents were used in the writing of the Scriptures by the New Testament writers. They were in use throughout the Christian community prior to the writings of the New Testament, in both oral and written form. This gives us a direct look into the beliefs and practices of those who knew Jesus firsthand.

The apostle Paul wrote praise to the first century Christians in 1 Corinthians 11:2: *I praise you for remembering me in everything and for holding to the teachings just as I passed them on to you.* These "teachings" were the "traditions" that were passed on.

One of these traditions was communion or the Lord's supper: *For I received from the Lord what I also passed on to you: The Lord Jesus, on the night he was betrayed, took bread, and when he had given thanks, he broke it and said, "This is my body which is for you; do this in remembrance of me. For whenever you eat this bread and drink this cup, you proclaim the Lord's death until he comes"* (1 Cor 11:23-26).

Another tradition was the death, burial, and resurrection of Jesus in 1 Corinthians 15:3-4: *For what I received I passed onto you as of first importance: that Christ died for our sins according to the Scriptures.* Here, Paul had "passed on" the tradition or teaching he had "received." Here we see that the gospel did not originate with Paul.

Some of the other passages that are based upon creeds, hymns or confessions are John 1:1-16; Rom 1:3-4; 3:24-26; 10:9-26; 1 Cor 8:6; 11:23-26; 2 Cor 1:8-10; 5:8-10; Gal 4:4-5; Eph 1:3-14; 2:6-22; Col.1:15-20; Phil 2:6-10; 1 Tim 3:16; Titus 3:4-7; Heb 1:3; 8-11; 1 Pet 1:3-9; 18-21; 2:4-8; 2:21-25; 3:18-22; 1 John 2:2; 4:2, 10; 5:1-5; and Jude 24-25. This written text was used along with the oral in the early Jewish church.

Qumran studies have shown that the written text played a significant role in Israel's culture that was predominantly oral. The written text began to emerge within Jewish Christianity, which was mission oriented and had established Christian synagogues called churches.

The Christian movement was growing rapidly, and these churches would need teachers for the growing movement and public reading was crucial. This made the move from the oral to the written text urgent. It would not replace the oral but it would catch up to it, and eventually overtake it.

By the time Luke wrote his gospel, he tells us: *Many have undertaken to draw up an account of the things that have been fulfilled among us, just as they were handed down by those who from the first were eyewitnesses and servants of the Word. Therefore, since I myself have carefully investigated everything from the beginning, it seemed good also to me to write an orderly account for you, most excellent Theophilus; so that you may know the certainty of the things you have been taught* (Luke 1:1-4).

The term "handed down" is a term for handing over a body of teaching to a disciple. That these were in written form is seen in Luke 1:3: *Since I myself have carefully investigated everything from the beginning it seemed good ALSO to me TO WRITE an orderly account for you.*

WAS JESUS' STORY BASED UPON PAGAN MYTHS?

Because of the sales of such books as the *Da Vinci Code*, it has become popular to claim that Jesus was simply patterned after pagan gods. This is a relatively recent idea. It began with Bruno Bauer's "The history of religions" school in the 1840's. He published a book that said the early church's "story of Jesus" was based on mythology. One of his students was Karl Marx, who was the father of communism, who taught that Jesus never existed.

By the mid twentieth century, the view that Jesus' story was simply a variation of the pagan myths lost support even among liberal theologians. But in recent years, this view has been revived with books claiming that many teachings about Jesus – including His virgin birth and resurrection – were taken from the mystery religions. For instance, "The story of Jesus and the teachings he gives in the Old Testament are prefigured by the myths and teaching of the ancient pagan mysteries" (Timothy Freke and Peter Gandy, authors of *The Jesus Mysteries*).

And "Christianity began as a cult with almost wholly pagan origins and motivations in the first century" (Tom Harpur, former Anglican priest in *Pagan Christ*).

One popular myth that is pointed to as a pattern of the Jesus story is Apollonius of Tyrana, who was a wonder worker, like Jesus. He healed people and cast out demons and raised the dead and prophesied, like Jesus. He was later worshiped by his followers, like Jesus. What is not mentioned in this comparison is that Jesus preceded this myth by at least 50 years, and then the biographer of Apollonius incorporated aspects of the life of Jesus into the biography he was writing. In fact, the Gnostic gospels date no earlier than the second century and have no concern about the historical Jesus but are a collection of strange and bizarre secret sayings, supposedly of Jesus, written long after the last apostle died. However, the tendencies of Gnosticism were already being refuted by the New Testament writers.

The key to the mystery religions is the seasonal vegetation cycle and the death and rebirth of nature. Over time, myths were developed to explain this "Mystery." We often hear sweeping generalizations to the effect that early Christianity borrowed from the pagan religions. But when the evidence is examined, we find that there was nothing to borrow. It is significant that there are no saviors before Jesus, while we do encounter other saviors soon after Jesus time.

There simply are no redeemers to pattern Jesus after; rather, we find that the post-Christian redeemers were patterned after the historical Jesus.

THE "SUPPRESSED" GOSPELS

The next question that books like the *Da Vinci Code* bring up is why the early church rejected or suppressed so many gospels to end up with only four? There are certain gospels popularized by Dan Brown's *Da Vinci Code*, and the "Jesus seminar" that are said to have been suppressed by the early church out of fear of competition. But like the notion that the story of Jesus was stolen from the pagan myths, this is simply a lot of hype and fluff with no substance.

These are the gnostic gospels. The word "gnosis" is Greek and means "Knowledge." The followers of this system called themselves "Gnostics" or "Knowers" or those with special understanding. Gnosticism had two gods – the good and unknowable god of light and an inferior god whom they equated with the god of the Old Testament: Yahweh, who they did not worship, but rather he was a god of darkness or evil.

All human souls had originally existed in a spiritual realm of light until a tragedy occurred. The lesser god created the physical world; however, he was very incompetent and made many mistakes. One of his huge mistakes consisted of leaving small sparks of divinity in certain human beings.

Matter was considered inherently evil and since these human beings were made of matter, these divine sparks of divinity would have to be liberated from the matter in which they were imprisoned. This would come about by gnosis or knowledge being imparted to these elect individuals, enabling them to discover the divine spark within them so they could nurture their "inner divinity." This knowledge was available only to the elect, as only they were capable of receiving it.

The lesser god wanted to hinder the elect from returning to the true god and being restored to the divine. This was done with the aid of evil powers called Archons. The gnostic Jesus came from the spiritual realm from a higher level than that of the inept Yahweh and closer to the true god. He came to reveal to the elect few their past, which they had forgotten. Within them was a divine spark that needed developing in order to lead them back to the realm of light.

In gnostic thought Jesus was a purely spirit being who could not take on a physical body because matter was evil. Therefore he could not die on a cross. He only had the appearance of a physical body.

This is called "Docetism," taken from the Greek word for "appearance" (Dokesis). So the resurrection had to be a spiritual one. All the gnostic gospels were written in the mid-to-late second century, around a hundred years after the apostles. This was far too late to be an influence on Christianity. The gnostic writings are nothing more than the gnostics taking Christianity, because of its popularity, and Gnosticizing it by taking Christian terminology and giving it a gnostic meaning.

It is claimed that the early church rejected these gnostic gospels because, under the Emperor Constantine, they wanted a divine Jesus. But the truth is that these gnostic gospels present a Jesus who was only divine without having humanity and thus could not die on a cross.

THE GOSPEL OF THOMAS

An example of the gnostic writings is the Gospel of Thomas, which claims to be a record of the secret teachings of Jesus that are only for those who are qualified to receive them. The opening line claims that these are the hidden words of Jesus spoken in private. Jesus came to reveal, through cryptic statements, to certain elect ones, how to escape the darkness of the world and join him in the realm of light above. The elect ones the gnostic Jesus came to awaken through enlightenment were human spirits with divine sparks of divinity that were trapped in physical, and therefore evil, bodies that needed to be released.

Saying 114 has a reference to Mary Magdalene: "Simon Peter said to them, 'Let Mary leave us, for women are not worthy of eternal life.' Jesus says, 'I myself shall lead her in order to make her male, so that she too may become a living spirit resembling you males. For every woman who will make herself male will enter the kingdom of heaven.'"

In the Greek and Roman world, women were considered inferior to men because they WERE men who had not fully developed. They were weaker and in a world dominated by power that made them subordinate to men. For men to dwell with God, they needed to be perfected and so did women. On the way to perfection, women had to become men. This is what the gnostic teachings of Jesus would give them.

The gospel of Thomas was written no earlier than 175 A.D.

ANOTHER IS THE GOSPEL OF JUDAS

It begins: "The secret account of the revelation that Jesus spoke in a conversation with Judas Iscariot." In this gnostic account, Judas is Jesus' greatest disciple who planned with Jesus his betrayal. The gnostic Jesus does not have a real physical body, but only an appearance of a body, and is not crucified.

APOCALYPSE OF PETER

Again, Jesus is not really human. Peter is speaking: "I saw him apparently being seized by them and I said, "What am I seeing, O Lord? Is it really you who they are taking? Are you holding on to me? Are they hammering the hands and feet of someone else?"

Then Jesus answers: "He whom you see on a tree, glad and laughing, this is the Living Jesus, but he in whose hands and feet they are driving the nails in his fleshly parts, his substitute. They

are putting to shame that which is his likeness, but look at him –
and look at me.

In the second treatise of the great Seth, 56ff, Jesus is speaking:
"It was another who drank the gall and vinegar. It was not I . . . it
was another, Simon, who carried the cross on his shoulders, it was
another on whom they placed the crown of thorns, but I was
rejoicing in the heights over all the reaches of the Archons . . .
laughing at their ignorance . . . and I kept changing my forms
above, transforming them from appearance to appearance." The
Apocalypse of Peter dates to the beginning of the fourth century.

THE ACTS OF PAUL

This teaches that in order to be a Christian, one must practice
complete abstinence from sexual relations, even within marriage!
Also in this book, Paul baptizes a lion that is eighteen feet tall.

THE INFANCY GOSPEL OF THOMAS

This is dated from the early second century. It begins with a
five-year-old Jesus playing by a stream of water on the Sabbath.
He makes a dam and gathers some muddy water and commands it
to be pure, and immediately it is. Then he takes some clay and
makes clay sparrows.

But a man walks by and warns him about making things and
thereby working on the Sabbath. The man reports Jesus to his
father Joseph, who comes and scolds him for breaking the
Sabbath. Upon which he claps his hands and the clay sparrows fly
away, thus getting rid of the evidence.

Then while he and another child are playing, Jesus has
gathered some pure water together and the child playing with him
takes a willow branch and scatters it. An angry Jesus cries out,
"You unrighteous, irreverent idiot. Those pools of water did
nothing to harm you! Now you will also be withered like a tree and
you will never bear leaves or root or fruit." And the child was
instantly withered (Infancy of Thomas 3:1-3).

Then in another account, a child bumps into Jesus on the
street. In anger Jesus cries out, "You shall go no further on your
way." At this the child falls down dead (Infancy of Thomas 4:1).

THE GOSPEL OF PHILIP

The *Da Vinci Code* caused a stir by claiming that Jesus and
Mary Magdalene were married and had a child. It is claimed that
the church has engaged in the greatest cover-up in history. The

main evidence for this is supposed to be the Gnostic gospels, especially the Gospel of Philip:

"The companion of the Savior is Mary Magdalene. But Christ loved her more than all the disciples and used to kiss her often on her (mouth). The rest of the disciples were offended by it and expressed disapproval. They said to him, 'Why do you love her more than all of us.'"

The papyrus is of poor quality and a few words are missing in the original. What made such a stir is the claim for the word "companion" by the *Da Vinci Code*: "As any Aramaic scholar will tell you, the word companion, in those days, literally meant spouse" (page 246).

But the gospel of Philip is not written in Aramaic but in the Coptic. Nowhere in the gnostic gospels does it say that Jesus and Mary Magdalene were married.

The main thing we learn from reading the gnostic literature is how radical their teachings were. They wrote at least a hundred years after the events were supposed to have happened. There is absolutely nothing to support the idea of Jesus being married.

The Church Father Irenaeus referred to Gnostics as Cainites who identified with Biblical villains. They believed the God of the Old Testament, Yahweh, who was the creator of the physical world, was evil. Therefore anyone he was against had to be a hero; such as Cain, Esau, Korah, the sodomites, etc.

The Bible has always had its critics. It is at the same time the world's most loved book and the world's most hated book. The cults, those corrupt offshoots of Christianity, all claim to "restore" to Christianity the truths that were lost. These "truths" were supposedly given to their leaders who claimed to receive them directly from God.

Charles Russell, founder of the Jehovah's witnesses, wrote his seven volumes of *Studies in the Scriptures,* and thus "restored" the true religion.

Joseph Smith wrote the *Book of Mormon, Doctrines and Covenants, and Pearl of Great Price,* and thus "restored" the true religion.

Mary Baker Eddy, the founder of Christian Science, wrote *Science and Health With Key to the Scriptures,"* and thus "restored" the true religion.

Herbert W. Armstrong published his magazine *The Plain Truth* and some books, and thus "restored" the true religion.

These are only a few of the many groups claiming to "restore" the true religion.

Some children with their school visited a blacksmith. When they saw his giant anvil, one of them asked, "Sir, how many anvils have you gone through?"

"This is the only one," he said. Then with a wink he added, "It's the anvil that wears out the hammers."

The critics of the Bible have hammered away for centuries, but it is their hammers that have worn out. 1 Peter 1:25 tells us: *But the Word of the Lord stands forever.*

It is the politically correct Jesus that the culture and media will praise. A Jesus that they can make after their own image whose words can be twisted to mean whatever they want them to mean. For instance, *"Judge not lest ye be judged"* is made to mean, "You condone my sins and I will condone your sins." It is the Jesus who can be manipulated and controlled that they will tolerate.

We live in an age when the wide road of tolerance for any idea that people want to be true has replaced the narrow road of truth, energized by a media that is hostile toward Christianity. Other religions are harmless because there is no confrontation with man's sinfulness, no "Repent or perish." These new ideas are cultivated in an atmosphere of Biblical ignorance.

Why were these gnostic writings rejected? For one thing they were not even written until later, but even if they were written earlier, you simply have to read them to discover why they were rejected. The more we read these "alternative gospels," the more we appreciate and thank God for the ones we have. It is the difference between the waters of life and the cesspools of this world.

DID CONSTANTINE MAKE JESUS DIVINE

The *Da Vinci Code* says that the Emperor Constantine stopped goddess worship, changed the day of worship from Saturday to Sunday, made Jesus divine, and established the Biblical Canon at the council of Nicaea in the early fourth century.

But the Council of Nicaea did none of these.

The divinity of Jesus had been affirmed for almost three hundred years by the time of Nicaea on May 20th 325. The Bishops and their congregations were worshiping Jesus and confessing Him as universal Lord. This was the stance of the church from the beginning, as we have seen from the writings of Paul, the four Gospels, and other New Testament writings.

Before Constantine, the church had already rejected the many Apocryphal writings that appeared by then. Throughout church history up to Nicaea, we have testimonies of the leaders of the church to the deity of Christ. "God Himself was manifest in human form" (Ignatius, 105 A.D).

Justin Martyr: "The Father of the universe has a son and he is even God" (160 A.D.).

Tertullian: "Christ our God" (200 A.D.) "He is not only man but God also" (Novation 235 A.D).

"Jesus Christ our Lord and our God" (Cyprian 250 A.D).

During the second century, the church leaders had already quoted the four Gospels, and only them, thousands of times in their writings, and the New Testament was cited more than 36,000 times. Constantine was consolidating his hold on the Roman Empire when a heresy developed among Arius and his followers.

They denied the deity of Christ, and Alexander, bishop of Alexandria, Egypt, declared Arius a heretic. Arius moved his followers to Palestine and there was calm. But Arius began to send letters to churches pushing his theology that Jesus was a created being. To Arius, to say that Christ was co-eternal with the Father was to presuppose two self-existent Beings, and this would deny monotheism. He could conceive of three Persons, but not as equals, sharing the same nature or essence. Over the next few years, the debate grew until it got the attention of Emperor Constantine. He saw that it would be a destabilizing problem for the Empire.

So he called together more than 300 bishops from around the empire. These bishops came to Constantinople; many traveled hundreds of miles. Many wore scars from being tortured for their faith years before, and they were not about to back down now. The bishops led by Athanasius stood with what was taught by the apostles in the New Testament. They were not going to compromise what had cost them and their brothers in Christ so much. They would rather go back to the torture racks.

Constantine's motive was driven by a desire to bring peace to the empire, and he allowed the church to declare what they had always believed. Whether Constantine was truly converted or was using the Christians to consolidate his power may be debated, but the fact that Constantine wanted peace in his Empire is beyond question. And he was not about to challenge those bishops whose backing he needed. He knew what they had gone through before for their stand for the truth and he knew that they would do it again!

In the *Da Vinci Code*, Dan Brown has Teabing say that Nicaea came down to "a relatively close vote at that." The actual vote of the bishops was 300 to 2!

DID THE MESSAGE OF THE BIBLE CHANGE OVER TIME?

The *Da Vinci Code* says of the Bible: "It has evolved through countless translations, additions, and revisions" (Page 231). It has been pointed out that the Gospel manuscripts don't agree in many details. But the truth of inspiration does not depend on a word for word agreement of all the manuscripts. When Jesus said in Matthew 4:4: *"Man does not live by bread alone, but by every word that comes from the mouth of God,"* He does not mean to imply that the writers would all use exactly the same words. For instance the four Gospel writers often tell of the same event, but used different words. When New Testament writers quote an Old Testament writer, they do not do it word for word.

They all say the same thing, though not in exactly the same words. Differences are complimentary rather than contradictory. Of course this refers to the original autographs not to translations. Translators can and do make mistakes, but these are corrected by the manuscripts that these translations are based on.

There may be different minor details or they may be put in a different order. Inspiration includes the different styles of each writer. To say that the Bible has evolved in the sense of constantly changing the meaning is totally misleading.

The manuscripts we have today are copies of the original autographs. Manuscripts were copied by hand, and, over time, errors have been inevitable.

Dan Brown in the *Da Vinci Code* says that the Bible we have today is but a copy of a copy of a copy, with accumulating errors along the way, giving the impression that what we have now is nothing like the original manuscripts.

Is there any way to know if this is true or not? There is, by simply comparing the more than five thousand copies of Greek manuscripts in our possession, going all the way back to about thirty years from the original writings.

We also have up to twenty thousand copies of translations in Syriac, Coptic, Armenian, Gregorian, etc. We have somewhere around thirty thousand handwritten copies of the New Testament.

Some scholars like to tell us that these manuscripts have more than 200 thousand variants. Often this is done to mislead the general public, who has no real understanding of what this means. They offer no explanation. What we are not told is that about 75 per cent of all variants consist of spelling differences and are insignificant.

The most common is the use of the Greek letter nu or n. This is the English equivalent to the difference between "a" and "an." There is no difference in meaning between "an elephant" or "a elephant." Sometimes it is a name, for instance, like John misspelled as Jon; it really doesn't matter.

The second greatest number of variants involves the order of words, such as "Jesus Christ" or "Christ Jesus," emphasizing a slightly different aspect. Sometimes words are interchangeable such as "when Jesus knew" versus "when the Lord knew." Or "sent from God" or "sent from the Lord," where both are true and it does not change the meaning.

The words "we" and "you" look very similar in the Greek and were often confused by the copyist. *You* or *We are the children of promise* (Gal 4:28), for example.

These insignificant changes make up 99 percent of the variants.

Some of the variants come from the copyist, who thought it was proper to clarify what the text already taught.

For instance, baptism always followed faith in Christ. But in Acts 8 the copyist was concerned whether it was clear that the Ethiopian eunuch believed in Christ before he was baptized. Verse 36 states: *When he asked: "What hinders me from being baptized?* The copyist added verse 37, which states that Philip said he could be baptized if he believed with all his heart, to which the eunuch replied that he believed that Jesus was the Son of God.

So the copyist highlighted a truth that other texts also taught. A copyist thought that Matthew 1:16 was not clear enough that Jesus was born of a virgin, so he added what was already taught throughout the passage, that Mary was a virgin.

Less than 1 percent of variants affect the meaning of the text to some degree, but none of these variants affect a single essential doctrine.

Variants can be found by a close analysis of the many manuscripts. Errors only occur in certain manuscripts and can be found by comparing all the manuscripts. What has been revealed is the fact that the New Testament remains virtually unchanged.

In 1947 the Dead Sea Scrolls were found in a cave in Qumran. These contained the entire Old Testament, except the Book of Esther. These hand-written manuscripts were a thousand years older than the ones we possessed at that time. After careful study it was found that there were no significant differences, other than a very small number of spelling variations.

Biblical inspiration (that is, the human authors were specially prepared by God and their writings were directed and controlled by God) applies only to the original writings (manuscripts known as autographs), and not to copying and translating. From the beginning there was a selecting process that was verified by those who were chosen and trained by Jesus to be His witnesses, and they could say: *That which we have seen and heard we proclaim also to you* (1 John 1:3).

We did not follow cleverly devised myths when we made known to you the power and coming of our Lord Jesus Christ, but were eyewitnesses of His majesty (1 Pet 1:16)

In John 16:13 Jesus told them, *"But when He, the Spirit of truth, comes, He will guide you into all truth. He will not speak on His own; He will speak only what He hears, and He will tell you what is yet to come."*

Thus the chosen disciples were the final authority on which writings were judged as Scripture. From the very beginning, the disciples were careful to preserve an accurate record of the words and deeds of Jesus, whom they believed was the Messiah, the Son of God. Matthew and John wrote as eyewitnesses. Irenaeus, who was a student of Polycarp, who had been a disciple of the Apostle John, tells us that Mark wrote Peter's account, while Luke wrote the testimony of *Eyewitnesses and servants of the word* (Luke 1:2). This would include the oral and written accounts of the Apostles.

In just a generation after the Apostles, every book in our present Bible had been recognized as authoritative by a church father. The Bible has been the most loved Book in history and at the same time it has been the most hated and attacked Book in history. It is no coincidence that Jesus Christ is the most loved and at the same time, the most hated figure in history.

The attack on the Bible has come from every direction of human wisdom. The deadliest attack of all has come in the last 100 years from the so-called higher critics. The German rationalists began this attack and it was soon taken up by the liberal theologians of Europe and America and has continued full force to this day.

At the beginning of the Christian era the attack was made by the admitted enemies of the Christian faith but in these modern days the attack has become far more subtle. Now it comes from within the church. The tares or weeds that Jesus warned about in Matthew 13:24-30 have infiltrated the churches and seminaries.

The divine origin of Scripture is being rejected within the church. This is being done by wolves in sheep's clothing. Much of the theological teaching today is dedicated to destroying the credibility of Scripture. Thousands of nominal Christians in these churches, bible colleges, and seminaries have their heads filled with doubts. It is strange that at one time these were called infidels and atheists but today they graduate from so-called Christian seminaries and teach future ministers.

There are two kinds of Biblical criticism. One is of great value and consists of Greek and Hebrew scholars, who, with great labor and patience, study the ancient manuscripts in order to determine the actual words used by the writers.

The other is Destructive criticism that sets out to prove that the Bible is full of errors no matter how much evidence there is to the contrary. They begin with a preconceived idea of history and have already determined their conclusions before they weigh all the evidence. They are already committed to a presupposed result. Every major doctrine of the Christian faith is attacked: The deity of Christ, His virgin birth, His atoning death, and resurrection are all relegated to myth. They pull this off by telling us that we can't confuse religious truth (which is based on faith – or make-believe) with historical truth. They say it is religiously true (based on faith) that Jesus rose from the dead but not literally or historically true.

That they would do their evil from within the church was foretold in 2 Corinthians 11:13-15: *For such men are false apostles, deceitful workmen, masquerading as apostles of Christ. And no wonder, for Satan himself masquerades as an angel of light. It is not surprising then, if his servants masquerade as angels of light. Their end will be what their actions deserve.*

When Jesus spoke of the apostasy of the last days and His disciples asked Him when this would happen and what would be the sign of His coming and the end of the age. It is no wonder that His first words were:

"Watch out that no man deceives you" (Matt 24:3-4). Satan's method is to deceive: *And if our gospel is veiled, it is veiled to*

those who are perishing. The god of this age has blinded the minds of unbelievers, so that they cannot see the light of the gospel of the glory of Christ who is the image of God (2 Cor 4:6).

Satan's work is to blind unbelievers to the gospel that God's people are to proclaim. He is the real enemy we are battling with: *For our struggle is not against flesh and blood, but against the rulers, against the authorities, against the powers of this dark world and against the spiritual forces of evil in the heavenly realms* (Eph 2:12).

The Bible tells us that those who attack the Bible are not the ones we ultimately struggle against. They are but front men; Satan always hides in the background. He knows his power was broken at the cross. Our real enemy is the motivating force behind the world system at war with God. Satan is the *ruler of the kingdom of the air, the spirit who is now at work in those who are disobedient* (Eph 2:2).

This is not a mere wrestling match but a struggle to the death, the eternal death of those who are in Satan's grasp. The passage goes on to list the enemies whom we struggle against: the rulers, authorities, and the powers, of this dark world – against the spiritual forces of evil in the heavenly realms. This is the *kingdom of the air* of Ephesians 2:2.

Here we have a hierarchy of evil spirit forces that we are at war with. Jesus said in Matthew 12:29: *"How can anyone enter a strongman's house and carry off his possessions unless he first ties up the strong man? Then he can rob his house."* Here the "strong man" is Satan. His "house" or dominion is the world.

He is the *god of this world* (2 Cor 4:4). His "goods" are the unsaved people of this world. He was "tied up" by Jesus at the cross. *"Now is the time for judgment on this world; now the prince of this world will be driven out"* (John 12:31).

God's people are called to enter Satan's house and steal his goods through the gospel. We must be willing to give up our comforts in order to carry the good news to those around us. *Then Jesus said, "Peace be with you! As the Father has sent me, I am sending you"* (John 20:20-21).

Those believers who know the Scriptures and their position "in Christ" will take his goods.

And with that Jesus breathed on them and said, "Receive the Holy Spirit. If you forgive anyone their sins, they are forgiven; if you do not forgive them, they are not forgiven" (John 20:23).

After giving us His work to carry on, He gives us the power to do it.

Only God can forgive sin, but He gives the believer the awesome responsibility and the great privilege of entering into this work in the sense of declaring the conditions of forgiveness. When we give out the gospel and they believe, their sins are forgiven, while the sins of those who do not believe are not forgiven. While we cannot forgive sin, we have the authority to declare their sins forgiven when they believe the gospel.

APPENDIX 4
Salvation: God's Masterpiece

The centerpiece of the Bible is God's marvelous work of salvation. It is God's shining jewel against the dark backdrop of man's sin and devastating fall. To fully understand salvation, we must begin with the fall and ruin of mankind. To understand the cure, we must understand the disease. To understand the remedy, we must understand the problem.

MAN'S FALL AND RUIN

Man's fall and God's remedy for it in a nutshell is: *For as in Adam all die, so in Christ all will be made alive* (1 Cor 15:22). The dreadful condition of man's fall is summed up in the words: "IN ADAM." The Bible reveals several things that are true of mankind because of their position "in Adam."

MANKIND'S STATE OR PERSONAL CONDITION

Mankind inherited Adam's sin nature. Romans 5:12 says: *Therefore just as sin entered the world through one man, and death through sin, and in this way death came to all men because all have sinned.* Adam acted as our representative and when he sinned his guilt was passed on to all of his descendants. Sin entered the world through Adam and both sin and its results spread to the whole creation. We are told in Psalms 51:5: *Surely I was sinful at birth, sinful from the time my mother conceived me.* Here we are told that while being formed in the womb the sin nature is being formed.

As a result everyone is born in rebellion against God, as we are told in Isaiah 53:6: *We all, like sheep, have gone astray, each of us has turned to his own way.*

Jeremiah 17:9 says: *The heart is deceitful above all things, and beyond cure, who can understand it?* And Matthew 15:19 says: *"For out of the heart come evil thoughts, murder, adultery and sexual immorality, theft, false testimony, slander."*

In these passages we see that it is not merely what we do, but what we are that condemns us. It is not so much that we sin but that we are sinners by nature. We do not become sinners because we sin, but rather we sin because we are sinners.

Through the fall, our hearts, the source of all our actions, have been polluted.

This condition is true of the entire human race descended from Adam: *The Lord looks down from heaven upon mankind to see if there are any who understand, any who seek God. All have turned aside, they have together become corrupt, there is no one who does good, not even one* (Psa 14:2-3).

As it is written: "There is no one righteous, not even one; there is no one who understands, no one who seeks God. All have turned away; they have together become worthless; there is no one who does good, not even one" (Rom 3:9-12).

Mankind's whole nature collapsed within him and he became self-centered. He has no real concern for God and does not seek Him. He became his own Lord and Master. Romans 3:18 sums it all up: *There is no fear of God in them.*

They have no reverence, no consideration, no respect for what God wants; only a resentment at any interference by God. All their actions are wrong because their motives are wrong. They are *dead in transgressions and sins* (Eph 2:1). Death in Scripture always means separation. The separation of body and the soul constitutes physical death. In this verse death refers to the separation of the sinner from God, the source of all value and meaning. God is now allowing them time to repent and come to Christ. But once physical death takes place, the full consequence of the separation from God will take its course.

Because of our innate warfare against God, apart from the new birth, we will never truly want to honor and please God. Though we will want to appease God through our "religion," but this is simply so we can sin without interference. This is mankind's "fig leaves." We want to cover our sins from God's eyes through our religion, but we do not want our sins taken away from us.

So God rejects our "religion" and all else from us. *The Lord detests the sacrifice of the wicked* (Prov 15:8). Nothing we do is pleasing to the Lord as long as we reject Christ's sacrifice for our sins and remain in rebellion: *"God's wrath remains on him"* (John 3:36). They are *by nature the objects of wrath* (Eph 2:3). It is not merely what we do but what we are (by nature) that makes us a child of wrath.

As man's nature was ruined, so also were all his relationships. He lost his dominion to the devil: *"The whole world is under the control of the evil one"* (1 John 5:19). Thus to be "in Adam" is to be under the control of the evil one. Satan became his master and ruler.

By virtue of Adam's submission the devil, he became the ruler of Adam's whole domain (the world). In John 12:31; 14:30; and 16:11 Jesus refers to Satan as the *Prince of this world*. Ephesians 2:2 says of unbelievers: *You followed the ways of this world and of the ruler of the kingdom of the air, the spirit who is now at work in those who are disobedient.* The unsaved world is separated from God, and all their thoughts, words, and deeds are motivated by Satan, who directs the course or mindset of this fallen world that is IN ADAM.

SATAN BECAME MAN'S GOD
The god of this age has blinded the minds of unbelievers (2 Cor 4:4).

SATAN BECAME MAN'S FATHER
God's revelation of mankind's terrible condition becomes worse and worse until it culminates in the personal relationship of father and child. Jesus said to a group of unbelievers: *"You belong to your father the devil"* (John 8:44).

Fallen mankind has the same close and intimate relationship with Satan that the believer has with the true God. It is not merely open and outward sins that reveal the darkness of our souls, but the everyday life of the so-called "good" person.

As Romans 3:11 tells us: *They do not seek God.* They live their lives apart from God. He is not in their normal thought pattern. Their actions are motivated without regard for Him. He is a non-factor in their lives. This is the dreadful plight of mankind and it required a drastic remedy.

GOD'S REMEDY FOR MAN'S FALL
The world "in Adam" was under condemnation, and God's relationship to the world was that of a Holy Judge. Sin had entered the world and demanded judgment from a Holy and Righteous God, and God could not draw near mankind without expressing His righteous wrath. Before God could save the world, this sin had to be removed so that God could draw near to mankind in mercy.

On the cross, the sins of the world, past, present, and future were judged in Christ. This in itself did not save the world but made the world savable. But it allowed God to draw near to mankind in mercy, rather than judgment, because sin had already been judged and God's holiness was satisfied.

Before Christ's death, God was on the throne as Judge because of our sin. But Christ removed the "sin barrier" that the first Adam had set up and changed God's throne of Judgment to a throne of mercy. Atonement and reconciliation refer to the same act of Christ on the cross. Between God and us was our sin. Christ made atonement (at-one-ment) by removing the sin barrier.

in Christ, God took the initiative to reconcile us to Himself. This does not mean that mankind is automatically saved, but that God can draw near with the offer of salvation – which must be accepted by the sinner by receiving Christ.

This brings us to another Biblical word, "substitution." Christ died as our substitute or "in our place." *Surely He took up OUR infirmities, and carried our sorrows, yet we considered Him stricken by God, smitten by Him and afflicted. But He was pierced for our transgressions, He was bruised for our iniquities; the punishment that brought us peace was upon Him, and by His wounds we are healed* (Isa 53:4-5).

". . . And I lay down my life for the sheep" (John 10:15). *When we were still powerless, Christ died for the ungodly* (Rom 5:6). *Who did not spare His own Son but gave Him up for us all* (Rom 8:32). *For there is one God, and One Mediator between God and man, the man Christ Jesus: who gave Himself a ransom for us all* (1 Tim 2:5-6).

But we see Jesus, who was made a little lower that the angels for the suffering of death . . . that he, by the grace of God, should experience death for every person (Heb 2:9).

Who himself bore our sins in His body on the tree (1 Pet 2:24). *For Christ died for sins once for all, the righteous for the unrighteous . . .* (1 Pet 3:18). *This is how we know what love is, Jesus Christ laid down His life for us* (1 John 3:16). *This is love, not that we loved God, but that He loved us, and sent His Son to be the atoning sacrifice for our sins* (1 John 4:10).

RECONCILIATION

For if, when we were God's enemies, we were reconciled to Him through the death of His Son, how much more, having been reconciled, shall we be saved through His life, not only is this so, we also rejoice in God through our Lord Jesus Christ, through whom we have received reconciliation (Rom 5:10).

Since we were reconciled to God when we were His enemies through the death of Jesus, we will be saved through His resurrected life now that we have been reconciled. While Christ's death provides our salvation, it is His resurrection life that sustains it and takes away the dominion of sin over us. We are continually kept saved by His Intercessory Life. And His resurrection life is imparted to the believer.

We are therefore Christ's ambassadors, as though God were making His appeal through us. We implore you on Christ's behalf: be reconciled to God. God made Him who had no sin to be sin for us, so that in Him we might become the righteousness of God (2 Cor 5:20-21).

Once believers are personally reconciled to God, they become ambassadors for Christ with the message of reconciliation.

IN CHRIST

The words "in Christ" take in the whole work of God in salvation. This phrase or its equivalent: "In Him," "In whom," "In the beloved" is found throughout the New Testament. It is found at least thirty times in the Book of Ephesians alone.

The First Adam was the representative of the human race, everything hinged upon him. His sin brought the race to ruin. Mankind fell under condemnation and Adam's race was cursed. By becoming Man, Christ became the Last Adam and became another representative of the human race. There are now two heads of the human race. Just as everything hinged upon Adam at the beginning, now everything hinges upon Christ for believers.

Instead of destroying the old creation, in Adam, God determined to build the new creation in Christ, out of the ruins of the old. All who accept God's salvation in Christ are removed from being in Adam, the sphere of condemnation, and placed in Christ, the sphere of Salvation. Just as the fallen creation shares everything with Adam so the believer shares everything with Christ.

Consequently, just as the result of one man's trespass was condemnation for all men, so also the result of one act of righteousness was justification that brings life to all men. For just as through the disobedience of one man the many will be made sinners, so also through the obedience of the one man the many will be made righteous (Rom 5:18-19). Here we have the two heads of the human race, the old creation in Adam and the new creation in Christ. *For as in Adam all die, so in Christ will all be made alive* (1 Cor 15:22).

Christ's Headship of the new creation is emphasized in Ephesians 1:22: *And God placed all things under His feet, and appointed Him to be the Head over everything for the Church.* The "church" here does not merely refer to the outward church, but to those who have been born again, not Christians in name only, but to those truly born again.

And in Colossians 1:18: *He is the Head of the body, the church; He is the Beginning and the First-born of the dead, so that in everything He might have the supremacy.* Here Christ is the Beginning and Head of the new creation and He has supremacy in the new creation as Adam had in the old creation. The new believer has entered a new sphere of existence.

Everything about the believer has drastically changed: *Therefore if anyone is in Christ, he is a new creation; the old has gone, the new has come!* (2 Cor 5:17). The person in Christ is a totally new creation. Their position and all their old relationships to Adam and the fallen race are forever passed away, and they now have a new position and relationship to Christ and the new creation.

As God, Christ represented God, and as Man, He is the Head of the new creation and He represents the believer. As we cannot honor God without honoring Christ, even so, God cannot honor Christ, our representative, without honoring the believer.

The Bible also sets forth this truth by the terms of law and grace: *For sin shall not be your master because you are not under law, but under grace* (Rom 6:14).

Here the two creations are referred to. The old creation "in Adam" is still under the law. The law must be fulfilled and will be fulfilled. The law says, "Do or die." If you do not fulfill the first part, you will fulfill the second part of the law.

But the believer in Christ has no relationship to the law. He failed to obey the "do" part of the law, but Christ fulfilled the second part of the law, the "die" part of the law on the believer's behalf. The believer is done with the law. Once the law carries out the sentence of death, there is no more it can do. The condemned one is done with the law, and the law is done with him. The law is satisfied by the death of the criminal.

This is brought out in Romans 7:4-6: *So, my brothers, you also died to the law through the body of Christ, that you might belong to another, to Him who was raised from the dead, in* order that we might bear fruit to God. For when we were controlled by the sinful nature, the sinful passions aroused by the law were at work in our bodies, so that we bore fruit for death.

But now by dying to what once bound us we have been released from the law so that we serve in the new way of the Spirit and not in the old way of the written code.

Here the believer is said to be *dead to the law by the body of Christ*. Through the death of Christ, the believer died to the law, because the law's penalty was carried out. Now the believer is removed from the sphere of the law and its penalty, he is dead and the law is satisfied and can never judge him again. The believer has left the sphere of the law and is joined to Christ and all his benefits.

He has entered the sphere of grace where God no longer deals with him according to what he deserves but according to what Christ deserves! The believer now no longer serves the law in order to attain salvation, which merely resulted in "dead works," because we cannot keep the law but now we serve God out of love and gratitude.

Now rather than serving the "letter of the Law," motivated by fear, the believer has received a new nature motivated by love, and now serves God in the spiritual realm rather than the fallen flesh. The Bible repeatedly emphasizes that the believer is "in Christ." *"And on that day you will realize that I am in my Father, and you are IN ME, and I am in you"* (John 14:20).

There is now no condemnation to those who are in Christ Jesus (Rom 8:1).

To the church of God in Corinth, to those sanctified (or set apart for God) *in Christ Jesus* (1 Cor 1:2).

It is because of Him that you are in Christ Jesus, who has become for us wisdom from God – that is, our righteousness, holiness and redemption (1 Cor 1:30). *Now it is God who makes both us and you stand firm in Christ. He anointed us, set His seal of ownership on us, and put His Spirit in our hearts as a deposit, guaranteeing what is to come* (2 Cor 1:21-22).

Praise be to the God and Father of our Lord Jesus Christ, who has blessed us in the heavenly realms with every spiritual blessing in Christ. For He chose us in Him before the creation of the world to be holy and blameless in His sight (Eph 1:3-4).

To the praise of His glorious grace, which he has freely given us in the One He loves (Eph 1:6).

Paul and Timothy, servants of Jesus Christ, to all the saints in Christ Jesus (Phil 1:1).

For the Lord himself will come down from heaven, with a loud command, with the voice of the archangel and with the trumpet call of God, and the dead in Christ shall rise first (1 Thess 4:16).

No one can read these words without be awed by the way the believer is referred to with the same intimacy that exists between the Father and the Son: "I *will remain in the world no longer, but they are still in the world, and I am coming to you. Holy Father, protect them by your name – the name you gave me – so that they may be one as we are one*" (John 17:11).

"*My prayer is not for them alone, I pray also for those who will believe in Me through their message; that all of them may be one: Father just as you are in me and I am in you, may they also be one in us, so that the world may know that you have sent me. I have given them the glory that you gave me; that they may be one as we are one*" (John 17:20-22).

While physically still in this world (the old creation), the believer is no longer OF this world, but forever united to Christ and part of the new creation: *I have given them your word; and the world has hated them, because they are not OF the world, any more than I am of the world*" (John 17:14). "*They are not of the world even as I am not of it*" (John 17:16).

Believers are so identified with Christ that the father loves them as He loves Christ: "I *have made you known to them and will continue to make you known in order that the love you have for me may be in them and that I myself will be in them*" (John 17:26).

When a sinner believes in Christ, he believes into Christ. He enters into a new existence where all the benefits of Christ's work are applied to him. Some of these benefits are legal and some are personal. These benefits do not spring from the believer's worthiness but solely upon Christ's worthiness. They are applied to the believer or credited to his account by the Holy Spirit. This corresponds to our modern banking system, where money can be transferred from one person's account into another's.

The judgment on Christ was credited to us. It went on our record that we died and, by dying, the righteous demands of the Law were carried out. It demanded obedience or death. We could not obey and our judgment was carried out on Christ in our place. It was credited to our account that we were punished for our sins

– carried out on Christ. Now the law has no more power over us. Once the law applies the death penalty, there is no more it can do.

Since Christ died for all of our sins, past, present, and future, the law is now powerless over the believer. His death, credited to us, releases us from the law and its penalty for sin. But God did not stop here. Not only did God erase the record of our sins, but Christ's righteousness was applied to the believer, thus making us as righteous as Christ Himself in God's sight.

Therefore no one will be declared righteous in His sight by observing the law; rather through the law we become conscience of sin. But now righteousness from God apart from the law has been made known, to which the law and the prophets testify. This righteousness from God comes from faith in Jesus Christ to all who believe (Rom 3:20-22). Here we see that no one can be justified by the deeds of the law because no one can keep the law.

The law was given to reveal to us that we are sinners and cannot earn our way to God. The knowledge that we are sinners is brought home to us as we try to keep the law (v. 20). Righteousness from God, wholly apart from the keeping of the law, can be attained by faith in Christ (21-22). This is brought out in Romans 4:5: *To the one who does not work but trusts God who justifies the wicked, his faith is credited as righteousness.*

Romans 3:21 tells us that this righteousness of God apart from the keeping of the law is witnessed to by the Old Testament (The law and the prophets). Paul expands on this by referring to Abraham being made righteous through faith: *This is why it was credited to him as righteousness. The words 'It was credited to him' were written not for him alone but also for us, to whom God will credit righteousness – for us who believe in Him who raised Jesus our Lord from the dead; He was delivered over to death for our sins and was raised to life for our justification* (Rom 4:22-25).

For if by the trespass of one man death reigned through that one man, how much more will those who receive God's abundant provision of grace and the gift of righteousness reign in life through the one man Jesus Christ. Consequently, just as the result of one trespass was condemnation for all mankind, so also the result of the one act of righteousness was justification that brings life to all men. For just as through the disobedience of the one man the many were made sinners, so also through the obedience of the one man the many will be made righteous.

The law was added so that the trespass might increase. But where sin increased, grace increased all the more, so that, just as sin reigned in death, so that grace might reign through righteousness to bring eternal life through Jesus Christ our Lord (Rom 5:17-21).

Here again the two heads of the human race are in view. By virtue of man's relationship to Adam, he is under death and condemnation; by virtue of his relationship to Christ, the believer receives life and righteousness. Adam brought sin while Christ brings righteousness.

The law was given that the *offence might abound,* that is, that we would become aware of the magnitude of our offenses. The law does not cause us to sin, but it makes us aware of our sins. As great as sin and its consequences are, God's grace through Christ is greater.

But if Christ is in you, your body is dead because of sin; yet your spirit is alive because of righteousness (Rom 8:10). Here we see that the believer's body is dying through the effects of its relationship to Adam, but their spirits are alive because of its relationship to Christ. The believer's body awaits its transformation at a later time, but until then their spirits have been made alive to God because of the crediting of Christ's righteousness to them.

Christ is the end of the law so that there may be righteousness to everyone who believes (Rom 10:4). Christ ended our need to keep the law in order to attain righteousness. By faith in Him, the very righteousness of Christ Himself is credited to the believer. *For God made him who had no sin, to be sin for us, so that in Him we might become the righteousness of God* (2 Cor 5:21).

This unbelievable exchange is called grace. A word that takes on a whole new meaning when used by the Biblical writers. Christ took our judgment and gives us His righteousness. This is the gift of God's unique love.

To be found in Him not having a righteousness of my own that comes from the law, but that which is through faith in Christ, the righteousness that comes from God and is by faith (Phil 3:9).

JUSTIFICATION

Justification includes both aspects of being released from the guilt of the law and being credited with Christ's righteousness.

Being justified freely by His grace through the redemption that is in Christ Jesus (Rom 3:24).

Therefore since we have been justified by faith, we have peace with God through our Lord Jesus Christ (Rom 5:1).

So also the result of one act of righteousness through him everyone who believes is justified from everything you could not be justified from by the law of Moses (Acts 13:39)

Justification, as with all the benefits applied to the believer, is absolutely perfect, and God Himself throws out the challenge: *Who will bring any charge against those whom God has chosen? It is God who justifies* (Rom 8:33)

REDEEMED

The word "Redemption" carries the thought of "buying" or "Purchasing." God saw us in the slave market of sin without hope, and Christ came and paid an incredible price to buy us and make us His own. The purchase price of our redemption is called a "ransom." *"Just as the Son of Man did not come to be served, but to serve, and to give His life a ransom for many"* (Matt 20:28).

Who gave Himself a ransom for all mankind (1 Tim 2:6). Because we are looking at these benefits individually, we will be considering many of the same verses with different aspects of salvation.

Being justified freely by His grace through the redemption that is in Christ Jesus (Rom 3:24).

Christ has redeemed us from the curse of the law, being made a curse for us (Gal 3:13).

But when the fullness of the time had come God sent His Son, made of a woman, made under the law to "redeem" them that were under the law, that we might receive the adoption of sons (Gal 4:4-5).

In whom we have redemption through His blood, the forgiveness of sins (Col 1:14).

By His own blood He entered once into the holy place, having obtained eternal redemption for us (Heb 9:12). Here we see that the Lord's redemption of the believer is a one-time act that remains in effect forever. The believer remains Christ's possession, purchased by Him forever.

For as much as you know that you were not redeemed with corruptible things, as silver and gold . . . but with the precious blood of Christ (1 Pet 1:18-19).

And they sang a new song, saying, "You are worthy to take the book and to open its seals: For you were slain, and have redeemed us to God by your blood" (Rev 5:9).

SANCTIFICATION

Sanctification means separation from something to something. It is closely related to redemption. By purchasing the believer, God has separated him from the old creation, in Adam, to the new creation in Christ. The believer is forever the possession of God. The word "saint" means "sanctified one" or "holy one."

The Bible presents two aspects of sanctification. The first is God's work in sanctification or "setting apart" the believer. This is done once and lasts forever. The second aspect is the believer's sanctification of himself to God.

The first aspect refers to our legal standing while the second refers to our daily walk. The believer is to sanctify himself. He is to set himself apart from the world to God in his daily walk. If he fails to do this, he will be chastised or disciplined by God.

The believer's sanctification of himself is imperfect and varies and fluctuates, but this does not change God's work, which is perfect and unchanging.

To all in Rome who are loved by God, and called to be saints . . . (Rom 1:7).

To the church of God in Corinth, to those sanctified in Christ Jesus, and called to be holy, together with all those everywhere who call upon the name of our Lord Jesus Christ – their Lord and ours (1 Cor 1:2).

Believers are saints by virtue of God's sanctifying them to Himself. *You also, as living stones, are built up into a spiritual house, a holy priesthood.*

Here the words "Saint" and "holy" mean the same thing: "Sanctified" ones, or ones who are "set apart to God and for God."

God's sanctification of the believer is eternal and unchanging as set forth in Hebrews 10:10: *And by that will, we have been made holy through the sacrifice of the body of Jesus Christ once for all.*

Because by one sacrifice he has made perfect forever those who are being made holy (Heb 10:14). This sanctification by God remains in effect forever.

To those who have been called, who are loved by God the Father and kept by Jesus Christ (Jude 1:1). Here the believer is called out of Adam to Christ. Called out of the old creation, to become God's own personal possession. Our salvation is "kept" or "preserved" by virtue of our being "in Christ."

WASHED

Here again we have a two-fold aspect. The first is an act done by God and is a one-time washing that cleanses the believer forever. The second aspect has to do with the believer's walk and is done by the believer through confession and repentance, and concerns his fellowship with God in this life.

The first aspect, God's work in washing the believer of his sins forever, is referred to in Titus 3:5: *Not by the works of righteousness that we have done, but according to his mercy he saved us, by the washing of regeneration and renewing of the Holy Spirit.*

And Revelation 1:5: *And from Jesus Christ, who is the faithful witness, the First born of the dead, and the prince of the kings of the earth, to him that loved us, and WASHED us from our sins in His own blood.* This is a once for all washing of our sin as the Holy Spirit applies the blood of Jesus Christ to the sinner.

The second aspect is seen in 1 John 1:9: *If we confess our sins, He is faithful and just to forgive us our sins and to purify us from all unrighteousness.* Here cleansing from daily sins, which affect our fellowship with God in our daily lives, is based upon confession of sins.

Both aspects are seen in John 13:4-11, where Jesus gives an illustration by washing His disciple's feet. Here Peter refuses the allow Jesus to do such a lowly act. But the Lord says that if Peter will not allow Him to wash his feet, He would have no part with Him (Referring to fellowship).

Jesus was illustrating our need for daily cleansing. Peter says, then in that case, Lord, give me a bath! Jesus answered that one who is bathed (referring to the one time washing of salvation) needed only to have their feet washed.

The illustration here is that the believer was washed completely at salvation. But during his daily walk here on earth he picks up defilement on his feet that needs daily cleansing. Jesus was referring to Peter's later denial of him when he would have to be cleansed and restored to Jesus fellowship and service. He would need his feet washed. But Judas could not be restored because there was no place for him to be restored to; he had never been saved in the first place.

REGENERATION – NEW BIRTH

Regeneration takes place within the believer personally. It is the impartation of eternal life. It is the new birth from above, whereby the believer becomes a child of God and receives a new nature from God.

This does not remove the old sin nature that we all inherited from Adam; it is the impartation of a new nature alongside the old nature. The believer has two sharply contrasting natures: One good, loving the things of God, and one evil and sinful.

And you were made alive, who were dead in your transgressions and sins (Eph 2:1).

When you were dead in your sins, and in the uncircumcision of your sinful nature, God made you alive with Christ. He forgave us all our sins (Col 2:13).

Here we see that the believer was "made alive" through the "new birth."

He saved us, not because of righteous things we have done, but because of His mercy. He saved us through the washing of rebirth and renewal by the Holy Spirit (Titus 3:5). Through faith in Christ, the Holy Spirit imparts the new nature to the believer. Receiving "eternal life" and being "born again" are synonymous in Scripture.

"That whosoever believes in Him will not perish, but have "eternal life." (John 3:15)

"I tell you the truth; whoever hears my word and believes on Him who sent me has eternal life and will not be condemned; they have crossed over from death to life" (At that very moment) (John 5:24).

"I tell you the truth; he who believes in me has everlasting life." (John 6:47)

Note the present tenses in these last three verses. Eternal life is not some future reward but a present possession of the believer the moment he or she believes in Jesus.

"I give them eternal life, and they shall never perish; no one can snatch them out of my hand" (John 10:28). Here we see that the believer has eternal life and will never lose it, it is guaranteed by God.

In John 17:2-3, Jesus prays to the Father and says about Himself; *"For you granted me authority over all people that I might give eternal life to all those you have given me. Now this is eternal life: that they may know you, the only true God, and Jesus Christ, whom you have sent"* (John 17:2-3). Here we see that Jesus Christ as the Last Adam was given authority over all people to remove them from Adam and give them eternal life.

Eternal life does not refer merely to duration of life. The unbeliever also has eternal duration, but it refers to quality of life – Knowing the true God and Jesus Christ in a personal way.

Yet to all who received him, to those who believe in His name, He gave the right to become the children of God – children born not of natural descent or of a husband's will, but born of God (John 1:12-13). The eternal life the believer receives is the very life of God Himself.

The believer not only escapes hell and goes to heaven when he dies, but God becomes his Father. Heaven is his home. As expectant parents joyfully prepare for the coming of their child, God has prepared a place for us in His home. We are His children! He loves us! Joy fills all heaven when a person comes to Christ, another child is born of God and God's heart leaps for joy! (Luke 15:3-7).

Heaven is not a place where we will just creep in feeling that maybe we don't really belong there, but a place where the Father longingly waits with hugs and kisses. *We are all the children by faith in Jesus Christ* (Gal 3:26). *For you have been born again, not of perishable seed, but of imperishable through the living and enduring word of God* (1 Pet 1:23).

His divine power has given us everything we need for life and godliness through our knowledge of Him who called us by His own glory and goodness. Through these He has given us very great and precious promises so that through these you may participate in the Divine nature and escape the corruption in the world caused by evil desires (2 Pet 1:3-4).

How great is the love the Father has lavished upon us, that we should be called the children of God! And that is what we are! The reason the world does not know us is that it did not know him. Dear friends, now are we the children of God, and what we will be has not yet been made known, but we know that when he appears, we shall be like Him, for we shall see Him as He is (1 John 3:1-2).

It is God's purpose to bring many children into glory: *In bringing many sons to glory, it was fitting that God, for whom, and through whom everything exists, should make the author of their salvation perfect through suffering* (Heb 2:10). Just as children are brought into the family through the suffering of childbirth, Christ suffered to bring us into God's family.

That Jesus might be the first-born of many brothers (Rom 8:29). This means that concerning Jesus' humanity, we become His brothers by birth through the Holy Spirit. Thus believers become the family of God with Jesus as the First-born or Head.

Both the one who makes us holy and those who are made holy are of the same family. So Jesus is not ashamed to call us brothers (Heb 2:11). So God who sanctifies believers, and believers who are sanctified, are of the same family of God.

He says, "I will declare your name to my brothers; in the presence of the congregation I will sing your praises." And again, "I will put my trust in Him." And again he says. "Here I am, and the children God has given me." (Heb 2:12-13). Here Christ, as Head of the new creation, the family of God, declares His Father to His brethren, and leads them in praises to God. What a wondrous sight this is! Jesus our great redeemer, leading the new creation amid a glorified universe in praises to the Father, energized by the Holy Spirit.

For those God fore-knew He also predestined to be conformed to the likeness of His Son, that he might be the First-born among many brothers (Rom 8:29).

Now if we are children, then we are heirs, heirs of God and co-heirs with Christ (Rom 8:17).

Here we see that God determined to share with His children all that He possesses. As the Firstborn or Head of the family of God, Christ receives these from God and distributes them to the rest of the family.

CHRIST IN THE BELIEVER

Not only is the believer in Christ, but Christ indwells the believer. *"On that day you shall understand that I am in my Father and you in me and I in you"* (John 14:20).

"And I have made you known to them and will continue to make you known, in order that the love you have for me may be in them and that I myself may be in them" (John 17:26).

I am crucified with Christ; yet I live: Yet not I, but Christ lives in me (Gal 2:20).

To them God has chosen to make known among the Gentiles the glorious riches of this mystery, which is Christ in you, the hope of glory (Col 1:27). The word here for "hope" is assurance. The assurance of our glorification is based on the fact that Christ indwells us.

When the sinner believes in Jesus, Christ enters into the believer and imparts His own life to him: *And this is the testimony: God has given us eternal life, and this life is in his Son. He who has the Son has life* (1 John 5:11-12).

THE FATHER IS IN THE BELIEVER
In Ephesians 4:6 Paul writes to the Ephesian believers: *And one God and Father of you all, who is over all and through all and in all.*

THE HOLY SPIRIT IS IN THE BELIEVER
Do you not know that your body is the temple of the Holy Spirit, who is in you, whom you have received from God? You are not your own; you have been bought with a price. Therefore honor God with your body (1 Cor 6:19).

"And I will ask the Father, and He will give you another Counselor to be with you forever – the Spirit of truth. The world cannot accept Him, because it neither sees Him nor knows Him, but you know Him for He lives with you and with be in you" (John 14:16-17).

UNION AND COMMUNION
Thus we see that the believer is in the triune God, and the Triune God is IN the believer. No greater words could describe the intimate, vital union that exists between God and the believer in the Lord Jesus Christ.

We have to distinguish between union with God and communion with God. Union with God is God's work and is perfect and eternal, while communion or fellowship involves the believer's cooperation with God. Thus the believer who is in Christ, that is, in union with Christ, is to maintain communion or fellowship with Him and bear fruit in his daily life.

"Remain in me and I will remain in you. No branch can bear fruit by itself; it must remain in the vine. Neither can you bear fruit unless you remain in me. I am the vine; you are the branches. If a man remains in me and I in him, he will bear much fruit; apart from me you can do nothing.

If you remain in me and my words remain in you, ask what you wish, and it will be given you. This is my Father's glory, that you bear much fruit, showing yourselves to be my disciples" (John 14:4-5, 7-8).

While the believer is "in Christ "as an eternal act of God, in his daily life he is exhorted to *Put on the new self, created to be like God in true righteousness and holiness* (Eph 4:24). In this passage the believer is to put into practice in his daily life the things that are already true of him. He is in Christ and Christ is in Him; he is born of God with a new nature. He is to put on this new self and live accordingly.

The believer could not do these things any more than the unbeliever could if these things were not already true of him by an act of God. The very fact that these things are true of the believer is the basis of God's exhortations to abstain from sin and do what is pleasing to God: *For you were once in darkness but now you are light in the Lord. Live as children of light* (Eph 5:8).

Here believers are exhorted to walk as children of light, not to become the children of light, but because they already are children of light. Some are afraid that if a believer is taught eternal security it will motivate him to sin. But this doctrine is the very basis to motivate us not to sin. They are teaching legalism. To them, salvation is always in doubt. Their service to God is based on fear. The Scriptures teach the very opposite. The believer's service to God is motivated by love because of what God has already done for them. Legalism says: "Do in order to be." Grace says, "Do because you already are." The Holy Spirit shames and convicts the believer with the fact that he is a child of God.

The believer is under grace, not law. His motivation comes from God's grace, not law. *For you did not receive the spirit that makes you a slave again to fear; but you have received the spirit of son ship. And by Him we cry, "Abba, Father!" The Spirit Himself testifies with our spirit, that we are God's children* (Rom 8:15-16).

THE DOWN PAYMENT OR FIRST-FRUITS OF THE SPIRIT

We know that the whole creation has been groaning as in the pains of childbirth right up to the present time. Not only so, but we ourselves, who have the first-fruits of the Spirit, groan inwardly as we wait eagerly for our adoption as sons, the redemption of our bodies (Rom 8:22-23). The first-fruits or down payment is God's guarantee that He will carry out the rest of His promises to the believer. The language here comes from the business world. God made a contract with the believer and signed the contract, pledging Himself to carry it out to completion.

The guarantee or down payment is the Holy Spirit Himself. While many of the benefits of salvation are now in the believer's possession, much of it is still promised. While he is already saved now, many of the benefits of his salvation are yet to be entered into. What the believer does possess now causes him to long for the completion of his salvation, the glorification of his body.

The believer's body has been purchased by Christ, but unlike many of the other benefits, he has not yet received his new body. What he now possesses saves him from the penalty of sin; the redemption of his body will save him from the effects of sin and its curse. 1 John 3:2 tells us: *Beloved now are we the Sons of God, but it does not yet appear what we shall be: But we know that when He will appear we will be like Him for we shall see Him as He is.*

In other words, we are now saved; we are removed from Adam and placed in Christ. Spiritually we are severed from the old creation, but physically we share in it, as we are told in Romans 8:10: *But if Christ is in you, your body is dead because of sin, yet your spirit is alive because of righteousness.*

Here we are told that the physical body is dead (literally "is dying") because of the effects of sin. This is because it is still related to Adam. But at the same time the believer has eternal life through the righteousness of Christ. The believer longs to be freed from the hindrances of his fallen body. He longs for a body that can fully express what God has done WITHIN the body. Until that time the believer lives in a constant struggle with sin and the old nature. While we can have daily victory through the Holy Spirit who dwells in us, we long to be completely free from this struggle.

SEALED BY THE HOLY SPIRIT

And do not grieve the Holy Spirit of God, with whom you are sealed for the day of redemption (Eph 4:30). The seal is God's sign of ownership, the sign of the completed transaction. Again the language is from the business world. He gives the down payment, which is the pledge that He will fulfill the rest of the contract.

And if the Spirit of Him who raised Jesus from the dead is living in you, He who raised Christ from the dead will also give life to your mortal bodies through His Spirit who lives in you (Rom 8:11). God paid the entire purchase price so the Holy Spirit can move into the body of the believer, and this guarantees that He will fulfill all the promises He has made.

God has moved into the believer (In the Person of the Holy Spirit) and lives there while He fulfills the rest of His pledge).

The down payment and the sealing of the Holy Spirit are vitally connected and are both presented in the following verses: *Now it is God who makes both us and you stand firm in Christ. He anointed us, set His seal of ownership on us, and put his Spirit in our hearts as a deposit* (or down payment), *guaranteeing what is to come* (2 Cor 1:21-22).

And you also were included in Christ when you heard the word of truth, the gospel of salvation. Having believed, you were marked in Him with a seal, the promised Holy Spirit, who is a deposit guaranteeing our inheritance until the redemption of those who are God's possession – to the praise of His glory (Eph 1:13-14).

PRIESTS TO GOD

You also like living stones, are being built into a spiritual house to be a holy priesthood, offering spiritual sacrifices acceptable to Jesus Christ (1 Pet 2:5).

But you are a chosen people, a royal priesthood, a holy nation, a people belonging to God, that you may declare the praises of Him who called you out of darkness into His wonderful light (1 Pet 2:9).

Revelation 1:6: *And has made us to be a kingdom and priests to serve His God and Father.*

Revelation 5:10: *You have made them to be a kingdom and priests to serve our God, and they will reign upon the earth.*

Here in these two passages it is literally "A kingdom OF priests."

MADE CITIZENS OF HEAVEN

"However, do not rejoice that the spirits submit to you, but rejoice that your names are written in heaven" (Luke 10:20).

Consequently, you are no longer foreigners and aliens, but fellow citizens with God's people and members of God's household (Eph 2:19).

But our citizenship is in heaven (Phil 3:20).

For he has rescued us from the dominion of darkness and brought us into the kingdom of the Son He loves (Col 1:13).

Into an inheritance that can never perish, spoil or fade – kept in heaven for you (1 Pet 1:4).

This work of God in translating believers from Adam to Christ, from the kingdom of Satan into the kingdom of Christ, begins the moment they believe in Christ and lasts forever. Heaven is already theirs. Their names are already written there on its citizenship roll. And because of Christ's work, they are already qualified to be there.

ALIENS AND STRANGERS IN THE WORLD

Because their citizenship has been changed to heaven, believers are no longer of this world, which is "in Adam" and under condemnation. *"They are not of the world even as I am not of it"* (John 17:16). By virtue of their being "in Christ," believers are no more of this world than Christ is.

Referring to the Old Testament saints we are told: *All of these people were still living by faith when they died. They did not receive the things promised; they only saw them and welcomed them from a distance. And they admitted that they were aliens and strangers on earth* (Heb 11:13).

New Testament saints are exhorted: *Dear friends, I urge you, as aliens and strangers in the world to abstain from sinful desires, which war against your soul* (1 Pet 2:11).

Here the believer is pleaded with as a stranger and pilgrim to this world system not to be ensnared by its lusts or desires that war against the new nature. One reason there are so many Christians who do not reach others for Christ is because they do not feel secure themselves. If a man thinks he is drowning, he is in poor condition to rescue anyone else. Before he can pull others out of the water, he must be sure of his own footing. The assurance that Paul had should characterize all believers: *Who shall separate us from the love of Christ? Shall trouble or hardship or persecution or famine or nakedness or danger or sword? As it is written: for your sake we face death all day long; we are considered sheep to be slaughtered. No, in all these things we are more than conquerors through Him who loved us. For I am convinced that neither death nor life, neither angels nor demons, neither the present nor the future, nor any powers, neither height nor depth, nor anything else in all creation, will be able to separate us from the love of God that is in Christ Jesus our Lord* (Rom 8:35-39). Paul had the assurance that is so crucial for an effective life for Christ.

MADE WORKERS WITH GOD

"As you sent me into the world, I have sent them into the world" (John 17:18).

Again Jesus said, "Peace be with you. As the Father has sent me, I am sending you" (John 20:21).

We are therefore Christ's ambassadors (2 Cor 5:20).

Believers are citizens of heaven. They are sent on a mission to this world in which they are aliens and strangers. We are not to settle down here or be ensnared by this world's philosophy or mind-set but are to be single-minded in our mission.

We are to throw out lifelines to those who are still "in Adam" and part of the old condemned creation and bring them into the new creation in Christ. Someday we will leave this world and enter into all that Christ has done for us, and the eternal glory that God has prepared for us.

THE FATHER'S LOVE-GIFT TO CHRIST

"My sheep listen to my voice; I know them, and they follow me. I give them eternal life, and they shall never perish; no one can snatch them out of my hand. My Father, who has GIVEN THEM TO ME, is greater than all; no one can snatch them out of my Father's hand. I and my Father are one" (John 10:27-30).

After Jesus said this, He looked up toward heaven and prayed: "Father, the time has come. Glorify your Son, that your Son may glorify You. For you have granted Him authority over all people that he might give eternal life to all those you have given him." (John 10:1-2)

"I have revealed you to those you gave me out of the world. They were yours; you gave them to me and they have obeyed your word. Now they know that everything you have given me comes from you" (John 17:6-7).

"I pray for them, I am not praying for the world, but for those you have given me, for they are yours, and all you have is mine. And glory has come to me through them. I will remain in the world no longer, but they are still in the world, and I am coming to you" (John 17:9-11).

"Father, I want those you have given me to be with me where I am, and see my glory, the glory you have given me because you loved me before the creation of the world."

Believers have been given to Christ by the Father as His love gift for an eternal possession. They are held by the Father and the Son and none of them will ever be lost.

APPENDIX 5
The Uniqueness of Jesus

The figure of Jesus Christ stands unique and alone. Towering over all of history. No one made the claims that He did and backed them up as He did, proving the truth of His words: *"Heaven and earth will pass away, but my words will never pass away. He* knows all of our failures and weakness and still He loves us. He will nurse us through the sickness from the fall, until He leads us to the other side where there is glory and no sickness, death, or sorrow, and we will never fail Him again.

The sweetest words that ever fell on sinful ears are, *"For God so loved the world that He gave His One and only Son, that whoever believes in Him shall not perish but have eternal life"* (John 3:16).

A little girl and her mother were walking along the street. The girl picked up a fragment of a page of the Bible and read it out loud, *"For God so loved the world that He gave . . .*

That's all there was. The mother took it from her and read it again and handed it back to her. "It doesn't say what He gave," she said. The little girl studied it some more and said, "Oh, but mom, don't you see, just the fact that God loved us enough to give us anything must mean something." The mother nodded and they walked on in silence.

But God did not just give us anything. He gave us the greatest Gift that even God could give. He gave us His Son, a Savior, who would love us and care for us; who would wash us of our sins and who would never leave us nor forsake us.

In His most desperate hour, He was denied and forsaken by His disciples, but not once did He ever abandon them. We will be united with the One we were created for and we will fulfill our purpose according to His will for each one of us. We will never let Him out of our sight and the amazement at what He did for us at Calvary will never leave us.

Before He invites us to come to Him and place ourselves under His yoke, He has already given us the supreme demonstration of His love. *This is how God showed His love among us: He sent His one and only Son into the world that we might live through Him. This is love: not that we loved God, but that He loved us and sent His Son to be an atoning sacrifice for our sins* (1 John 4:9-10).

We are told in John 1:18: *No one has ever seen God: but God the One and Only, who is at the Father's side, has made Him known.* This means that from the beginning God has revealed Himself through His Son. In the Old Testament the Son was revealed in prophecies and types and shadows.

In Hebrews 3:1-3 we read: *In the past God spoke to our forefathers through the prophets at many times and in various ways, but in these last days He has spoken to us by His Son, Whom He appointed heir of all things, and through whom He made the universe. The Son is the radiance of God's glory and the exact representation of His Being, sustaining all things by His powerful word. After He had provided purification for sins, He sat down at the right hand of the Majesty in heaven.*

Here we see that the revelation of God in the Old Testament was given at different times and in various ways. God revealed himself to His fallen creation through Angels, visions, dreams, and Christophanies (Appearances of Christ as the Angel or Messenger of the Lord), before His incarnation as man.

God chose Israel that, through them, *All the peoples of the earth will be blessed . . .* (Gen 12:3). It was through this nation that God's special revelation in Scripture was given, gradually, piece by piece, until the revelation was full and completed with the coming of Jesus Christ who was God revealed in the flesh.

It was through His appointed followers that the New Testament was completed as a capstone of God's revelation of Jesus Christ. As the Old Testament revelation of Jesus Christ was the "shadow" of His image, the incarnation was the *Radiance of God's glory and the exact representation of His Being*. Jesus was the exact representation of the invisible God, and the Exact representation of which the Old Testament was a shadow, has now appeared in the Person of Jesus Christ. Jesus Christ is God's revelation of Himself in human form. In John 14:6 Jesus says: *"Anyone who has seen me, has seen the Father."*

God has taken upon Himself our humanity and entered into our sorrow and pain, and as the Last Adam and the "Firstborn" or HEAD of every creature, He who never sinned took upon Himself the responsibility of our sins and paid the price of our redemption. God entering into human history in the incarnation is much more than a mere philosophy.

It establishes the Christian faith on a historical foundation in Jesus Christ. As 1 John 1:1 tells us: *That which was from the beginning, which we have heard, which we have seen with our eyes, which we have looked at and our hands have touched – this we have proclaimed concerning the Word of Life.* Here John is speaking of the disciples' intimate contact with Jesus.

In 1 Timothy 3:16 Paul describes the same thing. *Beyond all question, the mystery of godliness is great: He appeared in a body, was vindicated by the Spirit, was seen by angels, was preached among the nations, was believed on in the world, and was taken up in glory.*

God was not content to leave His rebellious creation go its way into eternal darkness but embraced it with the bloody hands of the Redeemer. *And He made known to us the mystery of His will according to His good pleasure, which he purposed in Christ, to be put into effect when the times will have reached their fulfillment – to bring all things in heaven and on earth together under one head, even Christ* (Eph 1:9-10). All believers and all creation will be brought into a glorious relationship under the Headship of Christ. God has entered into His fallen, sinful creation, not as judge but as Savior. *"For God did not send His Son into the world to condemn the world, but to save the world through Him"* (John 3:17).

He came on a mission of love. If you have any idea what He went through for you, you would not be afraid to give yourself to Him. Anyone who has honestly faced themselves knows something is wrong; something is missing. There is a yearning, a longing for something we lost a long time ago in the Garden of Eden that time has not erased. It's a relationship with God that Christ came to restore.

We live in the period between Christ's first coming to bring eternal redemption and His second coming to establish His kingdom. History is rapidly moving toward that goal. As Christians we must take seriously the job that Jesus has given us.

After Jesus rose from the dead He appeared to His disciples and said to them: "As *the Father has seen me, I am sending you*" (John 20:21) And in Mark 16:15 Jesus said: *"Go into all the world and preach the good news to all creation."*

As head of the church, our commander and chief has left us marching orders.

This is to be a group effort. We are each to do our share. We are all to reach some people for Jesus. We are all to reach out to our own little world, our sphere of influence: our families, friends, people we work with, etc.

These are our first responsibility. We must make every effort to reach them for Christ. After Jesus spoke to the Samaritan woman at the well, she left and went into the city to tell them about Jesus. As the people were returning with her to see the one she told them about. Jesus and His disciples watched them as they were coming and Jesus said to them: *"Do you not say, 'Four months more and then the harvest?' I tell you, open your eyes and look at the fields! They are ripe for harvest"* (John 4:35).

Here Jesus is saying that unlike the earthly fields, the spiritual fields are always ready for harvest. The problem is with the reapers: *"The harvest is plentiful but the workers are few. Ask the Lord of the harvest, therefore, to send out workers into his harvest field"* (Matt 9:37-38).

Jesus said: *"While I am in the world, I am the light of the world"* (John 9:5). But when He leaves the world WE will represent Him and be the light of the world" (Matt 5:14). We all have a job to do, given to us by no less than the Son of God. This is our major, not our minor. Keeping a job or keeping house is our minor.

We each have a job that is bigger than we are. Jesus' interests have taken center stage in our lives, putting ours on hold. This is why He said: *"If anyone would come after me, he must deny himself and take up his cross daily and follow me"* (Luke 9:23).

The cross is not an ornament that we are to wear, but an instrument of death. Once someone picks up his cross it means their death. You do not pick up your cross and tell your friends you will be back later. You tell them "Goodbye, I'm going out to die." When we were baptized, we testified that we died with Christ. Our desires and interests have lost their charm. We testified that we rose to follow and serve another.

The cross speaks of death; this is what Paul meant when He said, *I have been crucified with Christ and I no longer live, but Christ lives in me. The life I live in the body, I live by faith in the Son of God, who loved me and gave himself for me* (Gal 2:20). Paul is saying that he died to himself and now Christ lives in him and now has center stage in his life.

Isaac Watts caught a glimpse of the drawing power of Christ on the human heart when He composed his masterpiece: *When I Survey the Wondrous Cross*:

When I survey the wondrous cross on which the prince of glory died.

My richest gain I count but loss and pour contempt on all my pride.

Forbid it Lord that I should boast save in the cross of Christ my God.

All the vain things that charm me most I sacrifice them to His blood.

See. From His head, His hands, His feet sorrow and love flowed mingled down.

Did e'er such love and sorrow meet or thorns compose so rich a crown?

Were the whole realm of nature mine that were an offering far too small.

Love so amazing so divine demands my heart, my life, my all.

In Luke 14:16-23 Jesus compares heaven to a great banquet: *"A certain man was preparing a great banquet and invited many guests. At the time of the banquet he sent his servants to tell those who had been invited, 'Come, for everything is now ready.' But they all alike began to make excuses. The first said, 'I have just bought a field, and I must go and see it. Please excuse me.'*

Another said, 'I have just bought five yoke of oxen, and I am on my way to try them out. Please excuse me.' Still another said, 'I just got married, so I can't come.'

The servant came back and reported this to his master. Then the owner of the house became angry and ordered his servant, 'Go out quickly into the streets and alleys of the town and bring in the poor, the crippled, the blind and the lame.' 'Sir,' the servant said, 'what you ordered has been done, but there is still room.'

Then the master told his servant, 'Go out into the roads and country lanes and make them come in, so that my house will be full. I tell you, not one of those men who were invited will get a taste of my banquet.'"

Note how the servant in this story is constantly told to "Go." This is a matter of great urgency to the master. "Go! Go! GO! That my house may be full!"

Jesus came to save the lost. *"For the Son of Man came to seek and to save what was lost"* (Luke 19:10).

Let us fix our eyes on Jesus, the Author and Perfector of our faith, who for the joy set before him endured the cross, scorning the shame . . . (Heb 12:2).

This was always on Jesus heart; He told the parables of the lost sheep, the lost coin, and the prodigal son (Luke 15:8-31). These show that God longs for sinners to come to Him. He told the parable of the sower in Matthew 13:18-23 to show the Father's concern that the gospel be given to sinners. God has not changed. Lost sinners coming to Christ is still His greatest concern. Proverbs 11:30 says: *The fruit of the righteous is a tree of life, and he who wins souls is wise.*

Daniel 12:3: *Those who are wise will shine like the brightness of the heavens, and those who lead many to righteousness, like the stars for ever and ever.*

Here we are told that those who bring others to Christ will receive special rewards. The wise Christian will take the long look: He will not live for the things that will pass away with this life. In Matthew 6:19-20 we are exhorted: *"Do not store up for yourselves treasures on earth, where moth and rust destroy and where thieves break in and steal. But store up for yourselves treasures in heaven, where moth and rust do not destroy, and where thieves do not break in and steal. For where your treasure is, there your heart will be also."*

If our treasure is down here, we will have little spiritual power. It is not necessary for the person to have many possessions to have his treasures here on earth. It is not what a person has, but what his heart is set upon. Abraham's heart was set on the heavenly city. The rich fertile plains of this world held no temptation for him. He had turned his heart away from this fleeting world and all its temptations and focused on something better. His heart was set on the heavenly city and he laid his treasure there.

Many of God's people make the mistake of looking for their reward here on earth and become discouraged. In Galatians 6:9 we are exhorted: *Let us not become weary of well doing for at the proper time we will reap a harvest if we do not give up.* The assurance of heaven will make us better servants down here. It should free us from the pursuit of earthly pleasures and comforts. Christians are soldiers on the battlefield in a foreign land. Soldiers do not build mansions on the battlefield. They do not sit under palm trees fanning themselves. We are here to make a difference for Christ.

The wise Christian will not concern himself with the passing pleasures of this world. He will not lay up treasures on earth that he will someday have to leave behind. He will lay up treasures in eternity where he will enjoy them forever. We must make up our mind that if we serve Christ, the world will call us fools, but God says we are wise. If we live for ourselves, and worldly things, the world will call us wise, but God says we are fools. We must make up our minds whose commendation we want, because we cannot have them both.

There was a missionary on a ship coming from Africa with broken health. He lost his wife and child in Africa and suffered greatly from disease. On the same ship was president Theodore Roosevelt returning from a hunting trip. When they arrived in America, he watched as the cheering crowds welcomed the president home. Then the lonely missionary thought, "Lord, I spent these years on the mission field. I lost a wife and child, and gave up my health, and nobody is here to welcome me. But the president comes home from a hunting trip and everyone is here to welcome him home."

As he was about to leave the ship, he could hear a voice whisper, but son, you're not home yet."

Those who win souls are wise because they invest their time in the most important thing in the world. Some day we must leave this world and give an account. Because we live in a materialistic world, we must be on guard that this materialism does not creep into our lives. It is sad that so many Christians will work harder at business than they do for the Lord who bought them with His blood.

It is to our great loss if we fail to live under the influence of eternal things. Many of us are digging in the dirt for the worthless things of this world when true untold treasure is waiting above our heads. Our minds are on earthly things and we live as though we are going to be here forever! We forget that our days are numbered and will vanish like the morning dew.

Making the most of every opportunity, because the days are evil, therefore do not be foolish, but understand what the Lord's will is (Eph 5:16). A clearer vision of Heaven will expose the emptiness of the things of this world. We will function better here if our hearts are THERE. We will have a truer perspective and a greater sense of value. We will not mistake the artificial trinkets that perish for the priceless treasures that will endure forever. We are to fix our gaze heavenward, to have a proper perspective of this life.

One day a little boy came running to his mother screaming that a bee was after him. She covered him with her apron until finally she said, "You can come out now." The little boy peeked out from behind her apron. "You see, the bee has stung mommy and has lost its stinger in mommy's arm and cannot hurt you now." He watched as the bee crawled harmlessly down her arm.

Jesus has removed the sting of death by taking the stinger into His own heart and making it harmless for us. In the 23rd Psalm David speaks of the believers *Walk through the valley of the SHADOW of death*. Death has lost its reality and terror; it is a mere shadow and has lost its sting. For those who belong to Christ, Death is not "A leap in the dark" or a "Journey into the unknown," but a journey home.

As believers we have already been raised with Christ and made to sit with Him in heavenly places (Eph 2:6). Our citizenship is already there (Phil 3:20).

As we wore ourselves out in sin before we were saved, we should now be wearing ourselves out for the Lord.

In Luke 15:10 we read: *"There is rejoicing in heaven in the presence of the angels of God over one sinner who repents.* This is such an important job that all heaven is watching.

As individual Christians we are not responsible for the whole world, but we are responsible to God for our own little world. Each of us lives in a world all our own. God wants that world. We all have our own sphere of influence, our place of contact, the place that God has entrusted to us, where we have contacts every day. There are those in your sphere of influence that no one else can reach but you. This gives our little lives great significance.

To those who have never trusted in Him, He invites you to do so now. The devil will try to convince you of one of two lies. The first is that you are good enough as you are. But we are all members of a sinful and fallen race. No matter how much you might resent this, you cannot escape your birthright. We were born sinners.

We must repent and turn to Christ in faith. These are two sides of the same coin. We were born the first time walking away from God and toward sin. Repentance is turning from sin to Christ. This is a complete about-face, a total change of direction for our lives. Once you were big and Jesus was little and now Jesus is big and you are little.

The second lie is that you are too bad for Jesus to receive you. You may think that you are the worst sinner who ever lived, and maybe you are, but Jesus loves you and died for you. Paul said he was the chief of sinners because he persecuted the Church, but

Jesus received him and says to all *—Whoever comes to me I will never drive away* (John 6:37).

There are two words here that should be highlighted: The first is "whoever," which means anyone no matter how sinful. And the second word is "never," which means He will never reject anyone who comes to Him. This matter of salvation must become personal. It is true that Christ loved the world, and gave His life for the world so that whoever comes to Him can have eternal life. However, you must be confronted with the fact that Christ loved you and will give you eternal life if you receive Him. The sinner He is confronting is you and the one who must repent and receive Him is you. This is a matter of Jesus and you facing each other. He is presenting you with the problem of the sin that stands between you and Him and His rightful claim to your life.

The problem is you, not just what you do, but the source that produces these actions – your heart must be changed. No ritual or good work can make up for what you are. Only a new birth from God who gives us a new nature can save us.

This does not make you unable to sin, because you still have your old nature from Adam. These two natures will struggle for mastery as we are told in Galatians 5:17: *For the sinful nature desires what is contrary to the Spirit, and the Spirit what is contrary to the sinful nature.*

While the believer still struggles with sin, a fundamental change has taken place. Instead of a lifestyle where we enjoy and love sin, we grow more and more to hate it. Paul sums it up in Romans 7:21-23: *So I find this law at work: When I want to do good evil is right there with me. For in my inner being* (his new nature) *I delight in God's law; but I see another law at work in the members of my body waging war against the law of my mind and making me a prisoner of the law of sin at work within my members* (his old nature).

"Law" is not used in the sense of a code of ethics, like the Ten Commandments, but in the sense of a compelling principle or force like the law of gravity. There is a law or force in Paul's mind compelling him to delight in obeying God (his new nature). But at the same time he finds another law or force (the old Adamic nature that delights in sin) that is at war with his desire to obey God and at times makes him a prisoner to the law or principle of sin at work in his body through the old nature, causing him to cry out in anguish: *What a wretched person I am! Who will rescue me from this body of death?* (v. 24).

In desperation the believer realizes that the enemy is not only in the temptations from Satan and the lure of the world, but within his own body; it is this enemy that is within the camp that gives power to those outside enemies. Then he remembers that he has a powerful champion who promised never to abandon him. Thanks be to God through Jesus Christ our Lord (v. 25). The One who saves us from the penalty of sin will also rescue us from the power of sin.

Paul goes on: *So then, I myself am a slave to God's law, but in the sinful nature a slave to the law of sin* (v. 25b). Even though the believer is confused and feels helpless against the onslaughts of the old Adamic nature (Or principle) of the enemy within, he cannot be at peace with his old nature.

His mind (the new nature) is forever a slave to do God's will. He is driven by a desire obey God and at the same time he seems hopelessly enslaved by the old nature. Romans 8:2 tells us: *The law of the spirit of life set me free from the law of sin and death.* Here again "Law" refers to a principle or force; as the law of gravity is overcome by the law of aerodynamics, so the greater law or principle of the Holy Spirit overrules the law of sin and death.

For what the law was powerless to do in that it was weakened by the sinful nature, God did by sending His own Son in the likeness of sinful man to be a sin offering. And so He condemned sin in sinful man, in order that the righteous requirements of the law might be fully met in us who do not live according to the sinful nature but according to the Spirit (3-4).

The law was powerless to make us good because of our sinful nature. The law could only command me to do what I could not do, but it was not able to help me obey. But the Holy Spirit could enter into the believer and indwell him because Jesus paid for his sins.

He condemned or judged our sins on the cross by taking them on Himself, and now the Spirit can come into us and empower us to do what the law commands. The power of the Holy Spirit, when yielded to, will overcome the principle or power of the old nature. Now the enemy within is overpowered by the Holy Spirit within us as we are told in Galatians 5:16: *Live by the spirit, and you will not gratify the desires of the sinful nature.*

The believer's victory over sin is not the result of super effort on our part. We can no more LIVE the Christian life than we can enter into it. We enter the Christian life through the new birth by faith in Christ. Paul brings this out in Galatians 2:20: *I have been crucified with Christ and I no longer live, but Christ lives in me* (In the Person of the Holy spirit). *The life I live in the body, I live by faith in the Son of God, who loved me and gave Himself for me.*

We are saved by faith and we live the Christian life, moment by moment, by faith. By faith we can lay hold upon God through Christ, and draw upon His power to live the Christian life. This is why Jesus said: *"Apart from Me you can do nothing"* (John 15:5). Our victory over sin comes by our allowing Christ to live out Him life in us.

Christ loving us and giving Himself for us does not stop at the cross. He not only gives himself FOR us but TO us forever. Once a person genuinely trusts in Christ, he enters into a union with Him that will span eternity.

I beheld the Mighty One, the Glorious Lord of Heaven,
Fire and lightning and thunder surrounded His throne,
With great joy the angels rushed to do His bidding,
They stood before Him covering their eyes from the
glory of His holiness.
His voice was as a mighty thunder as He spoke His
commands.

My heart trembled as I looked upon that scene,
Fearing that it might be known that a sinner such as I
Would dare to look upon the glorious Son of the living
God,
But with trembling boldness I raised my eyes to look
upon His
   face
And lo and behold my eyes met His, alas He was
looking directly
   at me!
My heart sank. This sinner had been seen looking upon
the Holy
   One.

He rose from His throne and started toward me.
Woe is me! I cried as fear gripped my heart.
I fled from Him to the valley of the lost, through the
fields and
   forest I ran.

And lo, He was close behind. I ran faster and faster,
  until I came to the hill of damnation and hid in a cave.
I waited to catch my breath, and for the pounding of my
heart to
 calm,

When I heard the footsteps of the dreadful, eternal Son
of God.
  Where are you, sinner, He said.
But His voice was no longer as thunder
  but as a gentle breeze on a summer day.
A great fear and trembling seized me
  As He stood in the mouth of the cave.

But soon my fear was replaced by great amazement
  as He the glorious One was covered with blood.
His face was marred and battered
I was astonished and appalled as I looked upon Him.
He reached out a bloody hand and pulled me from the
cave.

I fell down at His feet, "My Lord," I cried out.
"What brought you to such sorrow and shame?
Are you not the living God?" He smiled, "Yes I Am," He
said.
"Then what brought you to this," I cried. He lifted me to
my feet.
  And looked into my eyes. "You did," He said.
He picked me up in His arms soaking me in His blood.

And lo and behold, I was clean! My sins were gone!
"O blessed Son of God who went through this for me, "I
said.
He set me on my feet and bid me go and tell others the
amazing story that changed me from a rebel to a son.

CPSIA information can be obtained
at www.ICGtesting.com
Printed in the USA
BVHW04s1543070818
523711BV00002B/9/P